The Marabout and the Muse

STUDIES IN AFRICAN LITERATURE

▼▼▼▼▼▼▼▼▼▼▼▼▼▼▼▼▼▼▼▼▼▼

▼▼▼▼▼▼▼▼▼▼▼▼▼▼▼▼▼▼▼▼▼▼▼▼▼▼▼▼▼▼▼▼

The Marabout and the Muse
New Approaches to Islam
in African Literature

Edited by

Kenneth W. Harrow

Michigan State University

HEINEMANN
Portsmouth, NH

JAMES CURREY
London

Heinemann
A division of Reed Elsevier Inc.
361 Hanover Street
Portsmouth, NH 03801-3912

James Currey Ltd.
54B Thornhill Square
Islington, London N1 1BE

ISBN 0-453-08983-8 (Heinemann)

ISBN 0-85255-540-7 (James Currey)

Library of Congress Cataloguing in Publication Data
On file at the Library of Congress

British Library Cataloguing in Publication Data
The marabout and the muse: new aspects of Islam in African literature
1. Islam in literature 2. African literature—History and criticism
I. Harrow, Kenneth W. II. Series
896'.09382

Designed by Jenny Greenleaf

Printed in the United States of America on acid-free paper.
99 98 97 96 DA 1 2 3 4 5 6

Contents

▼▼▼▼▼▼▼▼

Notes on Contributors

▼▼▼▼▼▼▼▼▼▼▼▼▼▼▼▼▼▼▼▼▼▼▼

AHMED SHEIKH BANGURA: Assistant Professor of Modern Languages at the University of San Francisco. He has published in the *Canadian Review of Comparative Literature*. A chapter of his Ph.D. thesis, "Politics of Representation: Islam and the Sub–Saharan African Novel," was recently published in the *Yearbook of Comparative and General Literature*. His research interests include Third World literatures and Islam in African literature.

JEAN BOYD: Worked in Northern Nigeria for twenty-nine years (1955–1984) of which twenty-four were spent in Sokoto. She is the author of *The Caliph's Sister* (London, 1989), and the co-editor of *The Collected Works of Nana Asma'u* (forthcoming). She is a Research Associate at the School of Oriental and African Studies, London.

DEBRA BOYD–BUGGS: Assistant Professor of French and African Studies at Wake Forest University. She has published on Mouridism in Senegalese Fiction, Maraboutism, Nigerien literature, Senegalese literature, and African and African–American female poets.

BRETT BOWLES: Holds B.A. and M.A. degrees from the University of Virginia, and is a doctoral candidate in French civilization at the Pennsylvania State University. He has published an article on how French peasants have transformed the dominant discourse in nineteenth–century France, and is now studying the way oral epics are used to shape the modern image of nineteenth–century Senegalese.

SAMBA DIOP: Assistant Professor of French, State University of New York at Buffalo. Publications: *The Oral History and Literature of the Wolof People of Waalo, Northern Senegal*; articles on the African novel in French and English, on African oral traditions and literatures, on African cinema. Currently writing a book on *Nationalism, Nationality, Ethnicity and the African Francophone Novel*.

PATRICIA GEESEY: Assistant Professor of French at the University of North Florida. She has published articles on North African French–language literature and Maghrebian women immigrants in France.

CHRISTOPHER GIBBINS: A doctoral student in Comparative Literature at the University of Alberta, Edmonton. His primary interest is contemporary

Moroccan literature and film, but more broadly he is interested in analyzing the complex nature of cultural production in postcolonial societies.

THOMAS A. HALE: Professor of African, French, and Comparative Literature at The Pennsylvania State University. He is the author of *Scribe, Griot and Novelist: Narrative Interpreters of the Songhay Empire* (Gainesville, 1990) and *Les Ecrits d'Aimé Césaire* (Montreal, 1978), as well as co–editor, with Richard K. Priebe, of *The Teaching of African Literature* (1977; 1989), and *Artist and Audience: African Literature as a Shared Experience* (1979).

KENNETH W. HARROW: Professor of English at Michigan State University. He has published *Faces of Islam in African Literature* (Portsmouth, 1991) and *Thresholds of Change in African Literature* (Portsmouth, NH, 1994).

JOHN C. HAWLEY: Associate Professor of English at Santa Clara University. He is the editor of *Cross–Addressing: Cultural Borders and Resistance* (1996), and *Writing the Nation: Self and Country in the Post–Colonial Imagination* (1996), and has published in *Research in African Literatures*, the *Literary Griot*, *Ariel*, and elsewhere.

LIDWIEN KAPTEIJNS: Associate Professor of African and Middle Eastern history, and chairwoman of Women's Studies at Wellesley College. She has published *African Historiography Written by Africans, 1955–1973: The Nigerian Case, The Use of Slaves in Precolonial Western Dar Fur, Women and the Somali Pastoral Tradition, An Islamic Alliance: Ali Dinar and the Sanusiyya, 1906–1916, Mahdist Faith and Sudanic Tradition*, and *After the Millennium: Diplomatic Correspondence from Wadai and Dar Fur on the Eve of Colonial Conquest, 1885–1916*. She is currently working on a social history of colonial northern Somalia, with special reference to women and songs.

GEORGE LANG: Associate Professor in the Department of Modern Languages and Comparative Studies at the University of Alberta, where he teaches francophone literature and cultural studies. He is currently completing a comparative study of creole literatures.

SONIA LEE: Teaches French and African literature at Trinity College in Hartford, Ct. Published several articles on African literature and two books: *Camara Laye* (1983), *Les Romancières du Continent Noir, anthologie* (1994).

BEVERLY B. MACK: Associate Professor of African Studies at the University of Kansas. She has written widely on both royal and non–royal Hausa women. She has published *Hausa Women in the Twentieth Century* (with Catherine Coles), and *The Collected Works of Nana Asma'u, 1793–1864* (with Jean Boyd).

ALAMIN MAZRUI: Associate Professor in the Department of Black Studies at Ohio State University, Columbus, Ohio. His latest publications include: *The Swahili: Idiom and Identity*, co-authored with I.N. Shariff (1994), and *Swahili State and Society: A Political-Economy of an African Language*, with Ali A. Mazrui (1995).

MAGGI PHILLIPS: A Ph.D. candidate at the Northern Territory University, Darwin, Australia. She has had articles published in *Research in African Literatures* (on Black African Women's Writing) and CRNLE (reviews on Bessie Head and Ben Okri).

PRISCILLA STARRATT: Assistant Professor of History at the University of Wisconsin-Superior where she teaches African and Middle Eastern history and Women's Studies. From 1974–1989 she lived in Kano, Nigeria, and taught African history at Bayero University. There she did oral history research on religious history and studied contemporary Muslim women.

FAROUK TOPAN: Lecturer in Swahili at the School of Oriental and African Studies, University of London. He initiated the teaching of Swahili literature at the Universities of Dar es Salaam and Nairobi, resulting in the publication of *Uchambuzi wa Maandishi ya Kiswahili*. He has published two plays: *Mfalme Juha* and *Aliyeonja Pepo*.

In memory of

Youcef Sebti (d. 1993) poète assassiné en Algérie par les Islamistes

Nabila Djahnine (d. 1994) Algerian feminist, architect, victim of "fundamentalist" violence

That their voices not be silenced.

Jean Déjeux (d. 1993) died before his contribution to this volume could be written. He devoted his life to the study of Maghrebian literature.

Acknowledgments

▼▼▼▼▼▼▼▼▼▼▼▼▼▼▼▼▼

Many thanks to John Watson of Heinemann in his help in getting this project going, and to Jean Hay of Heinemann in seeing it through to the end. Jean's editorial suggestions and guidance were particularly useful. Elizabeth Harrow was a valuable editor of my own contribution, and David McHale assisted in preparing the References section, the Glossary, and the Notes on Contributors. I am grateful to Ali Mazrui for his suggestions concerning the title of this book.

Introduction

▼▼▼▼▼▼▼▼▼▼▼▼

Kenneth W. Harrow

Any study of Islam in African literature would have to be confined to certain aspects of the subject. In our first volume, *Faces of Islam in African Literature* (1991), a number of familiar texts and authors were treated: the literatures of geographic regions like Somalia, or linguistic areas like that of Swahili, were considered; broad regional assessments of the Islamic presence in West and in East Africa were offered; and comparative studies of major topics, like mysticism in African Islamic texts or the role of women in Islamic films or novels, were analyzed. In short, *Faces of Islam in African Literature* presented as much of an overview as one volume could reasonably contain, a task made urgent by the absence of any other studies of the subject.

This left many lacunae, some of which are filled by the essays in the present volume. The essays in *Faces of Islam in African Literature* did not examine the extensive body of works produced in a variety of important regions; they did not contain studies of a number of major authors; and they considered only a few of the many African language literary traditions. The list of what could and should be studied under the rubric of African Islamic literature is enormous. The present volume does not purport to complete the task of undertaking that study, but rather to continue the ongoing venture.

Thus, *The Marabout and the Muse* focuses on a limited number of topics of particular interest, with essays devoted especially to key areas, such as the Maghreb and Nigeria; to African language literatures; to notable authors like Nuruddin Farah and Assia Djebar; to crucial issues, like the entrance of Islamic orthodoxy into indigenous African texts; and to key concepts, like Hadith, jihad and *ijtihad,* with a glossary to explain these and other terms.

The most exciting aspects of Islam contained within this volume are the varied extracts, and accompanying analyses, of African language literatures, including Somali women's songs in praise of the prominent female figures of early Islam, a Wolof epic, and Hausa tales and poems. Many of the extracts are as yet unpublished; many of the areas, like Tuareg poetry, women's Islamic literature in northern Nigeria, or Arabic literature in Nigeria, have been neglected. A novel of major importance, Ibrahim Tahir's *The Last Imam* (1984), has gone largely ignored by the critical community. The contributions to this collection attest in a multitude of ways to the vitality of a set of traditions joined by a common sense of belonging to the world of Islam. And despite the significant diversity in texts being analyzed, many of the works will demonstrate how the tension between the path of purity and that of mixing continues to inform the development of Islamic literature in its manifold configurations, in Africa as well as in the other regions of the *dar al–Islam*.

The concern with purity is integrally tied to the notion of jihad, and jihad, as George Lang demonstrates in his essay on jihad and *ijtihad* ("interpretation"), was marked by complexity from the start. On the one hand, jihad may be taken as a holy war in the service of God's Word, and, on the other, as self–struggle in the service of individual amelioration. The "Hadith game," which he and Christopher Gibbins explicate (following the work of Fischer and Abedi 1990), is the term used to describe the manner in which the commentary on the Qur'an, and on Muhammad's life, gained legitimacy. In a sense, it was the process of development of the Islamic tradition, grounded in the discussions concerning the formation of the Qur'an and especially the Hadith (the sayings and acts of the prophet as handed down by his followers). The "game" is actually the process, or rules, of intellectual exchange, that shape the formation of the text of Islam itself.

The game is concerned with what we can call the textuality of Islam. The three rules, all of which involve reference to others engaged in the discussion, include dialectical debate (with awareness of the counterargument of any given historical period), hermeneutics (with an awareness of allusions, contexts, etc, in word usage), and dialogics (with an awareness of others against whom political assertions are made). This constitutes an "ethical" dialogue with others, according to Fischer and Abedi, and at its core is the recognition that exchanges that grant the differences between members of the community are part of the growth of the religious text. This is in contrast to an understanding of jihad that we can take as monological and that gives priority to force over persuasion. Force and persuasion are always present to certain degrees in the formation of any dominant system or tradition, but what the "Hadith game" tacitly acknowledges is that human transmission within the context of a divinely understood system is essentially heterogeneous, and ultimately heterodox, as long as time and distance separate the participants in the dialogue that constitutes the Islamic text.

All facets of the Islamic text ultimately come to share, to some degree, the dialectical, hermeneutic, and dialogical properties of the Hadith game. In Africa, that game is marked by regional differences and by long reaches of historical time. This volume marks the varied nature of the Islamic text in Africa, a text seen especially as politically engaged, verbally contextualized, historicized, and intellectually committed. In short, the Islamic text is now presented as an essential component of an African cultural and social environment with which it enters into full dialogue. This dialogue has been misperceived as entailing either the imposition of a foreign presence (cf. Sembène's *Ceddo* or Armah's *Two Thousand Seasons*) or as the continuation of an original, traditional African epistemology. In fact, the Islamic text has been formed in conjunction with other texts that were always already present before its formation. In Senegal, the Wolof epic is revealed by Samba Diop as an Islamic text in formation, an epic that is both an inherited tradition handed down by generations of griots, and one that visibly reveals the reshaping of already existent stories about both Biblical/Qur'anic figures, like Noah, and Wolof rulers like Njaajaan.

For George Lang, Christopher Gibbins, Sonia Lee, John Hawley, and Patricia Geesey, who consider the role of Islam in Maghrebian literature, the Islamic text in North Africa is no less marked by an ongoing struggle, or jihad, like that undertaken by the men and women of the Muslim world from the earliest years of the Muslim era. Assia Djebar, for instance, takes up the old stories of Aisha and Fatima. The principles of postmodernity—self–referentiality, heterogeneity, the non–privileging of voice or authority—are recast as aspects of the Islamic text from the outset, especially when viewed through the optic of the women of the Islamic world. Djebar's revisiting of the originary moments of Muslim history are given these qualities. For Lang, her interpretive encounter with the foremothers of Islam partakes of this postmodern temperament, as "heterogeneity and non–linearity are the prevailing modes."

For John Hawley, who writes about Driss Chraïbi, as for Abdelkebir Khatibi, the Maghreb speaks with a medley of voices. In *Maghreb pluriel* (1983), Khatibi measures this "plurality" in a number of ways. The horizon of its thought is described by traditionalism, by "salafism" (Khatibi 1983, 25), reconciling science and religion, and rationalism. The Arabic "civilization" that marks the Maghreb is defined as "intermediate," that is, intermediate between Hellenism and the Renaissance; intermediate culturally between late Roman secularism and medieval clericism; intermediate spatially between Africa and Europe on the one hand, and India and China on the other. Finally, and most significantly, Khatibi marks Maghrebian thought as existing on the margin, turning between Western metaphysics and Muslim theology. Marginal, dominated, accorded minority status—these colonized spaces serve as the point of departure for an enriched quality of thought that emerges not despite these handicaps, but because of the enhanced possibilities they contain. Specifically, he claims that the traps of self–sufficiency are to be avoided only by tracing the lineaments of a thought that is "minoritaire, marginale, fragmentaire et inachevée" (p. 18)—a thought that will not reject the other always located within oneself, a thought he gracefully terms "une pensée plurielle."

Hawley quotes Danielle Marx–Scouras who elaborates on this plural Maghreb: "The Maghreb . . . [is] a site where Africa, Europe, and the Middle East intersect—a potential stage for the interplay of cultural diversity, ethnic pluralism, and multilingualism." The conclusion to Marx–Scouras's quotation provides the key to the present volume: "[S]uch a cultural perspective espoused by writers such as Chraïbi, Khatibi, Abdelwahab Meddeb, Nabile Farès, and Tahar Ben Jelloun, denies fundamentalism its basis." For Marx–Scouras, fundamentalist monologism is opposed by postmodernist diversities. This opposition, however, can only be a starting point, not an end point, when considering Islam in Africa.

The basis for Marx–Scouras's argument is that the more sophisticated, and now we might add, postmodernist Islam of the above mentioned authors, opposes the originary myth of a monological Islam: "Maghreb Pluriel" becomes, in sub–Saharan Africa no less than in North Africa, "Islam Pluriel," and the Islamic text becomes dialogic, as well as dialectical and hermeneutically complex in the above senses. Such an approach permits the convoluted delineations of Islamic textuality in Farah, self–consciously postmodern, to find common ground with the traditional Wolof epics, recorded by Samba Diop, and Somali women's praise songs, recorded by Lidwien Kapteijns—testifying to the multitudinous influences of traditional African culture upon the transplanted religious scriptures of Islam. However, this vision also rests upon cultural essentialism: it ignores the same qualities of complexity at play in the formation and expression of "traditional" African culture as in the "original" Arabic bases of Islam. As Bakhtin conceives of it, heteroglossia leads to an indefinite recession when we reach out for the meanings of each word, each linguistic entity, each mode of expression. And at the same time that recessionary motion is halted at every instance of expression in which the choice of meaning is made, in which the value, horizon, addressee are all set for the transmission. From the indefiniteness of words, we pass to the certitude of the Word, reinscribed as a fixed meaning. The apparent conflict between fundamentalism and postmodernism that lies at the heart of every aspect of contemporary Islam in Africa today (as had been the case earlier in the century when "modernism" struggled to reform the traditional face of Islam), is only the rehearsal of a perpetually, partially blind struggle for textual dominion.

In order to understand this apparent conflict, with all its violence and passion, and even beauty, one must come to appreciate the itinerary of a

Driss Chraïbi, as detailed by John Hawley. Chraïbi's first novel, *Le Passé simple* (1954), was written in revolt against patriarchal Islam, and yet his most recent words affirm Islamic sources of inspiration: "There is something which has never evolved: Qur'anic law, Islam. It remains as it was; that is, for us in the Arabo–Islamic world, it is newly–born, it is the source. And for me, it is a force: it is my strength." The importance of this statement does not lie in its distance from *Le Passé simple*, but in its continuity with the Islamic text as a site for both monological and dialogical expression—both inevitably and simultaneously present.

The Hadith game can serve as a model for the Islamization of the plural African text. Although the three-part structure—dialectic, hermeneutic, dialogic—may be arbitrary, it would seem to correspond to a natural pattern in which the Islamic influence is felt to pass from an initial stage of historical entry and confrontation, dialects, to the stage of ideological and intellectual expansion, hermeneutics, to a final stage of accommodation/co–respondence with already existent traditions, dialogics. We can see something of this three part game in the development of the Hausa tale, the *labarai*, a number of which have been recorded and analyzed by Priscilla Starratt. In one particular tale, a number of conventions are observed: a traditional *bori* priest is pitted against a Muslim holy man, a *mallam*, in a contest staged by the ruler. The traditional priest divines the correct answer to a riddle set by the ruler, that is, what is there to be found in a particular house whose contents are known only to the ruler. In this case, it is a horse. When the *mallam* is asked the same question, he prays to Allah for guidance, and is provided with a different answer, a white bull with horns. The ruler, expecting to find the horse he had placed in the house still there, orders the walls of the house demolished. The order is carried out, and to the ruler's surprise a white bull is found. Though the ruler then waits years for the bull to change back to a horse, it remains a bull. Through this miracle, God insures the successful transplantation of the true faith to Katsina.

The dialectical confrontation between the Hausa *bori* priest and the Muslim *mallam* sets the stage—a stage setting frequently found in many African oral traditions where magical struggles of power are the central action. The first level of meaning emerges from this dialectical contest—God's greatness is attested to in the triumph of the *mallam*. The magical transformation of the beast suggests a further hermeneutical level, in which God's intervention entails greater issues of struggle—jihad—and interpretation, or *ijtihad*, the twin terms examined elsewhere by Lang. The subordination of the identities of the beasts to God's will, the demolition of the walls surrounding the miraculous transformation, all suggest the mystic meanings commensurate with the traditions of Islamic wisdom literature. Finally, the insertion of this timeless parable into the specific context of the *labarai* with the issue of the conversion of the Hausa at Katsina, and with the accommodation of the ruler to Islam in this important urban center of northern Nigeria where the major nineteenth–century jihads took place, all mark the tale's dialogical quality. The application of the Hadith game here suggests that the *labarai*, viewed as a Muslim text, contains both the message of the religious victory of Islam along with the intertextual elements of a pre–Islamic Hausa universe, intertwined in the language, structure, and expression of the tale.

The tale concludes on this note: "Islam entered our land. That's what I know." But along with the triumphant entry, the tale reminds us of the strength of the *bori* specialist; and in this version relocates the action of the tale from the initial site of Gobir to Katsina, indicating, among other things, the reterritorialization of the foreign into the familiar. Excavation into this tale of origins reveals the Hausa–Gobir palimpsest. Just as the Hadith game represented a dialogue within the Muslim community whose goal was to establish a settled version of a given truth, so, too, does the formation of the Islamic text across Africa represent a dialogue whose eventual outcome will be the formation of a body of works that will recognize themselves as representing what is Islamic within the African tradition. The aspects of Islam that then emerge should not be viewed as superficial additions, nor as deviations from a true Islam. Not only is Islam an African "heritage," one part of Ali Mazrui's "triple heritage," it has followed the same processes of the Hadith game in Africa, to a greater or lesser degree, as were followed elsewhere in the *dar al–Islam*, the realm over which Islam rules as the dominant faith. Islam, in many cases like those of the Hausa traditions, has become a newly created/creating faith and practice in Africa whose identity is expressed, preserved, and transmitted through those texts that have come to know themselves as Islamic.

If we return to the foundation texts of Islam, the Qur'an and the Hadith, we can observe how the process of canonization came into play. Portions of the Qur'an were initially given in oral and written form during Muhammad's lifetime, but the task of accepting and rejecting authorized chapters (suras), that is, creating an authorized version, did not occur until the reign of the third caliph, Uthman. Similarly, the transmission of the sayings and of the acts of the Prophet continued until the ninth century, by which point the proliferation of "Hadith" had led to thousands of ostensible sayings and deeds. In order to bring the proliferation to an end, the task of authenticating the true words and deeds was undertaken; the reasonable compatibility of the Hadith with the Qur'an was considered, as was the *isnad* ("chain" of narrators); six collections eventually emerged as authoritative.

We can now complete the application of the Hadith game to Islamic texts in African literature. A chain of transmitters, like the griots whose descendants continued to repeat the Wolof epic recorded by Samba Diop, passed on the songs, tales, epics, or sayings infused with Islamic elements. The epic may suggest there is a starting point for the process, with the life, say, of an important king. But we know the genre preceded the lifetime of the subject; that the word was always already imbricated in dialogical processes. With the interventions of the transcribers of these traditions, like our Diops or Kapteijns, the last version in the chain is fixed, and like the Hadith achieves a certain "right" of "copy"—a copyright. It acquires what is conferred with the publication of written texts, like the poems of Hawad, the Tuareg poet whose work is analyzed by Debra Boyd–Buggs: not only legal rights, status, and authority, but also the fixity of what marks the end of one kind of transmission and the beginning of another kind of commentary. The work of the many scholars in this volume should be viewed as links in the above traditions.

Islamic literature as treated in *The Marabout and the Muse* extends over a wide area. The flowering of women's literature in northern Nigeria for the 150 years from 1820 to 1970, is analyzed by Jean Boyd and Beverly Mack, whose essay includes numerous examples of early poetry. They direct their attention to themes of nurturing, admonishment, and education for the peoples of the Islamic caliphate in the colonial period, and to the defense of a distinctive northern Islamic identity in the postcolonial era. Two more specific studies deal with neglected areas of Nigerian literature: Priscilla Starratt presents examples of a rarely examined form of oral tales, *labarai*, and provides analyses of their blend of Islamic and Hausa literary elements; and Ahmed Bangura examines one of the most interesting, and unappreciated major novels of African Islamic literature, Ibrahim Tahir's *The Last Imam*. Bangura focuses his study on the character of a rigidly orthodox imam whose stance against pre–Islamic Fulani–Hausa beliefs and practices sets the standards for a new puritanism, one which his community views as being in contradiction with his own personal life.

African language literature cannot be considered without examining the roles of those responsible for transmitting it. Thomas Hale, in collaboration with Brett Bowles, continues his important study of the *griot* by examining the changing relationship between *griots* and Islam, especially in narratives about Islamic rulers who resisted colonialism in the nineteenth century. Recent work on Wolof epics suggests that *griots*, once rivals with scribes, are now playing an increasingly important role in the resurgence of

Islam in the Sahel. In the epic of the Waalo kingdom, the *griot* established the "chain" that leads from Noah to the twelfth–thirteenth century Wolof ruler, Njaajaan, and finally, to the nineteenth–century ending of that kingdom with the advent of French colonialism and the conquests of Faidherbe. The genealogy traced in the epic is considered by Diop in his essay that accompanies it. Working with Mariam Omar Ali, Lidwien Kapteijns presents a series of Somali *sittaat* or women's praise songs for the "mothers of the believers," the early women of Islam. Recordings made at extraordinary sessions of recitations of the *sittaat* in Djibouti have been transcribed and subsequently analyzed. Originally serving as the basis for Somali feminist sensibility as well as spirituality, the *sittaat* sessions now face an uncertain future due to the pressures of more culturally "pure" approaches derived from the Islamic heartland. Swahili oral literature provides the sources for Farouk Topan's analysis of songs from spirit possession cults collected during fieldwork in Kenya in the 1960s and 1970s. As with the *sittaat*, the songs are derived from practices whose participants feel obliged to reconcile with orthodox Islam—a reconciliation perhaps made easier for them inasmuch as it is men, this time, who are setting for themselves the task of sustaining and reinforcing a Muslim identity. Here it is the marriage of *dini* ("religion") and *mila* ("custom") that is effected. Finally, the mysterious spirit of the blue men of the desert, the Tuareg, is captured by the poet Hawad whose "nomadic" soul is expressed in calligraphy and verse. Themes of drought and abandonment reflect something of the condition of his people, while the deeper mystic roots are evoked in the Sufi poetry.

Also the quintessential nomad, inhabitant of the spaces between desert and coastline, Nuruddin Farah is a unique figure in contemporary African literature. His novels, including especially *Maps* (1986) and *Close Sesame* (1983), have returned the reader to the central issues bearing on Islam in Somali society. For Aliman Mazrui, Farah is Africa's answer to Salman Rushdie. Iconoclastic, individualistic, postmodern, self–conscious juggler of words and ideas, Farah is perhaps best positioned to bait the bears of fundamentalism: for Mazrui, Farah does not escape the trap of Western liberal critics of Islam, thus placing him in the same camp as others like Nawal el–Saadawi. Whereas Mazrui derives his criticisms from *Maps*, Maggi Philips uses *Close Sesame* to argue the opposite point. She contends that the novel's inspirational sources are the Qur'an: centering on the aged figure of the nationalist hero Deeriye, Farah investigates the protagonist's redefinition of faith in himself and in his love for God, transforming political polemic into an evocation of humankind's sacred potential. Concept and metaphor are constructed through a kind of "mosque of words," resulting, she claims, in a thoroughly Islamic novel based on the puzzles of creation and sanctity.

The last space considered in this volume is also "bicultural," as Abdelwahab Meddeb has put it, only this time it is not predominantly a case of traditional, indigenous African culture mixed with the outsider's Islam, but rather the Islam of the home and community face to face with the European presence: "We bear the glorious traces of Islamic culture and we know the cultural values created in the West" [1] (quoted in Déjeux 1986, 27). Yet, as Khatibi has indicated over and again in his powerful descriptions of the plural face of the Maghreb, the Berber and Arabic cultures are themselves multidimensional, marked by the uneven distribution of power and authority; the writer often comes to sense the deep presence of an Islamic identity only after being positioned as the outsider with respect to a dominant Western culture. Islam is thus at once the religion of the victorious invading Arabic armies; the faith carried by jurists and mystics; the rituals of the *umma*, given by Albert Memmi as the "mother–community" (qtd in Déjeux 1986, 27), and thereby the repository of long-standing indigenous practices; and finally the "family" ways, the familiar sense of self faced with the Other. In this broad way, the Maghrebian writer is Muslim, without necessarily sharing in the beliefs of the faith: "Most Maghrebian writers, born into Muslim families, consider themselves to be Muslim in this sense of (sharing) 'Islamness,' without this having any eventual bearing on their possible faith in a transcendant God, in their indifference to or their involvement in religious practice. Their unconscious mind and imagination were steeped and formed in a Maghrebian cultural context that is Islamic and not French or otherwise. . ." (Déjeux 1986, 27).[2] This said, Déjeux does go on to stress the cultural métissage that also characterizes the Maghrebian author.

For Christopher Gibbins, the métissage of which Déjeux speaks is no more than a starting point for our understanding of the Maghreb. Rather than permitting Algerian–francophone binarism to stand in for the entire Maghreb, Gibbins suggests we recognize the more particular history of each country, remembering that in addition to French colonial influences, there were also Spanish and Italian presences in Morocco and Tunisia, respectively, not to mention the earlier influences of Turkish, Vandal, Roman, and Berber peoples. Gibbins cites Khatibi's description of the Maghrebian landscape as plurilingual, including diglossia (between Arabic and its dialects), Berber, French, Spanish in the north and the south of Morocco (Khatibi 1983, 179). An examination of the writings of Khatibi, Fatima Mernissi, and Tahar Ben Jelloun leads Gibbins to conclude that the Islam they draw upon is also plural, "impure" from the viewpoint of a fundamentalist, and yet enriched by their diversity.

Driss Chraïbi's itinerary from rebellious son to "royal exile," as described in John Hawley's essay, embraces fully the complex exchanges of identity arising out of the meeting of Morocco and France. At the end of the itinerary, Hawley depicts Chraïbi's embrace of a newfound force in Islam, while at the same time this sentiment is born out of permanent exile. Chraïbi's early works correspond to a period in which much of the work of the major fathers of contemporary Maghrebian literature was lionized. One has only to think of Kateb Yacine's *Nedjma* (1956) as the defining novel of the 1950s. Now it would have to be Assia Djebar who enjoys the status as the dominant voice, and it is her novel, *Loin de Médine* (1991) that most evokes the challenge of Islam for the Maghreb in these troubled times. For Sonia Lee, Djebar's goal in this novel is to enter into the spirit of the transmission of the life of the Prophet, that is, to reconfigure the chain of words in the manner of the Hadith. This is accomplished by an imaginative reconstruction of the attestations of the major female voices, including especially those of Aisha and Fatima. Most importantly, however, is the dialogical presence of the female narrative voices that enters into the male spaces of the *isnad*. Buried, suppressed female voices are here returned to the textual center—joining Djebar's project with that of her feminist sisters. This results, according to Lee, in the foregrounding of language, the discourse of transmission, as the real subject matter of Djebar's novel. Patricia Geesey agrees with the feminist goals analyzed by Lee, and examines more closely how the novel is modeled on the paradigm of the Hadith. The historical processes that unfold in the creation of Hadith are replicated by Djebar, with the space between historical fact and fictional "re–visioning" and reconstruction receiving particular attention: Djebar does not subvert traditional Islam, but resuscitates the collective female voice, joining women to the practices of interpretation controlled by men. This follows not only feminist agendas, but postmodern ones of opening the past to the present. This is precisely what George Lang seeks to accomplish in his astute revisiting of the conventional division between action and contemplation, between the active struggle of jihad and the interpretive dynamic of *ijtihad*, essentially deconstructing the opposition. For Lang the interaction between meanings that gives rise to interpretation parallels the manner in which cultural differences are "folded and blended into the new hegemony in ways that its own agents may not even realize," thus echoing dialogical forms. It is no coincidence that Lang also considers Djebar, Chraïbi, and Mernissi in developing his paradigm.

In the end, just as Africa's cultural heritage may be seen as comprising multiple filiations, so, too, does this volume bear witness to Islam's pluralist heritage: in the examination of specific cultural practices, specific literary forms and traditions, we see emerging a view of Islam that sets pluralism against monoculturalism, and that locates these opposing poles at the heart of Islam itself. At the same time, the "fundamentalist" option is not simply dismissed as the retrograde, patriarchal side of Islam, but is recovered, retrofitted into the structure of the Hadith as the metaphor for contemporary fictional practice itself. The chain is not broken, but is reforged and extended.

Notes

1. "Nous portons les traces glorieuses de la culture islamique et nous connaissons les valeurs culturelles qui se sont réalisées en Occident."
2. "La plupart des écrivains maghrébins, nés dans une famille musulmane, se veulent musulmans dans ce sens de l'islamité, sans que cela préjuge de la foi éventuelle de chacun en un Dieu transcendant, de son indifférence ou de son engagement dans la pratique du culte. Leur inconscient et leur imaginaire ont été impregnés et formés dans un contexte culturel maghrébin qui est islamique et non dans un contexte français ou autre . . ."

Chapter 1

▼▼▼▼▼▼▼▼

Jihad, Ijtihad, and other Dialogical Wars in La Mère du printemps, Le Harem politique, and Loin de Médine

GEORGE LANG

> *Western audiences, out of ignorance, yield too easily to fundamentalist Muslim claims that Islam is prescriptive in simple ways. To argue otherwise requires knowledge of Islamic hermeneutics, dialectics, and dialogics.*
>
> FISCHER AND ABEDI, *Debating Muslims* (p. 147)

An initial disclaimer is imposed by the epigraph standing above. It would be remiss for me to allege deep knowledge of the intellectual traditions of Islam for the same reasons, discussed below, that the Berber Azwaw Aït Yafelman had only a rough grasp of Arabic prior to his conversion and immersion in the Qur'an: not that conversion is prerequisite to immersion in Islamic thought, only that knowledge is relative, and my own in this case that of an apprentice. Appreciating *La Mère du printemps* (1982), *Le Harem politique: Le prophète et les femmes* (1987), and *Loin de Médine* (1991) at their worth, nonetheless, requires willingness to engage with the argumentative and interpretive strategies they "borrow" from Islamic traditions. Such willingness is already a first step away from the ignorance referred to in the epigraph. That this step leads into a realm riven not only by the schisms heralded so tellingly in *Loin de Médine*, but also by conflict fueled by simple prescriptions on all sides comes, as they say, with the territory.

Of course Driss Chraïbi, Fatima Mernissi, and Assia Djebar belong to the traditions from which they "borrow." Two predicaments nonetheless arise from their special situation as Maghrebian writers in a postmodern age. On the one hand, their use of French tends to lull unwary francophones into neglecting the extent and the originality of their adaptations. On the other hand, their having adopted certain Western literary modes makes them suspect in conservative Islamic eyes. All three authors exploit in conscientious and consciously innovative ways the intellectual resources of Islamic rhetoric, jurisprudence, and historiography, but the transgressions of genre and discipline they commit might offend some exegetes of Islam. Even Fatima Mernissi's essay, the most conventionally procedural of the three, resides at a generic crossroad, and draws upon a personal vision. As she says, "This book is not a work of history. This book is intended as a memory-narrative (*récit-souvenir*): an opening towards the sites where memory wavers, dates become clouded and events blur, as in those dreams that give us force" (p. 19). Mernissi's description of her examination of misogyny in the sourceworks of Islamic historiography aptly fits both Assia Djebar's and Driss Chraïbi's novels. Though there are significant differences among them, each undertakes what might be called revisionist explorations of early Islamic history. Moreover, these three narratives are connected by an implicit thematic thread, one I have conceived of by way of the kind of pun common in French and now North American critical theory, though the terms in question are transliterations from the Arabic: jihad/*ijtihad* ("holy war"/"free interpretation")—distant cognates, aspects of one other, and not especially irreconcilable countenances of Islam.

Given the widespread pejorative acceptation of jihad, I must first offer some clarification about its history. Then I shall address *ijtihad*, of which Fatima Mernissi's essay is a consummate example, and which Assia Djebar uses to characterize her own "intellectual quest for the truth" of women's experience during the early years of Islam.[1] Finally, with the tools provided by this exploration of the dyad jihad/*ijtihad*, I shall explore the dialogics of transcultural conversion as exposed by Driss Chraïbi.

The notion of *ijtihad*, which has wide currency in Islamic political and theological debate, deserves nativization into English, since jihad and *ijtihad* each anchor one end of a dialogical continuum running from holy war through conversion, maieutic, and on to the hermeneutics of *ijtihad*. War is, after all, innately dialogical, but interpretation has an intrinsically agonistic side, and the continuum jihad/*ijtihad* has as well a particular configuration in the Maghreb, where texts are intensely transtextual—an expression preferable to "intertextual" to emphasize their invasive nature, a characteristic rooted in the history of the region and in the imperative practice of Islam, which began, after all, with God's edict to Muhammad at the first moment of revelation: *iqra!* (read/recite).

Jihad, like other derivatives from the root *j-h-d*, had the pre-Qur'anic meaning of striving, laboring, or toiling, and in the thirty-six instances where the word occurs in the Qur'an was used "classically and literally in [that] natural sense" (Ali 1977, 165), especially with reference to exertion and to commitment, one connotation conveyed by Assia Djebar's translation of *djihad* as "internal struggle recommended to all believers" (p. 6). That said, emergent Islam was certainly bellicose, as Chraïbi and Djebar illustrate in their novels, with some admiration on the part of the former for the virility of his antagonists, and on that of the latter for the tenacity of her heroines. Within *shari'a* or juridical tradition therefore crystallized a number of precepts and behavioral codes regarding the particular forms of striving that consist of war and confrontation. Whereas it is common to restrict jihad to types of aggression, as Mervyn Hiskett does in *The Development of Islam in West Africa* by glossing only *jihad al-sayf* ("jihad of the Sword, armed jihad") and *jihad al-qawl* ("a period of preaching that usually precedes resort to jihad by arms") (1984, 32), jihad has a much larger range. To cite one example from what one might call the moderate school, in the twelfth century A.D. the Spaniard Averroes (Ibn Rushd) devoted a chapter to jihad in his elegantly titled *Bidayat al-Mudjtahid wa-Nihayat al-Mustasid* ("The beginning for him who interprets the sources independently and the end for him who wishes to limit himself")—whose terms are of more than passing interest here, since a *mujtahid*, derived from the same root that gives *ijtihad*, is an interpreter, albeit a rational or philological one. A second more contemporary monograph in this vein is that by the twentieth century Egyptian reformist Mahmud Shaltut, whose *Al-Qur'an wa-al-qital* ("The Qur'an and fighting") was composed in 1940 when "this topic [was] of practical importance in our times, as wars [were] being fought all over the world"—though he pertinently added that "many adherents of other religions constantly take up this subject with a view to discredit Islam" (Peters 1977, 27). Despite their distance in time, both Averroes and Shaltut converge insofar as their emphasis falls on jihad as a social obligation largely assumed for defensive reasons, like the draft. Averroes's stance can perhaps best be explained by his adherence to the Malikite School, one of the four major currents of Sunni jurisprudence, and whose doctrines still have influence in the Maghreb. Its originator, Malik Ibn Anas (d. 795 A.D.), justified his attitude by citing the Prophet as saying, "Leave the Ethiopians in peace as long as they leave you in peace" (Peters 1977, 31). For his part, Shaltut, invoking the right to free *ijtihad*, established through his own readings of the Qur'an that meaningful conversion could not be obtained through compulsion, either "manifest" (by iron or fire) or "secret" (by awe-inspiring tokens). He consequently argued that jihad was essentially defensive, not intended to be coercive: "The Qur'an instructs us clearly that Allah did not wish people to become believers by way of force and compulsion, but only by way of study, reflection and contemplation" (Peters 1977, 31).

These moderate positions should be weighed against the "radical fundamentalist" critique that a purely defensive conception of jihad is necessarily defeatist, as in the following assertion: "writers on jihad who are defeated spiritually and mentally do not distinguish between the method of this religion in rejecting compulsion to embrace Islam and its method in destroying those material and political forces which stand between man and his God" (Moussalli 1992, 205). Such forms of jihad aim at altering any institutions that impede free adhesion to Islam: "Those who [see] jihad only as defensive [do] not understand Islam; it is true that Islam defends the land it exists on, but it also struggles to establish the Islamic system wherever possible" (p. 206). Seen in this light, Islamic radicalism partakes much more of the dialectic between free will and determinism than it might appear from the outside. Free adhesion to Islam, radicals argue, is not possible where materialist value systems and institutions prevail, nor where ideological hegemony is in the hands of non-Muslims. Politically subordinate to the West, which has forced them to compromising and demeaning terms, moderate Muslims have been tainted by "non-Islamic notions" and disoriented by "attacks of the orientalists" (p. 206): they are not free to choose Islam.

Somewhat ironically, Assia Djebar and Driss Chraïbi have set their novels "within the continuous surge of Islam at its dawn" (Chraïbi 1982, 145), the century when Muhammad's immediate successors were subduing the Arabian peninsula and North Africa, and jihad was not only aggressive but aimed like an arrow at the heart of the religious and political institutions standing in the way of conversion of non-Muslims: Bedouin polytheism and the Berber paganism and Christianity that subsisted in the rump of the Roman Empire still under the Byzantine regime. Djebar's lack of sentimentality over the explosive expansion of Islam by the sword and the fact that several of her heroines are accomplished military leaders on both sides of battle suggest that a critique of military jihad was far from her mind. In fact she posits jihad as another of the customarily male domains that her heroines can and should invade and occupy (along with prophecy, predication and poetry, as a collective profile of her manifold heroines reveals). The connection between Djebar's feminism and her sense of jihad is, to be sure, understandable in an author who was an early militant in the Algerian revolution and who, like her sisters, was repressed after independence. Jihad in its military sense too, Djebar implies, is a right of women by virtue of its practice by women at the hour of Islamic origin, though the "gaping holes in the collective memory" (p. 5) that have erased those moments of empowerment must be filled by committed fiction like her own.

As for Chraïbi's Berber hero Azwaw Aït Yafelman, preemptive conversion to Islam is the only possible defensive ploy to the irresistible invasion led by Uqba ibn Nafi, for whom jihad was first and foremost an agent of mass conversion: "Uqba did not consider himself a warrior and had never wanted to be one. His own war was a war of faith" (p. 148). Though Chraïbi does not seek to veil the military aspects of jihad, he sees it essentially as a convulsive purgation, one exemplified by Uqba's destruction of the corrupt city of Qayrawan, the fortress at the edge of the Tunisian desert from which Islam subsequently spread across North and West Africa.

> Uqba carefully visited the city of Qayrawan which General Houdaij had founded a few years before and which was so widely discussed in the Arab empire. He had it razed to the ground. . . .
>
> "Fell these trees for me," he ordered. "Open up the banks of the wadi. I want to see the full course of the water. Pull out the weeds. I don't want there to be a sole human from the past, not an animal, snake or scorpion. This is also part of our war. That is what holy war is" (pp. 159–60).

Not to be forgotten, however, is that jihad also brings "a few days behind it the chariots full of the greatest scientists of the century, doctors of law, professors, architects, builders, artists" (p. 148). As Chraïbi affirms in the interview just below, his prime interest is the genesis and the decline of civilizations, including the decay of Islam, certainly implied by the words attributed to Muhammad in the epigraph of *La Mère du printemps*: "Islam will become again the foreigner it began by being." In this regard Chraïbi is and sees himself as a faithful descendent of the Maghrebian historian Ibn Khaldun:

> As far as civilizations go, they are beautiful at the moment of their birth. And I know nothing that is as beautiful as birth, be it the birth of a child or the birth of Islam, for example. We see it born, this civilization, which-ever one it might be, and then enter adolescence, maturity and then its autumn—and here I am referring to my distant relative Ibn Khaldun . . . , the 14th century founder of modern sociology (Dubois 1986, 22).

On the surface, *La Mère du printemps* deals with Azwaw's strategic response to Uqba's jihad: his hasty conversion to the then nascent civilization. As radicals might suggest, and here Chraïbi would agree, there can be no civilization without an ideological hegemony of some sort, one established through jihad (by this or another name), and consolidated through conversion.

Neither Chraïbi nor Djebar falls back onto a defensive reading of jihad precisely because committed inner and outer struggle with and against other political forces is, for both, a feature of life lived to the fullest. In addition, each in their own ways and by means of literary devices one might call postmodernist, transforms the terms of the above-mentioned key controversy within Islam, the polemic between modernists accused of pandering to the West by recasting jihad as defensive, and radicals for whom jihad is an unrelenting struggle to implement the conditions in which all peoples are free to accept Islam. Unlike the cautious Islamist modernists who preceded them, Chraïbi and Djebar take jihad seriously and relate it back to its root meaning of intense struggle; unlike the radicals, they question the homogeneity of the Islamic system jihad is committed to bring into existence. Both suggest, in fact, that heterogeneity was part and parcel of submission to Islam from the beginning.

Ijtihad needs even more background explanation than jihad, since the former is far from common in English or French. It took approximately three centuries for Sunni Islam to develop consensus about its corpus, up to which point a definitive frame of reference for the Qur'an was not in place. Interpretation was open, though conflict was far from purely hermeneutic. In fact the great schism between Sunni and Shi'ite currents anticipated in the first pages of *Loin de Médine* dates from the second Islamic generation, and the Maghreb itself was the scene of intense military and doctrinal clash, starting with the appearance of the Kharijis around 740 A.D. More than the result of political rivalry, however, the subsequent hardening of doctrines—the closing of "the gate of *ijtihad*" (*bab al-ijtihad*)— might also be understood as an inevitable consequence of what one might call Islamic epistemology. Like the big bang, the revelation of the Qur'an triggered a proliferation and dispersion of meaning that threatened to expand forever. To cite one evocative passage on the matter: "The text of the Qur'an reveals human language crushed by the power of the Divine Word. It is as if human language were scattered into a thousand fragments like a wave scattered into drops against the rocks at sea."[2] Likewise, Chraïbi speaks of "the gigantic emotion, the bursting commotion at hearing the Divine word" (p. 145). Sealing off *ijtihad* meant at least confining the reverberating realm of reaction to the Qur'an within the closed circuit of extant Hadith, sayings about and by the Prophet, and previously certified *isnad*, the chain of mouth-to-mouth and eventually scribal transmission of traditions upon which the authenticity of Hadith was predicated.

Taught as a fundament of Islamic learning, the procedures of isnad verification can be conceived monologically as the proper stringing together of discrete utterances. In their remarkable *Debating Muslims: Cultural Dialogues in Postmodernity and Tradition*, Michael M. J. Fischer and Mehdi Abedi cast isnad into a more dialogical perspective:[3]

The entire structure of Qur'an and Hadith is a fun house of mirrors playing upon appearances and resemblances (*mutashabih*) that may or may not be grounded (*muhkam*), depending upon the perspective and knowledge of the interpreter. It is a structure necessitating a critical sense, but one ambivalently also permissive of uncritical belief and false leads (100).

As Fischer and Abedi go on to observe, dispute and argumentation, which are inevitable parts of "the Hadith game," must be understood

dialectically (i.e., aware of the range of counterarguments in a given historical period), hermeneutically (i.e., aware of the allusions and contexts, nuances and changes in word usage), and dialogically (i.e., aware of the political others against whom assertions are made). It is an ethical discourse in the sense that it is always conducted in a communicative environment that assumes persuasive dialogue with others, that attempts to persuade those others to join one's own moral and political community (p. 146).

Hadith interpretation is, in other words, inherently agonistic, struggle.

In *Le Harem politique* Fatima Mernissi makes clear that she is willing to play the Hadith game by the rules, and in fact insists upon it (pp. 48–49), since her goal is to demonstrate that there have been patriarchal distortions of isnad procedures in a series of injunctions against women, for example those concerning the veil or the ill-advisedness of women in politics (the latter she tracks to a disciple of the Prophet whom she catches out as having tailored the Prophet's words *post facto* for his own political purposes); or, again, those that ignore or otherwise censor the fact that Muhammad's youngest wife Aisha herself engaged in jihad, and against the Prophet's own cousin and son-in-law Ali, this at the very moment when the primary unity of believers was shattered by *fitna* (disorder). Mernissi's reasoning is founded on the major commentary on the Qur'an, that by al-Tabari (d. 922 A.D.), on treatises on the *nasikh* and *mansoukh* (Qur'anic verses that were replaced by subsequent contradictory revelation, apocrypha of sorts), and on the massive collection of Hadith by Bokhari (d. 852 A.D.), plus other central texts of Islamic science. Both Muslim and feminist, she directs her attack on misogynists within the community of believers, all the while remaining respectful of the principles of Islamic scholarship. In other words, as tempting as it might be to some Western feminists to adopt Mernissi's cause, it is essential to understand the logic of her jihad, her *ijtihad*. The edifice of her argumentation makes no sense without its ultimate reference to the Qur'an and to the Prophet.

Le Harem politique can be profitably read as a companion piece to *Loin de Médine*, itself a tapestry of Hadith and interweaving of strands of textual transmission. Despite her characterization of her own essay as dream and memory-narrative, Mernissi accepts the principles of rational and linear interpretation, and in fact turns the irrationality of patriarchal readings against them. Djebar, however, sets her "desire to interpret" (p. 6) within an implicit theory of information in which heterogeneity and non-linearity prevail. Classical Sunni *ijtihad* was a ratiocinative procedure whose aim was to establish consensus among scholars alone "competent to exercise [it]" (Hourani 1991, 68)—a status to which Mernissi provocatively lays claim not only as grounds for her refutation of aberrant (patriarchal) isnad, but as ipso facto proof of her defense of women's rights within Islam. For her part, Assia Djebar so closely ties the question of isnad to alternative lines of narrative development that her *ijtihad* falls beyond ratiocination. In the first place, by speaking of her personal will, she connects renewal of interpretation with inner struggle, a notion by no means alien to Islamic thought but suspect from the point of view of the *uluma* (the learned), whose goal was *ijma* (consensus), and who holds the monopoly on *ijtihad* as usually construed. Furthermore, by constructing a montage of substitute fictional episodes that various isnad generate, Djebar undermines the procedural rationality that was the premise of both classical *ijtihad* and modernist revisionism dating from the colonial period (like that of Mahmud Shaltut quoted above). Juxtaposition of alternative narratives has been familiar in French fiction since the *nouveau roman*, in fact before, but the application of this literary device to the Hadith—and, to mention only its first occurrence in *Loin de Médine*, to a scene as sanctified as Muhammad's death in the arms of Aisha—is nothing short of revolutionary. Unlike Salman Rushdie, whose representation of Muhammad's harem in *The Satanic Verses* was certainly provocative and also based in part on Hadith, Assia Djebar calls into question the very procedures of Islamic rationality.

Though I have so far left aside feminist aspects of *Loin de Médine* in favor of its originality within Islamic hermeneutics, this novel is another of Djebar's explorations of women's repressed potentiality and denied virtuality, and can and should so be read. In her preface, for example, Djebar explicitly links women's dispossession and disempowerment with the entropic disintegration of the Qur'anic revelation once conveyed into human hands:

> In the course of the period evoked here, which begins with the death of Muhammad, the fates of numerous women imposed themselves on my imagination: I have tried to resuscitate them. . . . Women in action "far from Medina," that is to say outside, either geographically or symbolically, the site of temporal power that irreversibly deviates from its original source (p. 5).

There is thus a double movement within *Loin de Médine*. On the one hand, Medina is portrayed as a site of temporal power from which women have been excluded; on the other hand, the men of Medina from Muhammad on as well as its women are condemned to a progressive degradation and loss of spiritual purity, a loss reflected in ever-widening circles of political rivalry and clashing interpretations of the past. Moreover, what one might call the Amazonian virtues of women's jihad, plus other powers traditionally monopolized by men (prophecy, predication and poetry), are only part of the full spectrum of women's experience. As is apparent in her other novels, Assia Djebar insists that love, desire, and familial fulfilment are also valid concerns, hence the increasing focus, as *Loin de Médine* develops, on the family around Muhammad, his wives and daughters as well as his friends and allies.

Foundational Islam was a family matter—albeit that of an extended polygamous family—and its future schisms were smoldering within Muhammad's household and network of family alliances. Whatever else it might be, *Loin de Médine* is a fictional application of gender criticism to the primordial family drama of Islam.

Muhammad left no surviving sons. As the author repeats several times: "if Fatima had only been born a son" (pp. 58–60). The consequences of Fatima's female birth were devastating for the future of Islam within the cultural context of Arab society in the seventh century A.D., since the patriarchy in question, Muhammad's, was therefore unable to assure its legitimate transmission in an unambiguous and unassailable manner. In a sense, there is no need to deconstruct the patriarchal heritage of Islam; it deconstructed itself.

> Six months after the death of Muhammad his favorite daughter Fatima died, she who, in the absence of the son of Muhammad (who was *abtar*, without a male descendent) transmitted through her own children—who were almost twins—a double male descendance —the principal tie through blood. It is as if the presence of the beloved daughter, once her father was dead, proved to be a blankness, an emptiness, almost a fault line (p. 58).

The language of this passage will ring familiar to readers of Kristeva and Irigaray, but its application to the genealogy of the Prophet's family is original, intentionally provocative, and cuts two ways. Most obviously (and this is the aspect likely to be picked up in the West), Djebar is harshly critical of the patriarchal nature of Islamic society. At the same time, though, she suggests that the family setting of nascent Islam is the ideal framework within which to construct fresh feminist perspectives, precisely because the impotence of the patriarchy (as conceived in its own terms) translated its void, blankness, emptiness, and inner fault (*un blanc, un creux, quasiment une faille*) (Djebar 1991, 58). In other words, Western feminists should know more, not less, about Islam, which has been embedded within a most fertile paradigm for thought about gender.

Among her heroines, Djebar is especially drawn to Esma the healer, "she who will sooth the abrasion" (p. 210). In Djebar's fictionalization Esma (wife of the first caliph Abu Bakr and thus Aisha's stepmother), intimate friend of Fatima (wife of Ali), is the pivotal figure who resides on "a border invisible then, a border that will open up, deepen, bring progressive dissension, then violence to Medina" (pp. 231–32). Esma thus replaces Aisha, the young and faithful wife (albeit a whore in Shi'ite tradition and troublemaker among misogynist currents in general), and Fatima, the loyal daughter (though wife of the somewhat dubious Ali, in Sunni eyes), as exemplary female figure because she, Esma, is "the only one to subsume the seething contradictions that will appear, the only one capable of surmounting them" (p. 219).

At this point *Loin de Médine* offers two distinct but compatible lines of interpretation. According to the first, the Great Dissension should be attributed to the corruption polygamy introduced into Islam: "as if the body of Islam had to divide, to give birth by itself to civil struggles and quarrels, all that as tribute paid to the polygamy of the Founder" (p. 59). According to the second, however, this issue is moot, in so far as Djebar displaces the focus of Islamic tradition from Muhammad and his successors to the women around him, who are portrayed as the true actors in the drama that is unfolding. As she says of her first heroine, the anonymous Yemenite Queen: "far from being reduced to the role of simple intriguer, she is the very soul of the machination" (p. 22).

Ijtihad per Djebar has consequences for both moderates and radicals, since the world of the first and second Islamic generations provides an interpretive frame without which the Qur'an itself can have no *social* meaning, precisely the reason why the Hadith and their understanding are necessary foundations of shari'a. Yet Djebar's foundational realm is not that of Muhammad and the early caliphs, but of the women around them. The epistemology underpinning this domain is, moreover, polyvalent; events are not amenable to definitive readings. It is as if the social fact of polygamy, which engendered the conflictual relationship among rivals for Muhammad's succession, has as its implicit counterpart the proliferation of diverse meanings activated by the revelation of the Divine Word to humanity, except that the male desire that has produced polygamy when agency is in male hands has as its complement an equally omnivorous and polymorphous female desire thus far occulted from history, but now almost prophetically revealed by (female) *ijtihad*.

Two final points about *ijtihad* and Djebar's allusion to it need be made. First, reopening "the gate of *ijtihad*" (*bab al-ijtihad*) is fraught with potential contradiction, as Olivier Roy explains.

> In fact, the reopening of *ijtihad* devalues the corpus in so far as commentary upon it is no longer the primary task of he who knows and especially in so far as the corpus is only a point of departure, even a mere reference, always in danger of being transformed into rhetorical reverence, into proverb, epigraph and interpolation, in short into a pool of quotations. . . . The call for the reopening of *ijtihad* does not lead to innovation, but pastiche (Roy 1990, 272–73).

Roy's critique pertains to militant intellectuals and not necessarily to creative writers, but its concluding admonition should be pondered. To what extent, one might ask, is *Loin de Médine* a bricolage, a pastiche of bits and pieces of early Islamic history without any relevance to legitimate *ijtihad*?

Those who would think so, undoubtedly the majority of Islamic scholars—the majority of whom are, it goes without saying, male—have an easy response at hand. Unlike Fatima Mernissi's *Le Harem politique*, which must be answered and has been contested in terms of the rational *ijtihad* it engages, *Loin de Médine* dispenses with the apparatus of argumentation and turns the multiplicity of isnad into a source of creative inspiration. It is as if Djebar has converted a juridical procedure, say cross-examination, into a literary device, certainly not unheard of in the West, but tantamount to heresy if law and religion overlap, as they do in Islam. If, on the other hand, it were argued, as Djebar would, that all interpretation participates in ambiguity and has since the instant of revelation when humans began to fall away "irreversibly from the original light," then there is no absolute certainty of interpretation: *ijtihad* is finally and truly open, irreversibly decentered. It is crucial to observe, nonetheless, that the corpus Djebar is decentering resides on *this* side of the Qur'an, of which she in no way impugns the authority and whose words paradoxically play but a minor part in the novel, present only in and of themselves, not subject to the fracture and mosaic relativization of Hadith, isnad, and chronicle. Put another way, the words of God remain what they have always been within Islam, absolute and transcendental, unlike human language, which is relative and circumstantial.

Approaches to *ijtihad* within Sunni and Shi'a are dissimilar yet, as is often the case in the Maghreb, Assia Djebar's *ijtihad* seems to sit somewhere between the two camps, and does so in a complex manner. For example, some Shi'ite scholars question that the "Sunni tenth century alleged theory of the closure of the gates of *ijtihad*" was more than pure casuistry, a "façade hiding a more significant social issue" (Mallat 1993, 34), or worse, a nineteenth–century Western orientalist fabrication pawned off onto modern Muslim jurists (Mallat 1993, 202). Assia Djebar does share the spirit of social critique that is the heritage of Shi'ia, since she explicitly links the repression of women's truth(s) with the closure of *ijtihad* and the crystallization of patriarchal interpretation of the rights of women within Islamic society. Still, Djebar's very claim *as a woman* to the right of *ijtihad*, to say nothing of the intellectual consequences of her metafictionalization of Islamic foundations, make her as suspect from a Shi'ite as from a Sunni position. Beyond their differences, Shi'ia and Sunni remain dubious about free *ijtihad*, since the *mujtahid* (or interpreter) is allowed his freedom solely in terms of a prior submission either to consensual rationality or to higher figures of authority. Hence the pejorative connotations sometimes attached to *ijtihad*, apparent in Mervyn Hiskett's glossary entry for it: "individualistic interpretation of the Islamic scriptures"—as opposed to *taqlid*, "unquestioning obedience to established religious authority" (pp. 328-29). Whoever says "individualistic" is not far from saying "eccentric" and eventually "erroneous." Djebar's use of the principle of ijithad to condemn the patriarchs who have closed off feminist readings of the Hadith could be seen by the latter as confirmation of the inherent dangers of undisciplined *ijtihad*, the very incarnation of *fitna*—disorder, as noted above, but also in some contexts "female beauty."

Driss Chraïbi's *La Mère du printemps* is, like *Loin de Médine*, based on historical chronicles and engages with them dialogically, although less obviously so.

Chraïbi has described the genesis of his novel in anecdotal terms: Coming across an issue of the travel magazine *Geo*, he reacted strongly to the photo of a Moroccan girl on the banks of Oum-er-Bia (*La Mère du printemps*, the Mother of Spring), the river that empties into the Atlantic and on whose banks Chraïbi himself was born. Offended by the exoticization of the young Moroccan, he decided to extract her figment from the post-colonial media stereotype and revive her, as it were, at the moment Islam reached the shores of the Atlantic.[4] Riparian images thus dominate the novel, and culminate in the sequence where Azzaw's wife dies, and his son Yassin and daughter are carried away by the invading Muslims.

Two literary impulses blend in *La Mère du printemps*. The lyric manner is sustained throughout, and exemplified by the lute melody the Berber Naquishbendi plays to greet the Bedouin conqueror Uqba ibn

Nafi when he finally reaches the end of land, his horse striding into the surf (p. 185). Yet the novel also partakes of epic and many of its passages are drawn from Arabic chronicles, in particular the works of Ibn Khaldun and writers associated with him, such as the fourteenth century A.D. Egyptian encyclopedist En-Noweiri. By "epic" I do not mean the Bakhtinian denotation of the term, predicated as it is upon a closure of time and a refusal of dialogism, rather the loose sense of epic as a poem encompassing history. In fact, Chraïbi goes to great length to make readers conscious of the multiple and ever-evolving contexts for language, especially striking in his first chapter (the epilogue, he calls it) which takes place in the historical here and now and where Berber and Arabic, both glossed and free-standing, are sprinkled into the French. This heteroglossic bent is no less present in the main sections of the novel, called *marées* or tides. In fact, Chraïbi insures that his text remains not only interlinguistically but intersemiotically eclectic by inserting both a page of Qur'anic text in the original and three different melodies in musical transcription. Chraïbi's employ of historical chronicle is, however, more covert than Djebar's, who foregrounds her sources and comments authorially upon them. For the Moroccan, the subtle use of literary traditions in Arabic, a language unknown to the majority of his readers, suggests that the story of Azwaw Aït Yafelman, a pure fiction, is grounded in collective historical truth as far as such can be known, though like Fatima Mernissi, Chraïbi warns his readers: "this is not a history book, but a novel" (p. 11).

It turns out, however, that both the passage quoted several pages above on Uqba's destruction of Qayrawan and those dealing with Uqba's arrival on the Atlantic shores have close parallels in En-Noweiri's fourteenth century chronicle. Chraïbi's text reads:

> Uqba had given the order to empty the beach. Not a single human allowed, except for him. Very slowly within the silence of men and the symphony of the waves, *he entered into the sea until the waters rose to the brisket of his horse* [my emphasis]. . . . "Lord of all the earth, of the seas and all humans, I take Thee as my witness: this is the end of the earth, glory be to Thee! Your kingdom has become again what it was at the beginnings."[5]

En-Noweiri has:

> Having continued his march, he came to the surrounding sea without having run into resistence, and he *entered into the sea until the waters rose to the brisket of his horse* [my emphasis]. . . . He cried: "Lord, if this sea did not stop me, I would go in the far countries and to the kingdom of *Zul-Qarnein*, fighting for your religion, and killing those who do not believe in your existence, or who worship other gods than Thee."[6]

Chraïbi's possible omissions from the tradition are perhaps as telling as the apparent parallels between the texts, of no great substance in and of themselves, since the scene of Uqba's arrival at the Atlantic, like the snakes and vermin Uqba banished at Qayrawan, are part of the oral heritage of the Maghreb.[7] In fact the orientalist Paul Casanova, who appended En-Noweiri's account to Ibn Khaldun's *Histoire des Berbères*, considered it a mere *roman*, a novel, with a fabricated eyewitness and much embroidered invention (Casanova 1926, 313), which suggests how widely the images of Uqba ibn Nafi had been diffused in North Africa by the fourteenth century.

The Qur'anic sources of *La Mère du printemps* include Suras 36 (*Ya-Sin*, a co-name for Muhammad alluded to throughout the novel, since Azwaw's son is given this name), 91 (the ecstatic *Shams* or Sun sura quoted on pp. 21 and 146), and 96 (*Iqraa*, the first revelation to Muhammad containing Allah's imperative to recite, quoted directly on p. 145). It is accordingly curious, given Chraïbi's propensity for Qur'anic citation, that he did not seize upon the potential of En-Noweiri's allusion to the Qur'an, one that is admittedly invisible in translation but patent to readers of the Qur'an, since Zul-qarnain, cited by En-Noweiri above and associated with Uqba ibn Nafi, is the major figure of the last part of the "apocalyptic" Sura 18, regularly read on Fridays, and "all that Islam has in the way of weekly liturgy corresponding to the Christian Eucharist" (Brown 1991, 69).[8]

I do not mean to attribute monumental significance to an omission that may not have been deliberate or even possible if it turns out that Chraïbi was unfamiliar with the En-Noweiri source. What I would like to do is briefly explore the Qur'anic sub-text of traditional depiction of Uqba because the episode of Zul-qarnein's three missions in Sura 18 treats the relationship between the ideal Islamic conqueror and the peoples to whom he introduces the faith, and by implication the modalities of conversion and transculturation under Islam.

The parable of Zul-qarnein, sometimes identified with Alexander the Great, posits three types of cultures: the first, in the land of the setting sun, represents a kind of default situation in which the ruler simply delivers Islamic justice with no cultural interface, and rules with God's full delegation though a just governor, referring ultimate judgment of human behavior back to God: "Whoever doth wrong, him shall we punish; then shall he be sent back to his Lord; and He will punish him with a punishment unheard of" (Qur'an 18:87).[9] In the land of the rising sun, however, Zul-qarnein encounters a "people for whom We had provided no covering protection against the sun" (18:90). In his wisdom, Zul-Qarnein "left them as they were," God alone "understanding what was before him" (18:91), the implication being that the customs of "primitive" peoples need not be judged by the same standards as those of the civilized. In the words of Abdullah Yusuf Ali, Zul-Qarnein "left primitive peoples their freedom of life" (Ali 1946, 753). Finally, Zul-Qarnein came across "a people who scarcely understood a word" (18:93), but who sought his protection against the incursions of the wild tribes of the Gog and Magog. In this last case, the powers conferred upon Zul-qarnein enable this people, different in speech and customs from his own, to muster their technological skills and construct a wall of iron against savagery. Zul-Qarnein takes no credit himself; rather he directs his subjects' attention to the might of God, and to the fact that even walls of iron will crumble on judgment day. Traditional readings emphasize the text's eschatological tenor, yet the sociological paradigm implicit in this sura underlies Ibn Khaldun's political theory predicated on the distinction between *badawa* (primitivism) and *hadara* (civilization), and on the forms of *asabiyya* (group solidarity) particular to each (Rabi 1967, 48–55).

We might ask whether Uqba fits better in the first or third category of the paradigm provided by the parable of Zul-qarnein. His sense of justice was certainly unmediated by what we might today call crosscultural sensitivity. At first glance he therefore conforms to the first model, that of absolute ruler over a people of his own culture. Yet the fact that the Berbers were "a people who scarcely understood a word" (Qur'an 18:93) of Arabic would seem to put Zul-Qarnein in the third category. Moreover, as Chraïbi repeats on several occasions, the advent of Uqba and of Arab Islam meant the arrival of higher civilization, literacy, jurisprudence and poetry, architecture, engineering, and medicine. Civilization and technology, in Zul-Qarnein's words and even in the Bedouin Uqba's mind, are "a Mercy from my Lord" (Qur'an 18:98). Although the radicalism of Uqba's jihad implies that Islamic civilization is predicated on publicly professed faith in Islam, his care to inculcate higher forms of knowledge in the new society he was founding recalls Zul-Qarnein's third case, that in which superiority of material capacity plays a pragmatically persuasive role in Islamization. True conversion, according to Mahmud Shaltut's above argument, cannot be obtained by either "manifest" or "secret" compulsion, but proceeds from conviction, something like Assia Djebar's *djihad* or "inner struggle." But sincerity of creed in a transcultural setting is not always easy to ascertain, as Chraïbi demonstrates first in the penultimate chapter with the pivotal scene of the encounter between the vanquished Berber chieftain Azwaw Aït Yafelman and the Arab conqueror Uqba ibn Nafi, and then in the final chapter with Azwaw's fully Islamic betrayal of the man who converted him.

The showdown between Azwaw and Uqba is the third of three set piece dialogues in the novel: the first is between Azwaw and Dada, the *sage-femme* who first helps him and then becomes his mortal enemy; the second between Azwaw and Azoulay, the Jewish seer who persuades the Berber to name his son Yassin, though with no explanation why. In relating the third and final staged dialogue, Chraïbi resorts to a narrative trick of some consequence because, unbeknownst to the reader at this point, the narrator, the muezzin Imam Filani, is none other than Azwaw himself thirty years later, now become deeply devout and renowned for his rousing calls to prayer (p. 203). Filani's account of the confrontation between Azwaw and Uqba is thus ironic, since he is in some sense a fusion of both characters: a former non-believer transformed by jihad and conversion as well as a true believer active in the Islamization of the Maghreb. The dialogue Filani records is thus between two inner voices long since confounded, so much so that Uqba speaks Berber, at least in Azwaw's memory. Seconds later, though, as Azwaw had planned and practiced for over two years, he breaks out into the Arabic of the Qur'an: "*Ya-Sin. Wal Qo'rani al-hakim!* Yes, thou [by implication Uqba] art indeed one of the true apostles" (Chraïbi 1982, 203; Qur'an 36:2–3). This purported oath of allegiance provokes the following revealing exchange:

> "Ha!" approved Uqba, who was still laughing. "So you have religion?" "Yes" replied Azwaw, sincere in his lie. "I am a Muslim like you. That is why my people did not take up arms against you." "Ha!" repeated Uqba with vigor. "How can that be? When did you become Muslim? Explain. And also: was it by chance you converted just before I arrived?" "No. I reflected at length, for months, maybe even years," Azwaw replied, "And I subsequently came to the religion of God." "Subsequently? As if dragged by wild horses? And all by yourself? Ha!" If anyone heard the laugh of Uqba ibn Nafi on that day, it was myself, Imam Filani [then Azwaw]. A full-throated laugh, radiant as the sun whose light was spilling down upon us. "You see," said the Emir, "I know all winds, just as I know all there is to know about men. . . . You are not a Muslim. You are *not* a Muslim! But you will be, thanks to me! And your people will be Muslims too, thanks to you."[10]

Emir Uqba's interrogation touches upon two essential points of doctrine. He realizes that Azwaw's conversion must be factitious. As he says: "One does not use a word, not the least, from God's Book as an item of trade, politics or exchange, as you have just done before me. I ought to have you killed" (p. 205). The Qur'an must remain monological, as it were, its meaning free from the mesh of human motives. At the same time, as Uqba also knows, one can no more convert in isolation than a camel can pass through the eye of a needle. One cannot learn, should in fact not even study the

Qur'an alone, but do so with a spiritual leader or guide who will convey the intricacies of the text and its sense as understood by the community of believers. As Fischer and Abedi put it:

> [According to Qur'an 2:1–6] the Qur'an is not self-explanatory, one cannot just read it and be guided. . . . One needs guidance so as not to be misled. Such guidance comes in various dialogic forms: in the teacher-student, Imam-follower, or student-student debating of dialectical argument-counterargument to clarify the basis for decision making. *One may not study alone, with the text alone* (pp. 111–12, my emphasis).

Hence Uqba's skepticism: *All by yourself? Ha!*

The paradox is compelling: conversion, the outcome of dramatic inner struggle, is dialogical. There can be no transformation of the self without an other. Nor can a society renew itself without contact with another, a principle implied in Sura 49: *[We] made you into nations and tribes that ye may know each other (not that ye may despise each other).*

As the interview cited above shows, Chraïbi's concern in *La Mère du printemps* was the birth of the Islamic Maghrebian civilization that arose, symbolically, from Azwaw's conversion. Uqba's jihad was based on physical force, but insofar as the conquest also transformed the material and intellectual life of the Maghreb, it worked "perceptible miracles," forms of secret compulsion (Shaltut in Peters 1977, 38). Islam, in Azwaw's mind, was "the key to the new era" (p. 57). Conversely, as Azwaw perceived, converting to the invader's religion was "the ultimate weapon" (p. 208) against jihad: "We will enter into these new conquerors, inside their soul, into their Islam, their mores, their language" (p. 138). Chraïbi did not, however, portray Azwaw as an ironic victor over his conqueror Uqba. Azwaw's conversion was procured by means of a reciprocal yet diverse, that is, dialogical apperception of an utterance by a converter and a convertee. In the words of Emerson and Holquist in their translation of *The Dialogical Imagination*, "at any given time, in any given place, there will be a set of conditions—social, historical, meterological, physiological—that will insure that a word uttered in that place and at the time will have a meaning different than it would have under any other conditions" (Bakhtin 1981, 428). For Azwaw the first vocable of the Qur'anic passage he disingenuously recited before Uqba, *Ya-Sin*, was above all the name of his long–desired first son Yassin (Azwaw having "succeeded" where Muhammad did not). Yet *Ya* and *Sin* were, he had learned in his study of the Qur'an, the letters that inaugurate Sura 36 and comprise one mystic title for Muhammad. Invested with personal resonance for the Berber, the words were nonetheless from a foreign tongue to which he became an apprentice in order to carry out his strategy of preemptive conversion. At the same time *Ya-Sin* referred metonymically to his own conqueror and converter, a "descendant" of the Prophet.

Chraïbi does describe Azwaw's self-imposed study of Arabic and the Qur'an in decidedly dialogical terms:

> With the help of Boucchous who had resided in Qayrawan and with several "learned" refugees, he learned Arabic—or at least some. Also, and especially, he learned by memory and by ear whole suras from the Qur'an, among them the most dazzling. He could not distinguish between a letter and a tree. But he persisted, like a Berber, meditated, compared words between his and their language, their differences of meaning and their correspondences about earth and on humans.[11]

Here Chraïbi, cleverly, is alluding to Muhammad's own legendary illiteracy prior to revelation, but in so doing he also describes the foundations of Azwaw's mediated grasp of the word that would trigger his conversion.

As for Uqba, the vocable *Ya-Sin* had the standard meaning it did within the rapidly expanding Islamic interpretative community (a meaning of which Azwaw would have had only an approximation): *Ya-Sin* gives rise to *insan*, "man" or "human," but is here understood to mean "the Leader of man, the noblest of mankind, Muhammad the Prophet of God" (Ali 1946, 1169). Yet as Uqba revealed to Azwaw, *Ya-Sin* had personal import for the Bedouin, since it is the first word of the first sura this faithful disciple had learned in his youth, and was imbued, for himself, with exceptional charisma.

> "Wait! The first sura I memorized in my youth begins with those words: '*Ya-Sin! Wal Qo'rani al-hakim!*'"

> His voice broke. I, Imam Filani, was looking at him. Thirty years later, a whole lifetime afterwards, I still do not know how that breach opened up within me at that very moment, and how through it poured the intense emotion of that man.[12]

Azwaw's conversion to Islam transpired at that instant, and though he later goes on to betray Uqba by means of a call to prayer, his adhesion to the new society jihad was creating and to the ideological hegemony necessary to that society was galvanized at that flash of communion.

I find Douglas Robinson's words in *The Translator's Turn* useful to sort out the social and the emotional aspects of the conversion Chraïbi depicts:

> Ideological control is wielded, and collective meanings therefore shared, precisely through the mediation of the body—though the society's ideological . . . programming of each individual's limbic system, seat of the emotions, habit, and rote memorization. We learn shared meanings by learning the proper (ideologically controlled) feelings that drive them;

and we share them with other people through the empathetic power
that bodies have over other bodies, emotional states over other emotional states (p. 10).

This analysis, taken a step further, leads back to jihad, since ideological
control, authority over interpretation, over *ijtihad*, is what is at stake in
social struggle. The "power that bodies have over other bodies" is not
solely empathetic, though, and the empathetic power of conversion is
two-faced. Nor does the matter remain at this point, since the single
interchange between Azwaw and Uqba, as definitive as it might have
been for both individuals, is only one link in a much longer chain. Uqba
not only converts Azwaw, but turns him into a converter: *But you will
be [a Muslim] thanks to me! And your people will be [Muslims] too, thanks
to you!*

Still, Azwaw Aït Yafelman eventually betrays Uqba ibn Nafi. Attached
to Uqba's forces as muezzin, Azwaw seizes a strategic moment decades later
to warn the rebel Berber forces led by Kusayla: "I betrayed my Emir. I
informed Kusayla in the only manner I could: from on high of the mina-
ret, qur'anically. Uqba and his Bedouins perished in the gigantic ambush
that had been laid for them. The only survivors were my tribesmen, the Aït
Yafelman" (p. 212).[13] Azwaw's long range strategy thus bears fruit. His
Berber tribesmen survive, not the invading Bedouins. But they have become irreversibly Muslim.

For Chraïbi, I am arguing, jihad is dialogical. Much more than mere
self-defense (per Averroes and Mahmud Shaltut above), it is, rather, an active engagement with an ideological enemy before, during, and after defeat, to the point in fact that one becomes confounded with the enemy:
"The war is no longer between Berbers and Allah's warriors, but strangely
enough between each Muslim and himself" (p. 198). Jihad is more of an
environment than a self-contained action; it is an interaction of parry and
blow, strategy and tactics, dialogue and dialectic, hermeneutic and conversion. Even from a "radical fundamentalist" perspective jihad is "a movement that operate[s] in stages and takes time and effort as well as organization. [It] can take the form of writing, assisting others, teaching,
self-discipline, and many others" (Moussalli 1992, 208). For Azwaw, conversion was dictated by military forces on the ground, but it became a kind
of jihad itself, one rooted in the ambiguities and potential modalities of the
transculturation defeat brings, a new field of battle as much inner as outer.
The assertion that conversion is based on free choice would thus make as
little sense to Chraïbi as to radicals, whose critique of the limits of free
agency within an alien ideological hegemony echoes, incidentally, much
contemporary Western cultural criticism.

To return, by way of conclusion, to Fatima Mernissi and Assia Djebar, each of these authors struggles, albeit in different ways, to revise and reverse misogynistic traditions of interpretation of the early years of Islam that have been subverted by the patriarchy to its own ends. Both avail themselves of the tool of *ijtihad*, long denied not only women but all believers who are not accredited mujtahid. Mernissi has chosen to work within the conventions of the Hadith game, but Djebar's grasp of *ijtihad* verges on *différance*, the Derridean concept Fischer and Abedi have begun acclimatizing into Islamic dialogics, and which they define as occurring when "an attempt to freeze one meaning through an initial writing or context can be undone by reviving alternative meanings" (1990, 152). *Différance* would seem to be a facet of *ijtihad*—and of jihad as well.

The framework of both radical and moderate jihad has habitually been a monological one in which mediating cultural idioms have been accorded no weight. Chraïbi's vision of the birth of Arabo-Berber civilization in the Maghreb is, on the contrary, predicated upon the intuition that cultural difference cannot be simply "erased" but is folded and blended into new hegemonies in ways that their own agents may not realize. There is thus "constant interaction between meanings, all of which have the potential of conditioning others"—Emerson and Holquist's gloss for the condition of dialogism (Bakhtin 1981, 426).

To repeat Sura 49: "[We] made you into nations and tribes that ye may know each other (not that ye may despise each other)." Jihad and *ijtihad* each offer dialogical forms of the transcultural knowledge of which the Qur'an speaks.

Notes

1. Translations not otherwise attributed are mine throughout. For discussion of the concept of *ijtihad*, see Hiskett (1984, 328), Hourani (1991, 68, 160), Roy in Kepel and Richard (1990, 272–74, 283), Mallat (1993, 29–34), Moussalli (1992, 215), and Peters (1977, 2–5), as well as Djebar's own allusion to it, my point of departure (p. 6).

2. Seyyed Hossein Nasr, quoted in Norman O. Brown, "The Apocalypse of Islam" (1991, 90). Of note is that both Brown and the duo Fischer–Abedi repeatedly refer to Joyce's *Finnegan's Wake* when discussing Qur'anic interpretation.

3. Although Fischer and Abedi's study is written from a Shi'ite perspective, its observations about Qu'ranic exegesis in general are illuminating, and I am especially indebted to the chapters entitled "Qur'anic Dialogics"; "Fear of *Différance*," on the Hajj; and "Postscriptual Perergon," on Rushdie's *Satanic Verses*.

4. This is what Chraïbi claimed at a public conference on April 14, 1994, Faculté St.–Jean, University of Alberta, Edmonton, Canada.

5. Sur la plage, Oqba avait ordonné de faire place nette. Pas un humain, excepté lui. Très lentement, dans le silence des hommes et la symphonie des vagues, *il entra dans la mer jusqu'à ce que l'eau baignât le portrail de son cheval* [my emphasis]. . . . Seigneur de toute terre, de toute mer et des hommes, je Te prends à témoin: ceci est la fin de la terre, gloire à Toi! Ton règne est redevenu ce qu'il était à l'origine (Chraïbi 1982, 190).

6. This is the standard French translation: "Ayant continué sa marche, il vint jusqu'à la mer environnent, sans avoir éprouvé de résistence, et il *entra dans la mer jusqu'à ce que l'eau atteignît le portrail de son cheval.* [my emphasis]. Il s'écria: "Seigneur! si cette mer ne m'empêchait, j'irais dans les contrées éloignées et dans le royaume de *Dou–'l–Carnein*, en combattant pour ta religion, et en tuant ceux qui ne croient pas à ton existence ou qui adorent d'autres dieux que toi" (Casanova 1926, 333).

7. In conversation after the conference mentioned in Note 4, Chraïbi confirmed that he had used Arabic chronicles, but insisted the ones in question had not been translated, so there might still be a more direct source than the one I am proposing. The En–Noweiri text translated into French is an appendix of the 1926 edition of Ibn Khaldun's *Histoire des Berbères et des dynasties musulmanes de l'Afrique septentrionale* (Casanova 1926). The passages on the destruction of Qayrawan are on pp. 327–28.

8. The French translation of En–Noweiri has the following footnote for *Dou–'l–Carnein*: "Le roi Dou–'l–Carnein s'avança vers l'Occident jusqu'au lieu du coucher du soleil, et vit cet astre descendre dans un puit rempli de boue noire. Cette histoire authentique est racontée dans le Coran, sourate 18" (p. 333) ["The king Zulqarnein went as far west as the setting sun and saw this body sink into a well full of black mud. This authentic story is recounted in the Qur'an, Sura 18"]. In any event, the association between Uqba and Dou–'l–Carnein is extremely appropriate for reasons discussed immediately below.

9. I am following Abdullah Yusuf Ali's translation, a heavily annotated bilingual text provided by the Islamic Propagation Centre. I have slightly modified his typography.

10. Ha! approuva Oqba qui souriait toujours. Tu es de la religion? Oui, répondit Azwaw, sincère dans son mensonge. Je suis musulman comme toi. C'est pour cela que mon peuple n'a pas pris les armes contre toi. Ha! répéta l'émir avec force. Et comment cela? Quand l'es–tu devenu: Explique–moi. . . . Et dis–moi: c'est juste avant que je n'arrive que tu t'es converti à l'Islam? J'ai beaucoup réfléchi, des mois sinon des années [a dit Azwaw]. Et je suis entré dans la religion de Dieu par la suite. Par la suite? A la queue des chevaux? Tout seul? Ha! . . .
Si quelqu'un a entendu le rire d'Oqba ibn Nafi ce jour–là, ce fut moi, l'imam Filani. Un rire à gorge déployée, rayonnant comme le soleil qui nous baignait tous. Vois–tu, dit l'émir, je connais tous les vents comme je connais les hommes... Tu n'es *pas* musulman. . . . Tu n'es pas musulman! Mais tu le seras grâce à moi! Et ton peuple le sera lui aussi grâce à toi (Chraïbi 1982, 205).

11. Avec l'aide de Boucchous qui avait séjourné à Kairouan et de quelques réfugiés "savants", il a appris l'arabe—ou peu s'en faut. Appris également et surtout des sourates entières du Coran, parmi les plus éblouissantes, de vive voix. Il ne sait pas distinguer une lettre d'un arbre. Mais il a veillé avec sa tête

de Berbère, médité, comparé les mots, de sa langue à leur langue, leur différence de sens ou leurs correspondences en regard de la terre et des hommes (p. 174).

12. Attends! La première sourate que j'ai apprise dans mon enfance commence par ces mots: "*Yâ–Sin! Wal Qo'rani al–hakim!* . . . " Sa voix se brisa. [Moi, l'imam Filani,] je le regardais. Trente ans plus tard, toute une vie après, j'ignore encore comment une fêlure s'était faite en moi, juste à ce moment–là, par où entrait l'émotion intense de cet homme (p. 206).

13. This episode also has antecedents in the chronicles of Ibn Khaldun and En–Noweiri, in so far as tradition has it that Uqba ibn Nafi fell to the treachery of Kusayla (Kusaïla), a Berber chieftain whose conversion to Islam had wavered (Casanova 1926, 211–12, 334–36).

Chapter 2

▼▼▼▼▼▼▼

Dismantling the Maghreb: Contemporary Moroccan Writing and Islamic Discursivity

CHRISTOPHER GIBBINS

Despite the proliferation of politically discerning material within contemporary postcolonial criticism there remains, at least in the North American and European spheres, the lingering assumption that the Maghreb constitutes a *culturally* distinct and cohesive unit. When Winifred Woodhull, for example, writes that "to avoid isolating Maghrebian literature on a disciplinary continent of its own, I have undertaken the feminist analysis of a number of the most frequently discussed texts in Algerian literature in French" (Woodhull 1993, xxiv), the subtle conflation involved, in which a geographical part is made to speak for an assumed cultural whole, is typical of the critical field in general. Such a conflation is the inheritance of a critical tradition that situated Maghrebian writing within the context of European (and especially French) colonialism.[1] Primarily concerned with economic and political questions, European colonialists had little or no interest in the cultural complexities of the sites in question; the Maghreb, as a consequence, "became" a cultural unit. Such a perspective quietly violates the diversity of the sites in question and needs to be challenged if critical justice is to be done to the cultural plurality that exists within the area.

I would like to approach such a "dismantling" through a consideration of the work of three Moroccan writers—Abdelkebir Khatibi, Fatima Mernissi, and Tahar Ben Jelloun. My ambition is not to re—entrench their work within a narrowly nationalist framework (which would be equally limiting and arbitrary), but rather, to attempt to indicate the complexity and diversity of expression that arises within a rela-

23

▼

tively localized context. I would also like to address an apparent lacuna within the critical field (a product, it seems to me, of that same colonial heritage): the rich Islamic textual traditions that permeate, in diverse ways, the writings of these three writers. So much emphasis is placed upon their francophone relations that those of their more immediate and local context are simply not seen. An Islamic tradition is most explicitly at work in the writings of Mernissi who summons forth the textual struggles of the *Mu'tazila*, for example; but it is equally present, albeit in different forms, in the works of Khatibi and Ben Jelloun, who draw upon the spiritual and ontological aspects of Arabic calligraphy in the first instance, and on the dialogical nature of Islamic exegesis in the second. Such an emphasis on my part does not seek to replace one cultural construct with another: I have no desire to "reduce" these writings to an essential Islamic quality. I do, however, hope to displace these texts from their "traditional" Maghrebian readings by illustrating the diversity of their writings, their "Islamic" component which functions outside of a colonized francophone discourse, and finally, the manner in which these writings, through their incorporation of and engagement with such Islamic discursive components as *mutashabih* [allegorical or figurative] as opposed to *muhkam* [clear in thought] understandings, themselves resist closed and unified significations.

Abdelkebir Khatibi: Calligraphic Poststructuralist

On the first page of his first novel, *La Mémoire tatouée* (1971), Khatibi introduces what will remain a key thematic preoccupation in his work: the complex intertwining of language, identity, and religious discourse:

> Born on Aïd el Kebir day, my name recalls a millennial rite and it happens, on occasion, that I picture Abraham in the act of slitting his son's throat. Regardless, even if I am not obsessed by the song of the slaughter, there remains at the root the nominal rupture; from the maternal bow to my conscious will, time remains fascinated by childhood, as though writing, by placing me in the world, repeated the shock of my initial flight in the fold of my obscure divided self. Regardless, I have a soul open to eternity (Khatibi 1971, 9).[2]

It is in Khatibi's wonderful study of Arabic calligraphy—*The Splendour of Islamic Calligraphy* (co–written with Mohammed Sijelmassi 1976)—however, that we find the most succinct articulation of this thematic nexus. It is perhaps the key text, therefore, to our understanding of the rich interplay in Khatibi's work between Islam, which is never critically acknowledged, and European poststructuralism, to which his writing is almost always aligned.

For Khatibi, Arabic calligraphy is far more than a decorative rendering of language: "Among people without a calligraphic tradition, beautiful handwriting can of course be found anywhere—in a private letter, for instance. But this comes from an expression of feeling not rooted in a general knowledge and technique of calligraphy. It remains an individual impulse within the totality of a culture" (Khatibi 1976, 22). For him, calligraphy means "an art which, in the pattern which it creates, implies a theory of language and of writing" (p. 20). He later adds that calligraphy denotes "an all–embracing cultural manifestation which, at its extreme and sometimes confused limits, structures the metaphysic of regular language" (p. 22). Calligraphy, in other words, is both form and content, signifier and signified, and therefore contains within itself a whole order of signification, one that embraces and encloses the self and the divine, intellect and inspiration. As Khatibi explains: "Excluded from a figural treatment of the divine or human countenance, [the Muslim artist] must return to the source of existence in writing, the fundamental theory which asserts that everything must pass through the sacred text and return to it again: the sacred text and the central principle" (p. 228).

Although Khatibi is here simply articulating for the reader the traditional sacred dimensions of Arabic calligraphy, I would suggest that the paradigm in place within this Islamic textual discourse is Khatibi's also, and fundamentally shapes the manner in which he conceives of the relationships between language and writing, and language and identity. Furthermore, it is a paradigm that he brings to French poststructuralism; contrary to the all–too–frequent insinuation that Khatibi's work has been "tainted," or polluted by French poststructuralist doctrines, it is French poststructuralist thought that has been "tainted" by an Islamic discourse in Khatibi's writings. Suggesting that Khatibi's construction of identity through language is derived from his contact with European philosophy (be it Heidegger, Wittgenstein, Derrida, or others) erases the rich Islamic cultural and theological milieu in which he was raised, and to which, I might add, he draws our explicit attention in *La Mémoire tatouée.*

The link between Khatibi's linguistic preoccupation and Islamic textual discursivity is reinforced when one reads that he is interested in exploring "the course of development of the letter, the written character, as it tends towards the hidden aspect of Allah"—or one might add, "towards the hidden aspect of self"—which Khatibi suggests lies at the heart of the nature of "the divine image of art in Islam" (Khatibi 1976, 11). When he later writes that the "absolute aim of art is, specifically, to endow with soul—a wandering soul, which reveals itself in the field of existence only to show the impossibility of a sojourn there" (p. 192), it becomes clear that he is no longer explicating a Muslim calligrapher's understanding of his world. Inspired by Islamic calligraphic reflections upon the relationship between language, aesthetics, and the divine (identity), Khatibi is actually expressing his deep affinity with these Islamic "principles."

I am not suggesting that Khatibi's work is to be understood as primarily religious, but, although he is seen by many as being first and foremost a poststructuralist thinker, it was his immersion in an Islamic textual heritage that prompted his exploration of poststructuralist linguistics, for he found there a continuation of an intellectual tradition that extended well over one thousand years into his own Islamic past. Khatibi is a poststructuralist calligrapher whose work reflects his view that in Islam, "writing is an absolute, *the* Absolute, the *Sanctum Sanctorum*" (Khatibi 1976, 35, emphasis in original).

Khatibi's preoccupation with language is shared by Fatima Mernissi, but, whereas he has "inherited" (so to speak) that aspect of Islamic thought that has focused primarily upon the signifier—"calligraphy . . . examines the nature of the language in which it resides," writes Khatibi (p. 20)— Mernissi's work is concerned with that which is signified; her writing is one that is deeply informed by Islam's dialogical tradition of interpretation.

Fatima Mernissi's Dialogical "Hadith Game"

Consistently confronted by the seemingly unanswerable hadith—"Those who entrust their affairs to a woman will never know prosperity"—every time she, or any one else, dared suggest that women had the right to participate in the affairs of state as full and equal citizens, Fatima Mernissi soon realized she had no choice but to fight fire with textual fire. Whether the hadith was recited by her local grocer or a fellow scholar, it was clear that the intention was always the same—to silence her. She asks, "what could I have said to counterbalance the force of that political aphorism, which is as implacable as it is popular?" (Mernissi 1991, 1). For Mernissi, as it is for millions of women throughout the Arab world, such systemic exclusion of women from the social and political processes is not simply unacceptable, but constitutes a betrayal of Islamic faith:[3] "if women's rights are a problem for some modern Muslim men, it is neither because of the Qur'an nor the Prophet, nor the Islamic tradition, but simply because those rights conflict with the interests of a male elite" (p. ix). Hence her decision to embark upon a study "of the religious texts that everybody knows but no one really probes, with the exception of the authorities on the subject: the mullahs and imams" (p. 2), for it is increasingly the case that they who control the texts, control the social and political agendas.

The scope of such an inquiry is enough to intimidate all but the most determined. Mernissi's textual excavation included (but was not limited to) the thirteen volumes of al–Tabari's *Tarikh* [*History*], the thirty volumes of his *Tafsir* (commentary on or explication of the Qur'an), and the Hadith collections of al–Bukhari and al–Nasi'i. It is in the work of al–Bukhari (194–256/810–870)[4] that the "implacable" hadith—"Those who entrust their affairs to a woman will never know prosperity"—is to be found. According to al–Bukhari—whose work is so highly esteemed that the mere presence of the hadith within his work makes it "*a priori* considered true and therefore unassailable without proof to the contrary"—it was Abu Bakra, one of the Prophet's closest Companions, who reportedly heard the Prophet pronounce the hadith upon learning that "the Persians had named a woman to rule them" (Mernissi 1991, 49). Summoning forth the rigorously scientific methodology of hadith collection and verification that insists that "the believing reader has the right to have all the pertinent information about the source of the Hadith and the chain of its transmitters, so that he or she can continually judge whether they are worthy of credence or not" (p. 35), and undaunted by the stature and authority of al–Bukhari's work, Mernissi asserts her right, as a Muslim woman, to ask: "Who uttered this Hadith, where, when, why, and to whom?" (p. 49). The tradition Mernissi is calling forth with such a statement is a dialogical one that is explored in great and fascinating detail in a book entitled *Debating Muslims* (1990) written by Michael Fischer and Mehdi Abedi. In their introduction to the chapter "Qur'anic Dialogics" they write that

> three sorts of dialogue are central to the reading of the Qur'an: dialogue in the colloquial sense of oral communication between two face–to–face persons; dialogue in the Greek etymological sense of cross–play between arguments; and dialogue in the sense of juxtaposition of points of view in a political struggle for hegemonic control of interpretation of how the world should be seen (be it, today, between fundamentalist Islam and liberal Islam, or between Islamic nationalisms and cosmopolitan secularism) (Fischer and Abedi 1990, 97).

Somewhat later, in a section that specifically explores "The Hadith Game," they write that

> the Qur'an intends to *provoke thought*, not lay everything out for passive reception . . .
>   Where this leads, of course, is to (a) the ultimate unknowability of much of the Qur'an, and thus to (b) an openness of interpretation that requires (c) moral struggle, as well as (d) access to the disciplines and traditions of interpreting the Qur'an. Four important guides are available: (1) the disciplines for laying bare the plain meaning of the Qur'an

(including most importantly the identification of which verses abrogate other ones, the historical circumstances of revelation, and grammatical analysis); (2) interpretive means of *tafsir* and *taw'il* (exegesis, prolepsis) and dialectical disputation (*bahth*); (3) "those firmly grounded in knowledge"[5] (*rasikhun fi al-'ilm*); (4) and the politics of the hadith game also played through dialectical disputation with *taw'il* and grammatical analysis (p. 115, emphasis added).

Firmly entrenched within this Islamic dialogical and exegetical practice, Mernissi's inquiry into the origins of that "implacable" hadith leads her to conclude that: (1) Abu Bakra must have had a phenomenal memory for he recalled the hadith in question twenty–five years after the Prophet's death; (2) the hadith in question was recalled at a very politically sensitive time for Abu Bakra, that is, after the "Battle of the Camel" in which 'A'isha, the Prophet's wife, was defeated in her challenge to the right of the Caliph 'Ali to rule, during which Abu Bakra had not taken sides and therefore needed to carefully dissociate himself from 'A'isha's actions; and (3) that according to the tradition established for hadith verification, Abu Bakra should not be accepted as a "good, well–informed" Muslim, for it is recorded that he provided false testimony in a trial that came before the second Caliph, 'Umar (Mernissi 1991, 49–61). What's more, Mernissi points out that the hadith, although admitted by al–Bukhari into his collection of "authentic" hadiths, "was hotly contested and debated by many" (p. 61) both before and after its inclusion.

More significant, in the context of this essay, than Mernissi's findings (which are striking enough for they undermine this most famous, and, for women, most paralyzing, of hadith), is her insistence upon her absolute right to challenge the hadith, and, in so doing, her alignment with Islam's rationalist dialogical tradition—"Islam was, at least during its first centuries, the religion of reasoning, responsible individuals capable of telling what was true from what was false," she argues (Mernissi 1991, 35).

It is also true, unfortunately, that the interpretation and the manipulation of the hadiths and of the Qur'an were, from the very beginning, intensely political matters. Indeed, the very need for the hadiths to be collected, and verified, rose out of the political turmoil following Muhammad's death and the drifting of the new Muslim community towards a civil war as opposing camps struggled for the right of succession. Mernissi credits the astonishingly rapid rise of false hadiths to this political instability, for those either in, or seeking power quickly understood the need for, and the obvious advantage of, being able to turn to a hadith that would confirm the "correctness" of their actions and the appropriateness of their rule. Al–Bukhari, who carried out the first comprehensive compilation of hadiths, accumulated over 600,000! After having examined them all according the established procedures of verification, he concluded that only 7,275 were authentic (Mernissi 1991, 44). Mernissi is forced to conclude that "since all power, from the seventh century [C.E.] on, was only legitimated by religion, political forces and economic interests pushed for the fabrication of false traditions" (p. 9). As disturbing as such a statement may be, even more troubling is her observation that "not only have the sacred texts always been manipulated, but manipulation of them is a structural characteristic of the practice of power in Muslim societies" (pp. 8–9). That practice of power has necessarily involved the suppression of the rationalist tradition so dear to Mernissi, a tradition that insists upon the rights of individual thought and tolerance towards individual interpretation.

In a chapter entitled "Fear of the Imam" in her work, *Islam and Democracy* (1992),[6] Mernissi insists that the defenders of a rationalist philosophy within Islam "appeared on the scene very early [in Islamic history] and continued . . . to be active throughout Muslim history" (Mernissi 1992, 33). The *Mu'tazila*, as these early Islamic rationalists were called, included "not only philosophers, mathematicians, engineers, doctors and astronomers, but also Sufis, who found in religious texts everything they needed to bolster the idea of the thinking, responsible individual" (p. 34). A classic example of such a mystical thinker is al–Hallaj (244–309/857–922) who insisted that "each person reflected divine beauty and as a result was necessarily sovereign" (p. 20). Such teachings obviously undermined the authority of both imam and caliph who, if such teachings were believed, would no longer be able to claim greater proximity to divine truth. The *Mu'tazila's* brief period of direct political influence—their thinking played a part in the fall of the Umayyad empire (41–132/661–750) and the rise of the Abbasids (132–656/750–1258)—quickly dissolved, however, for the Abbasids, in turn, came to insist upon absolute rule. Seeking to undermine the *Mu'tazila's* influence, the Abbasid rulers condemned "private initiative . . . as a 'foreign'[7] enterprise" and cultivated an alternative tradition based on *ta'a* (obedience), which banned reflection (p. 37). The fruit of that tradition can be heard today in the fundamentalist's insistence that "all calls for a rational relationship between the imam and his followers as well as any criticism of the leader [be] discredited as a rejection of Islam and a lack of respect for its principles and ideals" (p. 37). This opposition to all that is "foreign" is the object of inquiry in *Islam and Democracy*, and Mernissi comes to the startling conclusion that the "Orient is seized by terror, not because the Occident is different, but because it reflects and exhibits the very part of the Orient that it is trying to hide from itself: individual responsibility" (p. 16).

It is clear that what is at stake is not simply political structures, social control, and individual rights, but more profoundly, personal identity. The underlying question in Mernissi's work is, in fact, who is to determine the construction of identity in Muslim societies—the clergy, the state, or the individual. What is fascinating in Mernissi's work is the realization of how profoundly textual the construction of that identity is, regardless of its author. Mernissi's challenge to current political and religious structures, as radical as it is, is mobilized within a strong Islamic discursive tradition. Consider, for example, the following passage from *Islam and Democracy*:

> Two ways lay open to the Muslims [confronted with arbitrary rule]: the way of rebellion . . . which leads to violence and murder; and the way of *'aql*, glorifying reason . . . [and which] intellectualized the political scene. . . . In the modern Islamic world only the violent, rebellious way is being taken by those who loudly proclaim their wish to rule. The rationalist tradition is apparently not part of their Muslim heritage. That is why outlining it and thinking about it is so critical (Mernissi 1992, 32).

Paradoxically, it would seem that Mernissi's methodology is remarkably similar to that of a fundamentalist's. Where, he, the fundamentalist, turns towards one tradition, she calls upon another; where he draws upon certain hadiths and certain interpretations of the Qur'an, she counters with others. On the one hand, she seeks affirmation of her Muslim female identity within the sacred texts, but on the other, she insists upon the Muslim right to interpret those texts, on an individual basis—her Muslim identity, in other words, is both divinely decreed, *and* individually and humanly constructed. The difference is that Mernissi's work embraces the paradox as a source of spiritual and intellectual richness, one that lies at the heart of the Islamic dialogical discourse. For the fundamentalist, such a paradox can never be admitted for his theological tradition insists upon *mukham* only, as opposed to *mutashabih*, and seeks to impose his reading of the text as its "true" and indisputable meaning.

An identity such as that posited by Mernissi's dialogics, rooted as it is in the signified, may strike one as being rather more stable than Khatibi's more metaphysical struggle with the signifier itself. Nevertheless, it is as vulnerable to manipulation and distortion—as millions of Arab women know only too well—for interpretation is, as Mernissi is herself aware, a linguistic affair. A wonderful example of her awareness of the constant interplay between the "moral struggle" and the "grammatical analysis" alluded to by Fischer and Abedi appears in *The Veil and the Male Elite*. In the debate of the true meaning of the Qur'anic verse, "Give not unto the foolish [*al–sufaha*] (what is in) your (keeping of their) wealth, which Allah hath given you to maintain" (Sura 4, verse 5), the great Islamic scholar al–Tabari (225–310/839–923) sought to resolve the question linguistically. Under dispute was the interpretation of the word *al–sufaha*, the foolish, for there were those who insisted that the term included women and children, so as to exclude them from the laws of inheritance. Rather than (or, perhaps, unable to?) address the issue directly on principled grounds, al–Tabari argued that "*sufaha* only excludes those who have not achieved maturity in the sense of discernment, and . . . excluding women from inheritance is to introduce a specification by sex that does not exist in the Koranic text. . . . According to [al–Tabari]," Mernissi continues, "if Allah meant that women were foolish, he could have used the appropriate plural form" (Mernissi 1991, 128). Mernissi is incensed that "never at any time does al–Tabari take a stand on a principle" (p. 128), but admits that "it remains to us as believers to find the best way to understand the word *sufaha*" (p. 127). Furthermore, she recognizes that "because of their wish to master their subjectivities, the *fuqaha* (religious scholars) were reduced to simply accumulating various cases and opinions concerning them. Since they gave to each person the right to have an opinion, the end result is a literature of juxtapositions of opinions" (p. 128). It is the consequences of the fundamentalist denial of this "juxtaposition of opinions" that Tahar Ben Jelloun so forcefully explores.

Sexual and Textual Plurality:
The Fictions of Tahar Ben Jelloun

Tahar Ben Jelloun's most popular novels—*L'Enfant de sable* (1985) [*The Sand Child* (1987a)] and its sequel *La Nuit sacrée* (1987b) [*The Sacred Night* (1989)]—are, at their most immediate level, poetic and brutal accounts of the repression of women within a fundamentalist Islamic context. There can be no doubt that it is fundamentalism that is at issue in these two novels: on the second page of *The Sand Child*, for example, the narrator comments that "the strident noise of the badly recorded call to prayer emitted five times a day from a loudspeaker is no longer a call to prayer, but an incitement to riot" (Ben Jelloun 1987a, 2);[8] in *The Sacred Night* the challenge is articulated far more explicitly: "I detest people who exploit [the Qur'an] like parasites and limit freedom of thought," states Zahra, the novel's protagonist, "They're hypocrites. . . . They invoke religion to crush and to dominate" (Ben Jelloun 1989, 73).[9] One must be careful not to confuse these passionate attacks upon fundamentalist "hypocrites" with a comprehensive assault upon Islam, however. On the contrary, I think that Ben Jelloun's novels express an almost desperate plea for the preservation of the Islamic dialogical tradition, the presence of which in his novels is often mistaken for postmodern literary techniques.

That Ben Jelloun's work is associated with contemporary postmodern writing is in part due to the narrative preoccupation with gender confusion. In *The Sand Child*, it is revealed that Muhammad Ahmed, son of Hajji Ahmed, was not, after twenty years of deceit, a man but was, in fact, a woman (Zahra). Tormented by "a religion which is pitiless for a man who has no heirs. It dispossesses him in favor of his brothers, while the daughters receive only one-third of the inheritance" (Ben Jelloun 1987a, 9–10),[10] Hajji Ahmed decided that his next child would be male, regardless. This simple conceit functions very simply, and very graphically, to highlight the social inequity between men and women in fundamentalist Islam. Ahmed's overwriting of Zahra's gender acts as a perfect metaphor of the consequences of those socioreligious forces that ultimately seek to deny the female gender altogether. As one of the characters says in *The Sand Child*, "there's such violence in our relationships that a crazy story about a man with a woman's body is a means of carrying that violence to its limit" (Ben Jelloun 1987a, 124).[11]

This "erasure," in itself an act of violence, acquires horrific proportions in *The Sacred Night* when Zahra's brutal and fanatical Muslim sisters (as she herself calls them) suddenly appear. In one breath they mobilize both the patriarchal and the fundamentalist discourses (illustrating, of course, that the two are inseparable) in their justification of the circumcision they have come to perform upon her. The patriarchal nature of their discourse is, I think, obvious:

> You were never our brother and you will never be our sister. We have expelled you from the family in the presence of men of religion and witnesses of good faith and high virtue. . . . You made us believe that you were a statue, a monument radiating light, bringing honor and pride to the house, whereas, in fact you were only a hole wrapped in a scrawny body, a hole just like mine and your six ex–sisters (Ben Jelloun, 1989, 150).[12]

The fundamentalist aspect is perhaps more explicit in a passage that follows shortly after:

> We're going to get rid of that sex you hid. Life will be simpler. No more desire. No more pleasure. You'll become a thing, a vegetable that will drool until you die. You can start praying. You can shout. No one will hear. Since your betrayal we have discovered the virtues of our beloved religion. Justice has become our passion, truth, our ideal and obsession, Islam our guide. We render to life that which belongs to it. And we prefer to act in love and family discretion. Now, in the name of God, the Merciful, the Compassionate, Just and All–Powerful, we open our little case (p. 151).[13]

Following the course of a perverse and twisted logic, Zahra's "Muslim sisters," on the one hand, seek to eliminate the "blasphemous" confusion Ahmed/Zahra's gender vacillation represents by insisting that his/her gender *must* be a singular one; on the other hand, that act of insistence—the clitoridectomy—is one that would actually erase that gender altogether: the female becomes that which must be cut away. This violent act is all the more (brutally) ironic when one realizes that it was the inheritance laws cultivated by a fundamentalist ethic—extensively discussed by Fatima Mernissi and identified by her as lying at the heart of gender discrimination within Islam for the laws fail to recognize women as proper and full human beings[14]—that gave rise to the "abomination" that is Ahmed/Zahra in the first place. At work within these seemingly contradictory impulses is a perceived double threat posed by Ahmed/Zahra: the first is the destabilizing of the rigid gender lines upon which any patriarchal structure is based; the second is a fear of difference and more specifically, the difference that is female sexuality within a patriarchal society. In the context of Ben Jelloun's two novels, the assault upon Zahra's sexuality must be seen not "only" as an attack upon her gender, but also upon a whole Islamic mystical tradition. Georges Bataille writes that "eroticism always entails a breaking down of established patterns, the patterns . . . of the regulated social order basic to our discontinuous mode of existence as defined and separate individuals" (Bataille 1962, 18). Furthermore he notes—and he is, of course, far from being alone in this assertion—that "there are staggering similarities and even corresponding or interchangeable characteristics in the two systems, erotic and mystical" (p. 226). Such a correspondence is, I believe, at play within Ben Jelloun's novels.

In *The Sand Child*, for example, a character observes: "So many books have been written about bodies, pleasures, perfumes, tenderness, the sweetness of love between man and woman in Islam— ancient books that nobody reads nowadays. Where has the spirit of that poetry gone?" (Ben Jelloun 1987a, 122).[15] A fascinating triangle is established in this passage in which bodies, Islam, and poetry are intertwined. Within such a configuration eroticism becomes an integral component of religious expression, a sentiment expressed by Zahra in *The Sacred Night*:

> No longer was I a creature whose skin was but a mask [says she of her love-making with the Consul], an illusion designed to deceive a shameless society based on hypocrisy and the myths of a twisted religion, an illusion devoid of spirit, a delusion fabricated by a father obsessed with shame. To be reborn and to live I needed to forget, to roam, to find grace distilled by love (Ben Jelloun, 1989, 128).[16]

Zahra's sexual "transgressions," therefore, are not to be seen as provocatively heretical behavior but rather as participation in a poetic and sensual mysticism repressed within orthodox Islam.

As both Bataille and Mernissi (in *Islam and Democracy*) suggest, such expressions of eroto–mysticism are threatening to an orthodox social order because they are rooted in individual experience. As Mernissi makes clear, such experiences, by definition, fall outside the control of religious and political rulers. Zahra unequivocally aligns herself with such individualistic expression: "I invoke the right of free thought, the right to believe or not to believe. It's nobody's business but my own" (Ben Jelloun 1989, 73),[17] she declares. A similar sentiment is expressed by the storyteller in *The Sand Child* when he responds to those who consider Ahmed's "distortion" of a line from the Qur'an as an heretical act: "if, at the moment when he undergoes a crisis, he takes some liberty with a line, a single line, we should be able to forgive him. Besides, we are not his judges. God will take care of that" (Ben Jelloun 1987a, 79).[18]

A famous example of such an intrinsic bond between individual expression and Islamic mysticism, already noted earlier, is al–Hallaj, who, you will recall, "insisted that the human being is the depository of *hagg*, 'truth,' and that each person reflects divine beauty and as a result is necessarily sovereign" (Mernissi 1992, 19–20). Not surprisingly, al–Hallaj is referred to in both *The Sand Child* and *The Sacred Night*. In the former he is invoked as one who incorporates an ideal of religious expression—"I wanted to say to them: The Islam that I carry inside of me cannot be found; I am a man who has lived alone, and religion does not really interest me. But if I talked about Ibn Arabi or al-Hallaj, I would certainly have got myself into trouble" (Ben Jelloun 1987a, 112–113).[19] In *The Sacred Night* it is with Zahra, appropriately enough, with whom he is associated: "I have renounced the world," Zahra declares, "withdrawn from it in the mystical sense, rather like al–Hallaj" (Ben Jelloun 1989, 76).[20] Ahmed also writes of his passion for certain mystical poets (Ben Jelloun 1987a, 77), and Zahra refers to the Qur'an as an exquisite poem (Ben Jelloun 1989, 73). For Zahra, as for the mystics before her, the Qur'an is above all a poetic text to be negotiated and interpreted on an individual basis. Obviously, such an approach rejects the definitive readings fundamentalist imams insist upon (that is, *their* readings), but rather calls for a dialogical relationship with the text.

Furthermore, Ben Jelloun's playful manipulation of gender through the character of Ahmed/Zahra becomes a textual embodiment of Fischer and Abedi's assertion that the entire structure of Qur'an and hadith is a fun house of mirrors *playing upon appearances and resemblances (mutashabih)* that may or may not be grounded *(mukham)*, depending upon the perspective and knowledge of the interpreter, [and that] it is a structure necessitating a critical sense, but one ambivalently also permissive of uncritical belief and false leads (Fischer and Abedi 1990, 100; emphasis added).

As the Consul says to Zahra upon learning the secret of her past: "it recalls our mystical poets, for whom appearance was the most perverse mask of truth" (Ben Jelloun 1989, 125).[21] Indeed, the novels coyly suggest parallels between the storyteller and Muhammad, the storyteller's story and the Qur'an. In *The Sand Child*, the storyteller says: "My stories come to me, inhabit me, and transform me. I need to get them out of my body in order to make room for new stories. I need you. I make you part of my undertaking. I carry you on my back and on the ship. Each stop will be used for silence and reflection. No prayers, but an immense faith" (Ben Jelloun 1987a, 8).[22] If the storyteller is associated with Muhammad, it follows that the story told is associated with the Qur'an. Such a textual parallel is indeed suggested:

> The storyteller, sitting on the mat, his legs crossed like a tailor's, took out a great notebook from a briefcase and showed it to his audience. The secret was there, in those pages, woven out of syllables and images. . . . I read the first sentence and understood nothing. I read the second paragraph and understood nothing. I read the whole of the first page and was illuminated (p. 5).[23]

What is merely hinted at in this passage is made explicit later in the novel: challenging the storyteller's telling, an audience member stands up and insists that

> The storyteller is pretending to read from a book that Ahmed is supposed to have left behind him. That is untrue! Of course the book exists, but it is not that old notebook, yellowed by the sun, which our storyteller has covered with that dirty scarf. Anyway, it isn't a notebook, but a cheap edition of the Koran. It's very peculiar—he looks at the verses and reads the diary of a madman, a victim of his own illusions (p. 49).[24]

Ben Jelloun's novels, in other words, are profoundly informed by the Qur'an's dialogical discourse and it is that dialogical tradition, and the threat that fundamentalism poses to it, that *The Sand Child* and *The Sacred Night* are textually engaged with. Ben Jelloun's novels incorporate and replicate the "fun house of mirrors" that is the Qur'anic exegetical tradition within the very fabric of their narratives; each novel becomes a mise–en–abyme of the Qur'anic dialogical process—a metadialogue. Hence the many challenges to the storyteller's discursive authority and the presence of so many voices within the novels battling to be heard. Such plurivocality is to be found, for example, in Chapter Four of *The Sand Child*, "The Saturday Gate," in which a number of "readers" challenge the veracity of the storyteller's, and of each others', tales: "The wind of rebellion blows among you!" the storyteller exclaims happily, "You are free to believe or not to believe this story. All I wanted was to kindle your interest" (Ben Jelloun 1987a, 28)[25]—echoing Fischer and Abedi's comments that "the Qur'an intends to provoke thought." Elsewhere, the storyteller is challenged by "a tall thin man" who tells the gathered crowd that the storyteller's tale is actually his own and that the storyteller is not telling his audience all there is to really tell (Ben Jelloun 1987a, 47). And towards the end of the novel, the storyteller's voice disappears altogether as three additional characters—Salem, Amar, and Fatuma—each offer their versions of how Ahmed/Zahra's story comes to an end. What is at issue, of course, is the intrinsically ambiguous and shifting nature of "truth"; each voice insists that her, or his, story is the true one, and each voice is allowed to challenge and to speak. As the Consul says, "nothing is ever completely clear or completely obscure. The way I see it, everything is complex, and the truth is closer to the shadow than to the tree that casts the shadow. . . . You know from your own experience [Zahra] that clarity is a delusion. How can anything be clear and definable in the relations between two people?" (Ben Jelloun 1989, 124–25).[26] Or, one might add, between two texts, two genders, and two cultures.

Conclusion

Less concerned with the consequences of European colonialism upon Morocco than they are with their more immediate and more local Islamic cultures, the writings of Khatibi, Mernissi, and Ben Jelloun challenge the latent colonial supposition that the Maghreb is a cultural unit, but they do so in an unexpected manner. Not only does their work sidestep the question of cultural unity derived from a shared colonial experience, but it embraces, insists upon, and draws extensively from, an Islamic discursivity that is plural and, from a fundamentalist's viewpoint, "impure." Each in their own way undermines any notion of an "authentic" Islamic culture. As Khatibi says, "bilingualism and plurilingualism are not, in these regions, recent events. The maghrebian linguistic landscape is still plurilingual: diglossic (between Arabic and dialects), Berber, French [and] Spanish in northern and southern Morocco" (Khatibi 1983, 179).[27] For all three writers it is precisely the plurality and diversity of Islam that is enriching, as suggested by the Consul in the above quote.

In *The Splendour of Islamic Calligraphy* Khatibi writes:

> Muslim art obviously did not rise up, whole and entire, in some miraculous transmutation. A survey of its full extent reveals metaphysical and cultural influences which are necessarily diverse and numerous. Islamic art is by no means centred upon Mecca, nor on Timbuctoo; it presents a varied landscape, without any precise centre. . . . Each culture has its own particular joys, displacing the other on the ground of its difference. Creativity flourishes when the seeds are scattered far and wide (Khatibi 1976, 226).

Just as, one might add, local Moroccan cultures were displaced by the colonizing Islamic Arab army, they too, in their turn influenced the Islam brought to them, transforming it—whether it be, most notably, through Berber or Andalusian traditions—into something new and even more diverse. Fatima Mernissi points out that the *Mu'tazila* drew upon ancient Greek, Persian, and Indian philosophies and sciences and "enriched by original scholarship, produced the flowering of Muslim thought" (Mernissi 1992, 36). The philosophical musings of Khatibi, the fictions of Ben Jelloun, and the dialogical nature of Mernissi's polemics are all embodiments of that diversity and it is through the celebration of such plurality that they "dismantle" the idea of *a* Moroccan, let alone *a* Maghrebian, Islamic culture.

Notes

1. For example: "this territory, i.e., North Africa, has been the object of consecutive waves of linguistic, economic, religious and political domination, the last of which has been the French colonial presence" (Mehrez 1990, 106). Abdallah Laroui challenges this kind of essentialising when he writes that "we must distinguish a long period during which the Maghrib is a pure object and can be seen only through the eyes of its foreign conquerors. When narrated directly and uncritically, the history of this period ceases to be anything more than a history of foreigners on African soil" (Laroui 1977, 10).

2. "Né le jour de l'Aïd el Kébir, mon nom suggère un rite millénaire et il m'arrive, à l'occasion, d'imaginer le geste d'Abraham égorgeant son fils. Rien à faire, même si ne m'obsède pas le chant de l'égorgement, il y a, à la racine, la déchirure nominale; de l'archet maternel à mon vouloir, le temps reste fasciné par l'enfance, comme si l'écriture, en me donnant au monde, recommençait le choc de mon élan, au pli d'un obscur dédoublement. Rien à faire, j'ai l'âme facile à l'éternité" (Khatibi 1971, 9).

3. A point, I might add, consistently overlooked in the many commentaries upon Mernissi's work which, more often than not, understand her within an exclusively Western feminist framework.

4. All dates have been recorded in the following manner: A.H./C.E., i.e., Anno Hejira/Common Era.

5. They are here quoting Al-Raghib al-Isfahani, a twelfth-century exegete.

6. *Islam and Democracy* can be considered, in many respects, as a "sequel" to *The Veil and the Male Elite,* for the theological and historical foundations estab-

lished in the latter are extended in *Islam and Democracy* to address the issue of individual freedom.

7. Mernissi is referring to the fact that the *Mu'tazilites* embraced all knowledge, including Greek, Persian, and Indian philosophies, which they translated into Arabic.

8. "Le bruit strident de l'appel à la prière mal enregistré et qu'un haut-parleur émet cinq fois par jour. Ce n'était plus un appel à la prière mais une incitation à l'émeute" (Ben Jelloun 1985, 8).

9. "J'ai horreur de ceux qui exploitent [le Coran] en parasites et qui limitent la liberté de la pensée. Ce sont des hypocrites. . . . Ils invoquent la religion pour écraser et dominer" (Ben Jelloun 1987b, 79).

10. "Un religion [qui] est impitoyable pour l'homme sans héritier; elle le dépossède ou presque en faveur des frères. Quant aux filles, elles reçoivent seulement le tiers de l'héritage" (Ben Jelloun 1985, 18).

11. "Il y a une telle violence dans nos rapports qu'une histoire folle, comme celle de cet homme avec un corps de femme, est une façon de pousser cette violence très loin, à son extrême limite" (Ben Jelloun 1985, 160).

12. "Tu n'as jamais été notre frère et tu ne seras jamais notre sœur. Nous t'avons exclue de la famille en présence d'hommes de religion et de témoins de bonne foi et de haute vertu. . . . tu nous as fait croire que tu étais une statue, un monument donnant la lumière, ramenant l'honneur et la fierté dans la maison, alors que tu n'étais qu'un trou enveloppé d'un corps maigrichon, un trou identique au mien et à celui de tes six autres ex-sœurs" (Ben Jelloun 1987b, 158).

13. "On va te débarrasser de ce sexe que tu as caché. La vie sera plus simple. Plus de désir. Plus de plaisir. Tu deviendras une chose, un légume qui bavera jusqu'à la mort. Tu peux commencer ta prière. Tu pourras crier. Personne ne t'entendra. Depuis ta trahison nous avons découvert les vertus de notre religion bien-aimée. La justice est devenue notre passion. La vérité notre idéal et notre obsession. L'islam, notre guide. Nous rendrons à la vie ce qui lui appartient. Et puis nous préférons agir dans l'amour et la discrétion familiale. A présent, au nom de Dieu le Clément et le Miséricordieux, le Juste et le Très-Puissant, nous ouvrons la petite mallette" (Ben Jelloun 1987b, 159).

14. See in particular Chapter Seven, "The Prophet and Women," of *The Veil and the Male Elite* (1991).

15. "Tant de livres ont été écrits sur les corps, les plaisirs, les parfums, la tendresse, la douceur de l'amour entre homme et femme en Islam . . . , des livres anciens et que plus personne ne lit aujourd'hui. Où a disparu l'esprit de cette poésie?" (Ben Jelloun 1985, 158).

16. "Je n'étais plus cet être de vent dont toute la peau n'était qu'un masque, une illusion faite pour tromper une société sans vergogne, basée sur l'hypocrisie, les mythes d'une religion détournée, vidée de sa spiritualité, un leurre fabriqué par un père obsédé par la honte qu'agite l'entourage. Il m'avait fallu l'oubli, l'errance et la grâce distillée par l'amour, pour renaître et vivre" (Ben Jelloun 1987b, 138).

17. "J'invoque à présent le droit à la liberté de penser, de croire ou de ne pas croire. Cela ne regarde que ma conscience" (Ben Jelloun 1987b, 79).

18. "Si, au moment où il traverse une crise, il prend quelque liberté avec un verset, un seul verset, sachons le lui pardonner! Et puis nous ne sommes pas ses juges; Dieu s'en occupera" (Ben Jelloun 1985, 107).

19. "J'ai eu envie de leur dire: l'Islam que je porte en moi est introuvable, je suis un homme seul et la religion ne m'intéresse pas vraiment. Mais leur parler d'Ibn Arabi ou d'El Hallaj aurait pu me valoir des ennuis" (Ben Jelloun 1985, 146).

20. "Moi j'ai renoncé. Je suis une renoncée dans le sens mystique, un peu comme El Hallaj" (Ben Jelloun 1987b, 83).

21. "Cela nous ramène à nos poètes mystiques pour qui l'apparence était le masque le plus pervers de la vérité" (Ben Jelloun 1987b, 134).

22. "Ce sont les histoires qui viennent à moi, m'habitent et me transforment. J'ai besoin de les sortir de mon corps pour libérer des cases trop chargées et recevoir de nouvelles histoires. J'ai besoin de vous. Je vous associe à mon entreprise. Je vous embarque sur le dos et le navire. Chaque arrêt sera utilisé pour le silence et la réflexion. Pas de prières, mais une foi immense" (Ben Jelloun 1985, 16).

23. "Le conteur assis sur la natte, les jambes pliées en tailleur, sortit d'un cartable un grand cahier et le montra à l'assistance. Le secret est là, dans ces pages, tissé par des syllabes et des images. . . . J'ai lu la première phrase et je n'ai rien compris. J'ai lu le deuxième paragraphe et je n'ai rien compris. J'ai lu toute la première page et je fus illuminé" (Ben Jelloun 1985, 12).

24. "Notre conteur prétend lire dans un livre qu'Ahmed aurait laissé. Or, c'est faux! Ce livre, certes, existe. Ce n'est pas ce vieux cahier jauni par le soleil que notre conteur a couvert avec ce foulard sale. D'ailleurs ce n'est pas un cahier, mais une édition très bon marché du Coran. C'est curieux, il regardait les versets et lisait le journal d'un fou, victime de ses propres illusions" (Ben Jelloun 1985, 70).

25. "C'est le vent de la rébellion qui souffle! Vous êtes libres de croire ou de ne pas croire à cette histoire. Mais, en vous associant à ce récit, je voulais juste évaluer votre intérêt" (Ben Jelloun 1985, 43).

26. "Rien n'est vraiment clair, rien n'est absolument obscur. Je dirais que tout est complexe et que la vérité est plus proche de l'ombre que de l'arbre qui donne cette ombre. . . . Vous savez [Zahra], puisque vous l'avez vécu dans votre corps, que la clarté est un leurre. Qu'est-ce qu'il y a de clair, de définissable, dans les rapports entre deux êtres?" (Ben Jelloun 1987b, 133–34).

27. "Le bilinguisme et le plurilinguisme ne sont pas, dans ces régions, des faits récents. Le paysage linguistique maghrébin est encore plurilingue: diglossie (entre l'arabe et le dialectal), le berbère, le français, l'espagnol ar nord et au sud du Maroc" (Khatibi 1983, 179).

Chapter 3

▼▼▼▼▼▼▼▼

Women's Words:
Assia Djebar's Loin de Médine

PATRICIA GEESEY

> *Woman must put herself into the text—as into the world and into history—by her own movement.*
>
> Hélène Cixous

Born in the coastal city of Cherchell in 1936, Assia Djebar is Algeria's most renowned and prolific woman novelist and film-maker. Her literary career began in 1957 with the publication of *La Soif;* three more novels followed and then, a ten-year period of near silence. Djebar returned to public life in 1977 with the production of her first film, *La Nouba des femmes du Mont Chenoua.* Her return to fictional narrative in 1980, with *Femmes d'Alger dans leur appartement,* heralded a change in the thematic and stylistic nature of her writing. Clarisse Zimra quite rightly observes that the key to understanding the significance of the hiatus in Djebar's trajectory lies in the work that signaled her return to writing (1992, 69). *Femmes d'Alger dans leur appartement* is a collection of short stories, followed by a meditation on Eugène Delacroix's painting of the same name. The story that shares the volume's title clearly presents a thematic turning point in Djebar's work. The new concern is with women's words and women's voices: the aural manifestation of a feminine solidarity. As a character in "Femmes d'Alger dans leur appartement" observes:

> I see only one way for Arab women to release everything: to speak, to speak without stopping about yesterday and today, to speak among ourselves, in all the gynecia, the traditional ones and those of the housing projects. To speak among ourselves and to look. Look outside, look out from the walls and the prisons! The woman-gaze and the woman-voice. . . . The voice that searches in the open tombs! (p. 68).[1]

This passage sets the tone for Djebar's subsequent narratives in which women speak out not only as individuals, but also blend their voices to form a polyphonic chorus that will resist the pressure to return to what Djebar has elsewhere identified as a state of silence imposed by the heritage of cultural traditions and colonialism.

One of Djebar's most recent narrative works is *Loin de Médine* (1991), subtitled "Filles d'Ismaël." This novel marks a transition from her previous works as the primary concern is no longer women in contemporary Algeria, but rather women's lives in seventh-century Arabia—more specifically the women in the Prophet Muhammad's circle. Islam has never before been closely studied in Djebar's works. Indeed, even in *Loin de Médine*, the focus is not on the religion introduced by Muhammad at this historical moment; rather Djebar concentrates on depicting the experiences and relaying the testimonials of women who were in contact with the Prophet and his close followers. As Zimra points out, the work is not only a "meditation on history" (1992, 69), but a carefully orchestrated "re-reading" and "re-phrasing" of historical chronicles of the early years of Islam, written by men such as Tabari, Ibn Hisham, and Ibn Saad.

Djebar's objective in undertaking this re-reading may be linked to Adrienne Rich's comments on gendered reading in "When We Dead Awaken: Writing as Re-Vision," still a seminal essay on feminist interpretation: "Re-vision—the act of looking back, of seeing with fresh eyes, of entering an old text from a new critical direction—is for us more than a chapter in cultural history: it is an act of survival" (1972, 18). Djebar's goal in looking at these male-authored histories is to first uncover women's obscured presence and then highlight their voices in the construction of early Islamic historiography. Her narrative covers a two-year period, from the last days of the Prophet, through the first caliphate of Abu Bakr, ending with the installation of Umar as the second caliph (632–34 A.D.). The process of "re-vision" will enable her to perform an act of "resuscitation" and "exhumation." Both terms are key notions for Djebar: "In the course of the period evoked here, which begins with the death of Muhammad, multiple women's destinies have stood out for me: I have sought to resurrect them. . . (p. 5).[2]

In *Loin de Médine*, Djebar's project of re-reading highly regarded historical chronicles of the first centuries of Islam and then performing an interpretive act that elaborates on the glimpses of women's presence and women's words demonstrates a conscious manipulation of the discourses of both historiography and fictional narration. Given this technique, Djebar's text may be categorized as what Linda Hutcheon describes as "historiographic metafiction" in *A Poetics of Postmodernism* (1988). Hutcheon's work on historiographic metafiction underscores the "theoretical self-awareness of history and fiction as human constructs," thereby establishing a narrative framework for "rethinking and reworking the forms and contents of the past" (1988, 5).

Djebar's choice of quotes from historical chronicles as epigraphs to introduce the prologue, illustrates her awareness that her efforts to resurrect women's words from the first century of Islam links her narrative to an established historical tradition. As Anne Donadey suggests, Djebar's use of epigraphs has the purpose of legitimizing her text in relationship to the works existing prior to her own, while at the same time subverting that very relationship (1993, 109–110). In *Loin de Médine*, epigraphs are used only on two occasions; at the very beginning of the work, and once again to present the section dealing with the caliphate of Umar. To introduce the entire work, two epigraphs are cited. The first is from the Persian author Firdawsi's (c. 940–1020 A.D.) *Shah-nameh* [The Book of Kings]. Her choice of citation indicates that she is seeking to ground her own text in a tradition of epic and legendary narration that knowingly covers familiar territory: "All that I will say, all have already recounted; all have already covered the garden of knowledge" (p. 7).[3] The second epigraph is from the nineteenth-century French historian Jules Michelet: "And then there was a strange dialogue between him and myself, the one who revived him, and the old time put back on its feet" (p. 7).[4] The notion of a dialogue, particularly one that takes place among women, is crucial to Djebar's project in *Loin de Médine*. Dialogue is present as her characters—historically accurate as well as fictional ones—converse with each other, recounting events and conversations that have linked them to the Prophet's presence. As an example of historiographic metafictional narrative, *Loin de Médine* problematizes the notion of how the past has been transmitted in and through the earliest extant texts—oral and then written—of early Islam. The use of Michelet's suggestion that the historian resuscitates the past through narration, reveals the interpretative nature of historical discourse.

According to Hutcheon, "Postmodern fiction suggests that to re-write or to re-present the past in fiction and in history is, in both cases, to open it up to the present, to prevent it from being conclusive and teleological" (1988, 110). Djebar's re-reading of the early history of Islam provides an understanding of the role played by women and their discourses in the transmission of historical accounts during Islam's first century. *Loin de Médine* challenges the reader to reconsider the notions of fact and fiction, as well as oral and written transmission of women's words. Djebar notifies the reader in the preface that fiction will be the material used to fill "the gaps of collective memory" (p. 5). The objective of this essay is to analyze the blurring of boundaries between historical fact and fictional creation, and to assess her use of women's voices to accomplish this reconstitution. The key to Djebar's project lies in her technique of mixing fictional with historical narrative, and in her insistence on the role of oral transmission in the early years of Islam.

In the *avant-propos*, Djebar observes that the voices of several *rawiyates* (sing. *rawiya*) interject their commentaries into the reconstitution of the period she examines. The *rawiyates* are female transmitters of statements made by Muhammad and his companions. Their testimonies appear as threads in the tapestry of women's presence and women's words that the author weaves in *Loin de Médine*. Djebar states that she is most concerned in this text with "reviving" the voices of these women transmitters because their presence has been fragmentary, only momentarily evoked in the male-authored chronicles of the first decades of Islam. These individuals were: "Scrupulous transmitters of course, but already naturally inclined by habit, to occult all feminine presence . . . " (p. 5).[5] The figure of the *rawiya*, the woman who is an active agent of oral transmission, becomes the crucial figure in Djebar's reconstructive project.

Djebar uses the symbolic and literal structure of *isnad* and Hadith transmission as her discursive models. The Hadith are sayings attributed to Muhammad and brief narratives about his life and those of his companions, transmitted orally and then written down after the death of the Prophet. Women's relationship to the Hadith are unique as they appear both as the subjects, and authors of these attributed sayings. In her study *Women and Gender in Islam* (1992), Leila Ahmed contrasts the later absence of women's discursive power with the fact that in the early years of Islam, women were the "authors of verbal texts," later transcribed by men and instituted as some of the founding discourses of Islam (p. 82). In *Loin de Médine*, there are several instances in which the narration is directly modeled on the Hadith paradigm: "Twenty or so years later, Abderahmane son of Hassan ibn Thabit will report to Mondir ibn Abid, who will report it to Osaïma ibn Zeid who will report it to Mohammed ibn Omar—and it is in this very precise transmission that the *isnad*, or Islamic chain will be accepted by the tradition experts. . . " (p. 194).[6]

The chain of women's words portrayed in *Loin de Médine* consciously evokes the *isnad*, or chain of transmission that must be established to authenticate a Hadith. After the Prophet's death, the science of *isnad* was crucial because it was one of the most important sources of spiritual and temporal guidance for the community of believers. Employing techniques comparable to a modern-day interviewer, Hadith transcribers and collectors had to verify the sources of every Hadith. By clearly establishing the chain (*isnad*) of transmitters back to a close companion of the Prophet, subsequent believers could be assured of the Hadith's validity. In *The Veil and the Male Elite: A Feminist Interpretation of Women's Rights in Islam* (1987), the Moroccan feminist-sociologist Fatima Mernissi observes that what makes the *isnad*'s authenticity so vital, is the fact that in the early centuries of Islam, believers were expected to judge for themselves the credibility of the Hadith in question (p. 35). Therefore, all pertinent information regarding the chain of transmission, including the biographies of those individuals who formed the links of the chain, was required in order to allow the faithful to reflect upon and to interpret the Hadith's relevance and validity. In the introduction to *The Veil and the Male Elite*, Mernissi herself exercises this fundamental right of the individual believer to evaluate a Hadith when she performs a detailed reconstruction of the *isnad* of a certain Hadith regarding the incompatibility of women and secular power. She observes that the significance of the Hadith for women's status in Islam is immeasurable. Many Hadith, for example, deal with issues that closely affect women and their rights and duties as believers. Mernissi notes, as do other Muslim feminists, that many of the Hadith authenticated in Al-Bukhari's (b. 810–870) collection may be originally attributed to the Prophet's wives, to Aisha in particular (1991, 35). The historical reality of the women in the Prophet's circle as sources of these traditions is the inspiration for Djebar's project. In order to authenticate Hadith, it is inevitable that numerous accounts of the same incidents or communications of Muhammad will surface. According to the historian Albert Hourani, throughout the first centuries of Islam, the method of distinguishing false Hadith from authentic ones was considered to be an important science. He points out that false Hadith were dangerous as they might be created in order to serve political ends (1991, 70-71). It may be said that the authentification process was a "reading" or interpretative strategy that sought to distinguish "fact" from "fiction." In this way, Djebar's appropriation of the Hadith model as a paradigm for re-reading women's words in early Islam entails the problems of separating fiction from fact, as well as enjoining an act of reading that is also an act of reconstitution of the chain of women's voices.

In her discussion of the Hadith and women's status, Mernissi notes that these traditions provide a "veritable panorama of daily life in the seventh century, a vivid panorama extremely varied because there are various versions of the same event" (1991, 34–35). The recognition that the Hadith present a multiplicity of narrations, or "readings" of the same events, parallels the polyphonic nature of Djebar's presentation and "re-visioning" of events that are discussed in the Hadith and in the chronicles by Tabari, Ibn Saad, and Ibn Hisham.

In *Loin de Médine*, Djebar uses a plurality of narrative voices, an *isnad* to represent the multiplicity of points of view and voices. The entire narrative is structured around the theme of "la voix." Introduced by a prologue and concluded by an epilogue, the four main divisions of the novel are further broken down into accounts of individual women, several of whose stories are narrated in the first person. Alternating with these narrative segments are italicized passages, *rawiya*, entitled first, second, and third, and passages entitled "voix." The fourth transmitter is Aisha, wife of the Prophet, whose story is narrated in third-person, and in her own, first-person narration. In the passages entitled "voix," and *rawiya*, the use of italics and first-person narration underscore the presence of direct transmission, seemingly transcribed from the oral. In the segments that detail the lives and specific incidents of certain women, the third-person narrating voice is that of the author herself, performing her "re-reading" and "recounting" of the women whose presence is momentarily remarked in the chronicles of early Islam. In an interview with Clarisse Zimra, Djebar explains her dedication to the project of reviving and re-interpreting women's history and presence in early Islam. She states that her purpose in *Loin de Médine* is to "answer back," to give a response to "official history." Djebar points out that this text is evidently a "piece of committed literature" (Zimra 1993, 126). Consequently, the author's own voice may be "heard" in those passages in *Loin de Médine* where the third-person narrator comments upon the role played by the women of the Prophet's entourage and the relevance of their actions and words in the history of Islam. It is this same voice that comments upon the incidents related in the historical texts and offers alternate interpretations and possibilities for the women's actions and words recounted. In these narrative passages, the author's voice opens a dialogue between "factual" and "fictional" readings.

The first re-reading presents the account of a Yeminite queen, Islamized with her people during the Prophet's lifetime. Shortly before Muhammad's death, the woman is widowed and captured by a rebel Bedouin leader who has set himself up as a false prophet. At her people's surrender to the rebels, the woman is a part of the spoils of war and becomes the wife of the false prophet. History, according to Djebar, does not make it clear whether the queen is a victim or the one who seduced the conqueror of her tribe. From the chronicles of the era, it is known, however, that the young queen helped assassins to gain access to the sleeping rebel. "The fiction would be to imagine this woman as cunning, since the weapons of femininity remain, in these circumstances, the only ones left intact" (p. 20).[7] The conscious evocation of fiction in completing the portrait of this woman's nearly eclipsed role in history, demonstrates that

Djebar's "re-visioning" and resuscitation is ultimately linked to an attempt to rewrite history. Djebar insists on the ambiguity surrounding the Yeminite queen's actions as this uncertainty about the women's role in authenticated history allows for a "re-reading" of her words and actions: "Ambiguity above all envelopes the character of the Yeminite with the lamp. She disappears into oblivion: without honors, without other comments. No trail prolongs her. Her candle has gone out: silence closes over her" (p. 28).[8]

The entire structure of *Loin de Médine*, reflects a careful attention to a harmony of patterns, alternating third-person "recounting" with first-person "transmission." The resulting textual orchestration of women's voices and women's narratives echoes the format of Djebar's *L'Amour, la fantasia* (1985), and, like this preceding work, creates a fantasia-like medley in which the voice of each single *narratrice* derives strength from the collective.

In "Ecritures féminines algériennes: histoire et société," Simone Rezzoug observes that the portrayal of women's solidarity through collective speech is a frequently occurring literary device in contemporary Algerian women's writing. The act of women writing, she notes, is seen as one that transgresses women's socially and culturally defined limits in much of the Maghreb. Rezzoug suggests that women who speak out or who write must therefore foreground their texts in a commitment to participation with the mainstream community: "contemporary Algerian production [. . .] solicits the recognition of the feminine voice *within and not against* a masculine community" (1984, 80). It may be suggested, then, that Djebar's effort to establish a link between her "revision" project and the pattern followed by Hadith transmission and authentification, seeks legitimization in retracing the narrative steps back to the original women's words and presence. In this fashion, *Loin de Médine* is not a "subversive" re-reading that overturns any patriarchal limitations or interpretations on women's status in Islam, but rather it posits a relationship between her fictional narrative and an established body of texts—oral and written—whose interpretation has normally been controlled by men, that is, by the masculine community referred to in Rezzoug's study.

If, as Rezzoug believes, many Algerian women writers prefer to blend their voices with those of a collective and not to appear to be speaking out alone, then the multiple voices that narrate *Loin de Médine* create a chain of transmission that is strengthened with the addition of each *rawiya*.

The strongest voice of the women from the past who are resurrected to recount their stories in Djebar's work is Aisha, the Prophet's favorite wife, who is generally considered to be one of the most reliable voices among the first transmitters of Hadith. Djebar creates a portrait of Aisha, who, like the author herself, performs " . . . a slow exhumation which runs the risk of appearing dusty, flimsy fog" (p. 300).[9] She gives consistency to her memories *by* and *through* their telling to an audience of children: nieces and nephews included. In Djebar's description, Aisha recognizes the necessity of her reconstitution to offset the growing testimony of "eux" [masculine them] who are already relating *their* version of events and statements. "What can she, all alone, do against so many words, so many speeches that will flow? She evokes. She relives. She remembers. First for herself and for her audience of children . . . "(p. 300).[10] The triple gesture of evoking, reliving, and remembering signifies the character's affirmation of her own discourse, made public through recitation. Aisha's recounting will eventually lead to her becoming a source for Hadith and a most important link in the *isnad* (it should be remembered that the root of the word Hadith is the verb *haddatha*, to recount). By preserving and transmitting her accounts of the past, Aisha, as portrayed by Djebar, ensures that her vision of history will be recorded as a counterweight to later reinterpretations and revisions.

As a historical character, Aisha's presence in the novel is characterized by a sense of factual, not fictional development. A great deal is known about the historical Aisha since accounts of her deeds and words survive in Hadith and chronicles of the period. In *Loin de Médine*, all but a very few of the speeches, comments, and gestures attributed to her character are read as "fiction." However, not all of the female characters in the novel are representations of individuals who truly existed. In the list of characters and their relationships that is included as an appendix to the narrative, an N.B. is added to indicate that among all the major characters portrayed, only that of Habiba, referred to as the second *rawiya*, is "totally imaginary" (p. 311).

Habiba's story is narrated in an italicized passage entitled "Deuxième rawiya," and it begins the second major division of the text, "Soumises, Insoumises." The oppositional notion of "submissive, unsubdued" used in the feminine form highlights the thematic development to come in the women's narratives presented in that division. The character of Habiba is relayed by an anonymous, first-person female narrator. Her sister, another *rawiya*, has just died and the anonymous narrator feels incapable of continuing in her late sister's role as a transmitter. Soon, Habiba arrives in Medina; she is a woman in her fifties, without either a home or close male relatives to shelter or supervise her. She asks that she be called Habiba, a friend, since she prefers to make no claim to any other name. She establishes her position as a marginalized woman, without either family or a name in a society that highly values both. The anonymous narrator declares that Habiba will become the second *rawiya* and that "it will be she who will continue the chain, I sensed it right away: a woman arriving in

Medina without children, without a husband, and without a nephew" (p. 93).[11] To prepare for her role as *rawiya*, Habiba visits the women of Medina who have the most recollections to relate to her. She eventually stays two years in the company of the Prophet's wife Maïmouna, the one married most recently before his death, because she especially knew how to "evoke the past" (p. 98).

Given the fact that, according to Djebar, Habiba occupies the unique position of being the only totally imaginary principal character in *Loin de Médine*, it is significant that her words and deeds are depicted as transgressing established precepts for women's behavior. She is described as "the wanderer," free to move about, even at night, to visit homes and the tomb of Fatima, the Prophet's beloved daughter. As Djebar does not have to account for "facts" related by the chronicles, Habiba's behavior is a recreation of how the process of becoming a *rawiya* might have been undertaken. Habiba's position as a marginalized woman even within the feminine circle of Medina, empowers her to take on the role of a collector and a transmitter of other women's life-stories and of Hadith precisely *because of* her marginal status. As Hutcheon notes, "the protagonists of historiographic metafiction are anything but proper types: they are the ex-centrics, the marginalized, the peripheral figures of fictional history . . ." (1988, 113–14). The character of Habiba occupies critical space in the factual versus fictional history paradigm. As she has no family ties, she can be seen as having no political scores to settle in her collection and transmission of Hadith. The neutrality of this imaginary *rawiya* guarantees that her accounts, if she had truly existed, would have been above reproach.

The transgressive, ex-centric, and even "powerless" (in the temporal sense) position of the fictional character of Habiba prefigures the marginalized role to be assigned to women in general in the centuries of Arab-Islamic history to come. Her character portends the fate of the Algerian author Assia Djebar herself: exiled, living alone, collecting women's words to be preserved and recounted to a larger audience and to succeeding generations. As a fictional character, Habiba the second transmitter, bridges the gap between the historical discourse of the chronicles Djebar is "re-reading," and the fictional elements that enter into a dialogic relationship with both of these forms of narrative. Creating a kind of intertextual tapestry of women's real and imagined words, and women's historical presence, *Loin de Médine* operates on a level of intertextuality that Hutcheon identifies as being unique to historiographic metafiction. It reveals "a formal manifestation of both a desire to close the gap between past and present of the reader and a desire to rewrite the past in a new context" (1988, 118).

In the epilogue to the work, Djebar consciously evokes the ties between present-day Arab–Muslim women and those whose lives are recounted in the work. Indeed, the author has declared in her interview with Clarisse Zimra that the true inspiration for *Loin de Médine*, may be found in the tumultuous events in Algeria in the late 1980s, including the riots of 1988 and the Muslim reaction to the publication of Salman Rushdie's *The Satanic Verses* in 1989, (1993, 123). During these incidents, men and women protested in the streets in Algerian cities, many falling victim to the army's violent repression of the demonstrations. In the novel's epilogue, Djebar emphasizes the two distinct tendencies of women's words as they have been represented and relayed in the narrative: "parole de la contestation" (Fatima) and "parole de la transmission" (Aisha) (p. 299). The overall future of "la parole féminine" is assured through the two veins. But what if, Djebar suggests, the "voice of transmission" one day encounters and fuses with the "voice of rebellion" (p. 300)? The resulting fusion would be an Arab–Muslim woman who both speaks out and who has recourse to direct action. In *"Filles d'Agar," dit-elle*—the second part of the epilogue—Djebar presents a final, free-verse chorus of voices—those of yesterday harmonizing with those of today. By choosing this heading for the epilogue instead of "filles d'Ismaël," Djebar evokes Hagar, the Egyptian servant and concubine of Abraham, exiled into the desert with her infant son Ishmael, ancestor of the Arabs. Her objective here is to create a link between all descendants—the daughters of Hagar—who have originated in the deserts of Arabia. As Djebar points out in a footnote, the root of Hagar's name is the same word in Arabic for "hegira," or emigration. Hagar was "She who emigrated"—Ishmael's mother and hence the first woman "from Medina." The chain of words, transmitted generation to generation, parallels that of the birthright of exile and wandering, extending back through "celles de Médine," those women who left that city with the Prophet, all the way back to Hagar, and continuing today in those women who make the return journey—the haj—back to Medina.

Does Djebar's writing in *Loin de Médine*, then, represent a kind of pilgrimage back to the earliest sources of women's voices in Islam? In resurrecting the voices and stories of women who played important roles in families, society, and even in politics during the first several decades of Islam in Arabia, Djebar has sought to fill in the gaps of collective memory through a fusion of historical and fictional sources. The resulting polyphonic orchestration provides for the creation of a chain of women's voices stretching through many generations, across the varied lands that now make up what is often collectively referred to as the Muslim–Arab world. The chain of voices in her narrative derives its legitimacy and authenticity from its appropriation of the Hadith paradigm, preserved through the science of *isnad*, retracing the path of the spoken words back to their original source. Djebar's project in *Loin de Médine* re-enacts the triple gesture of Aisha, *rawiya* par excellence: "she evokes. She relives. She remembers" (p. 300).

Notes

1. "Je ne vois pour les femmes arabes qu'un seul moyen de tout débloquer: parler, parler sans cesse d'hier et d'aujourd'hui, parler entre nous, dans tous les gynécées, les traditionnels et ceux des H.L.M. Parler entre nous et regarder. Regarder dehors, regarder hors des murs et des prisons! . . . La femme–regard et la femme–voix . . . La voix qui cherche dans les tombeaux ouverts!"

2. "Au cours de la période évoquée ici, qui commence avec la mort de Mohammed, de multiples destinées de femmes se sont imposées à moi: j'ai cherché à les ressusciter . . ."

3. "Tout ce que je dirai, tous l'ont déjà conté; tous ont déjà parcouru le jardin du savoir."

4. "Et il y eut alors un étrange dialogue entre lui et moi, entre moi, son ressusciteur, et le vieux temps remis debout."

5. "Transmetteurs certes scrupuleux, mais naturellement portés, par habitude déjà, à occulter toute présence féminine. . . ."

6. "Vingt ans plus tard, ou davantage, Abderahmane fils de Hassan ibn Thabit rapportera à Mondir ibn Abid, qui le rapportera à Osaïma ibn Zeid, qui le parrortera à Mohammed ibn Omar—et c'est dans cette transmission bien précise que *l'isnad*, ou chaine islamique, sera accepté par les traditionnistes . . ."

7. "La fiction serait d'imaginer cette femme rouée, puisque les armes de la féminité demeurent, en ces circonstances, les seules inentamées."

8. "L'ambiguïté enrobe surtout le personnage de la Yéménite à la lampe. Elle disparaît dans l'oubli: sans honneurs, sans d'autres commentaires. Nul sillage ne la prolonge. Sa chandelle s'est éteinte: le silence se referme sur elle."

9. ". . . une exhumation lente de ce qui risque de paraître poussière, brume inconsistante."

10. "Que peut–elle, et toute seule, contre tant de mots, tant de discours qui vont affluer? Elle évoque. Elle revit. Elle se souvient. D'abord pour elle, et pour son public d'enfants . . ."

11. "Ce sera elle qui continuera la chaîne, je l'ai aussitôt pressenti: une femme arrivant à Médine sans enfant, sans mari, sans neveu."

Chapter 4

▼▼▼▼▼▼▼

Daughters of Hagar: Daughters of Muhammad

SONIA LEE

Trained as a historian, Assia Djebar has been concerned with the missing voices or what she calls the blank spaces of history, in which the presence of women, along with that of other traditionally suppressed voices, lies buried. *Loin de Médine* (1991), the subject of the present essay, constitutes the first step of Djebar's inquiry into Islam's collective memory, and that through the mediation of women's discourses. The text is composed like a mosaic whose center is the historical and mythical figure of Muhammad the man and the prophet, transmitter of God's word. From the divine transmission, then spun out the human chain of transmitters of traditions.

Loin de Médine begins with the death of the Prophet and ends with that of Abu Bakr, first caliph of Islam. In the foreword, Djebar admits that her novel is in fact a collection of narratives, visions, and tableaux, sometimes fictional but most often drawn from the works of the first historians of Islam and in particular Ibn Hicham, Ibn Saad, Tabari and the Hadith. In fact, the protagonists (with the exception of the second *Rawiya*) are all historical figures and contemporaries of the Prophet. Consequently, Djebar's narrative constantly oscillates between the actual and the possible, thus underlying the real subject matter of the novel, i.e., the discourse of transmission as it reflects the problematic of Islamic collective memory with regard to women. Language is a primordial issue in the Arab world, starting with the Qur'an which for Muslim believers is the actual word of God, but the ultimate poetic text for all Arabs, be they Muslim or not. Furthermore, the archaic language of the early historians and that of the *Hadith* is the locus of many semantic ambiguities, and this in turn has given rise to a plurality of interpretations. Djebar's text itself is thus a further poetic variation on this long chain of interpretations.

The novel's extensive paratext encodes the intent of the author, a modern transmitter who tells us that the poetry of the ancient text with all its ambiguities, nuances, and rhythm inspired her desire for truth or *ijtihad*. "The iridescent richness of the original text, its rhythm, its nuances, and its ambiguities, its very patina, in a word, its poetry, the only true image of a period, has spurred my desire for Ijtihad"[1] (Djebar 1991, 6). The antithetical opening sentences of the short liminal paragraph of the prologue set the text in its inquiring mode: "He has died. He is not dead," meaning that the Prophet is dead but that his spirit lives on. This short assertion is quickly followed by a brief description of the Prophet's death in the arms of his favorite wife, Aisha, thus underlining the primordial role of women in early Islam. "He dropped his head slightly, on one side, against Aisha's breast"[2] (p. 11). We should remember that Islam's first convert was Khadija, Muhammad's first wife, and that it was in her arms that he found refuge after the agonizing fear of the first revelation. In turn, it is in Aisha's arms that he breathed his last.

There is no dispute as to the importance of women in Muhammad's life. What has become more problematic is the recognition of the importance of the role granted to women in Islam. Conflicts arose after the death of the Prophet because of his inability or unwillingness to resolve the dilemma of his succession. Interestingly, the ensuing schism, which was to tear the fabric of Islam into two irreconcilable factions at the death of Ali, was sanctioned by the Prophet's most beloved women: Aisha, his favorite wife, and Fatima his cherished daughter. Djebar's text is anchored in the antithetic discourses of these two women. Their dual voices and presence are inscribed in the first and last parts of the text, thus framing the plurality of women's voices and stories that constitute the background of the novel in a contesting mode. As a modern transmitter, Assia Djebar recalls and reinterprets the opposing discourses of Aisha and Fatima.

> Therefore, Word of contestation and at the other extreme, Word of transmission: that of the mystical daughter on a nocturnal side, and that of the wife on the verge of becoming a woman of power and of influence, on the side of dawn[3] (p. 299).

Fatima, the cherished daughter of the Prophet, is referred to in the text as "The one who said No to Medina." Her story occupies the end of the first part of the novel entitled "Freedom and Defiance." The only surviving daughter of the four children that Muhammad had with his first wife Khadija, Fatima was married to Ali Ibn Abu Talib, cousin and adopted son of the Prophet. From the very beginning, Ali was a candidate for the Prophet's temporal succession, and he did in fact become the fourth Caliph of Islam before being murdered. It was his death that provoked the great Islamic schism between the Shiites, who are Ali's followers and the Sunnis, embraced by Aisha.

Fatima's story is steeped in contestation. Motivated by a keen sense of justice and sustained by her father's love, she expresses her dissidence in the name of her principles. Djebar insists a great deal on the father–daughter connection, and Fatima's "No" echoes that of her father, the "No" he uttered on her behalf, in public and at the mosque, *his* mosque.

> It was first the father, the father of the beloved daughter–may God's salvation be upon him and may His divine mercy protect him–, it was he who was the first in Medina to say "no." He repeated "no" in front of everyone. . . . This refusal, in front of the faithful, in the middle of the mosque, *his* mosque[4] (p. 68).

He said "No" to Ali's desire to take a second wife. And yet, how could he when the Qur'an allows four wives? Sura 4:3. In fact, Muhammad did not forbid Ali to marry, but required him to divorce Fatima first. The disagreement came from Ali's choice, the young Jouwayria, daughter of Abu Jahl, rich Mecca merchant and fierce enemy of the Prophet. He was killed by the Muslim forces at the battle of Bedr in the second year of exile. However, after his death, Jouwayria and her entire family converted to Islam. So why the refusal of the prophet? Why blame the young woman for the sins of the father? Djebar hints that the real motive is to be found in fatherly love and Muhammad's paternal sensibility. She imagines Fatima's anguish at the thought of Ali's marriage. "Ali wants to marry": the little sentence slowly worked its way into her mind . . . like a drop of cold poison"[5] (p. 72).

Djebar imagines Fatima searching for her father and trying to remember which wife's turn it is to enjoy her husband that day. The author chooses to place him at the house of Um Salama, his fifth wife, well-known for her jealousy. She imagines Fatima's silent protest at the law that condones men's desires, the law that she calls a destiny, and that brings so much unhappiness to women, even to his father's wives, even though he is renowned for his fairness and his tenderness toward his harem. Revolted by what she sees as the destiny of all Muslim women, she awaits her father's decision, the one who has always been a conciliatory agent in her numerous marital conflicts with Ali. But this time, the father does not preach patience and conciliation. He says " No" in front of the whole community. He speaks with his heart as a man, as a loving father: "–my daughter is a part of me! What hurts her hurts me! what casts her down, casts me down!"[6] (p. 68). This metonymic affirmation of Muhammad and his daughter will fuel Fatima's protest when, at the death of the Prophet, she is to be dispossessed of her inheritance. To this emotional speech, and maybe to strengthen it or to better convince his all–male audience of newly converted Muslims, the Prophet adds, " I fear that Fatima may have come to question her faith. . . !"[7] (p. 75).

Why would Fatima be questioning her faith? Is it because Ali's intended is the daughter of the enemy of God, or is she questioning Islam, this new religion which seems to disregard women's feelings? The reasons for the Prophet's verdict are ambiguous at best, vacillating between fatherly love and personal and political animosity toward the intended bride's family. What is clear, however, is the author's intent in her interpretation: she states that fourteen centuries have passed since that famous "No" and "Since then, it seems that no father, at least in the Islamic community, not one single father ever rose up and offered such a passionate defense of his daughter's peace of mind"[8] (p. 69).

Why is it, asks the author, that Muslim fathers do not care enough for their daughters to question polygamy? The possibility of four wives allowed by the Qur'an is simply just an option, not an obligation. In fact, some have argued that it was meant to curb the polygamous habits of the Arabs since the Holy book specifies that one may take more than one wife only on condition that they be treated with total equality—a quasi impossibility in view of the frailties of the human heart. Muhammad himself remained monogamous until the death of his first wife, whom he loved dearly, even though she was some twenty years his senior. Interestingly enough, it was as a Muslim that he became a polygamist. What interests the author is obviously the father–daughter connection already explored on the personal level in *L'Amour, la fantasia* (1985). Djebar seems to feel that Muhammad's legendary love for Fatima should have served as a model for Muslim fathers, an opportunity to improve their society, and to act upon the wisdom of the Qur'an. But instead of listening to their heart, they chose to perpetuate the law of their fathers, thereby yielding to their desire to preserve male prerogatives.

At the death of the Prophet, Fatima was his only living heir. All his other children had died before him, his three sons in infancy. Therefore, it can be said that Arab women are the daughters of Hagar, who was entrusted by God with the future of the sons of Ishmael.[9] Muslim women, in turn, are the daughters of the Prophet, and as such have been dispossessed of their inheritance through the dispossession of Fatima. As Muhammad died without designating an heir, the community of the believers had to choose a leader and did so amidst confusion and political dissent. Abu Bakr, Aisha's father and the faithful friend of the Prophet was chosen first Caliph of Islam over Ali, the only direct heir and blood relative of the Messenger of God. Djebar revisits this famous political development to underline Fatima's difficult relationship with the men of Medina and what she saw as a betrayal of her father's intent. Fatima protested the decision of the Prophet's companions, but it was the issue of her personal inheritance as Muhammad's daughter that caused her to break with the successors of the Messenger. Abu Bakr, as Caliph of Islam, denied her her share of inheritance because the Prophet had once said: "As for us, who are prophets, one does not inherit from us! That which is given to us is given as a gift!"[10] (p. 79). Fatima contests the decision and argues that this saying of the Prophet does not involve temporal possessions. She refuses to submit to the law of the new Caliph and, like her father before her, and speaking in his name, says, "No," publicly arguing that Abu Bakr's denial of her share of the inheritance is based on a misinterpretation of her father's words. It was furthermore a betrayal of Islam, since it was the Qur'an which had, for the first time in the history of the Arabs, allowed women to inherit from their fathers, Sura 4:2. Thus, Djebar interprets Fatima's resistance as symbolic of the beginning of the dispossession of Muslim women through a willful misconception of the Qur'an and the *Hadith*.

> Fatima, she who was stripped of her rights, the first at the head of an endless procession of women whose disinheritance—often brought by their brothers, their uncles, even their very sons—would represent an effort to become the law, in order to little by little block the intolerable feminist revolution within Islam in this Christian seventh century![11] (p. 79).

Strengthened by what she knows to be the truth, Fatima invokes the morality of spiritual Islam over the expediency of temporal power. She, too, can quote her father, who said, "Seek the contentment of Fatima, for that is my contentment. Fear what angers Fatima, for that is what angers me!"[12] (p. 84). But Abu Bakr, the faithful companion of the Prophet and father of Aisha, will choose compromise over justice; now that he is Caliph, he must enforce the law of Medina and it seems that the law of Medina comes before that of God. Fatima will not forgive him and wounds him with these terrible words: "Every time I pray I complain to God about you!" (p. 84). She is soon to take her grievance directly to the supreme authority, for she dies a few months after the Prophet. Her dying words are words of defiance, for she is happy to leave this world of men and their failings:

> I feel myself leaving your world at last and that I am going to be rid of all your men! since I have witnessed so many of their failings, since I have so often had the occasion to plumb their hearts, henceforth I finally reject them all![13] (p. 86).

Fatima's words of protest will not die with her, for her words and her spirit live on and her speeches are still venerated texts for the Shiites. After her, and starting with her two daughters, each generation was to produce what Djebar names "a rare breed of Muslim women: obedient to the will of God and fiercely rebellious against power"[14] (p. 299). In view of the rise of fundamentalism, Fatima's demanding voice takes on an urgent poignancy today. Were she alive now, the Prophet's daughter would no doubt incur the wrath of the Imams since she would refuse their politics and would hold them to the Text.

Fatima carried her revolt to the grave for she had left instructions that no one from Medina was to be allowed in her mortuary chamber, thus crystallizing her opposition to Medina's orthodoxy. Consequently, not even Aisha, the Prophet's beloved, was allowed to pay her respects, a humiliating breach of etiquette for this very traditional society. Djebar interprets the fact that no exception was made in the case of Aisha, as evidence of the tension that may have existed between the two women. Fatima the mystic and Aisha the worldly held antinomic discourses, and regrettably for Muslim women, entertained different aspirations.

For Djebar, Aisha is "on the side of dawn" (p. 299) meaning perhaps that she is on the side of life and of truth. She was a woman of power, not only as one of the Mothers of the Believers (as Muhammad's widows are called), but also as the preferred one, thus enjoying a higher status in the Sunni community. However, it is not her political intervention and her famous opposition to Ali's caliphate which interests Djebar in this text. Her politics were most likely the result of her filial and clanic allegiances, and as such remain a strictly historical issue. It is rather her role as a transmitter, for, according to Nabia Abbott, Aisha's most reknowned biographer, she "ranks with such leading traditionalists of the school of Medina as Abu Hurairah, Ibn'Umar, and Ibn al'Abbas. She is credited with 2,210 traditions, of which 1,210 are said to have been reported direct from Muhammad" (Abbott 1942, 201). For Djebar, she is "first among the rawiyates. She, the transmitter par excellence of the deed. She, (who was) at the well–spring of the living Word. Of each and every feminine Word, and bearing on the essential"[15] (p. 292). It must be noted, however, that through the centuries, the veracity of many of Aisha's "sayings" have been questioned by the masters of Islamic tradition because some traditions attributed to her may have been invented or manipulated to serve the particular political purpose of the scribe.

In her excellent article, "*The Mothers of the Believers in the Hadith*," Barbara Stowasser comments that "In the contemporary Muslim world, the question of *Hadith* authenticity serves as one of the touchstones which define and separate a number of ideologically different Muslim approaches to religion and law" (Stowasser 1992, 1). Djebar, in relying on authenticated sources, side–steps the issue of veracity and concentrates rather on the issue of collective memory. The transmitter is not an innocent story teller, but an anachronistic creator of the past: and to quote the wisdom of Birago Diop's *Amadou Koumba*, "When Memory goes to fetch dead wood, it brings back the kindling of its choice"[16] (Diop 1961, 1). What did Aisha choose to remember of her life with the Prophet? Mostly details of their daily life since, for her, the Messenger of God is first and foremost a man and a husband. Djebar tells us, "She recounts. She never invents: she recreates"[17] (p. 300).

So does Djebar herself: she does not invent, but revisits the *Hadith*, hoping to get a glimpse of the truth through another interpretation of the texts, a feminine reading of the past. Djebar feels a kinship with Aisha's desire to speak, to use words in order to relive her life, to set the record straight against "them"—all those who claim to remember and to know the facts. How can they possibly know what she knows? She was the privileged one, the favorite, the beloved, the only one of the Prophet's wives to come to him as a virgin and to have been the source of several revelations. And yet, her "sayings" have been so often dismissed or manipulated in keeping with the political or religious conflicts of the time. Thus the author, as a Muslim woman and as an artist, feels compelled to use Aisha's spoken words to recast anew the favorite's most trying hour, namely, the very famous "affair of the slander or of the lie" (*al–ifk*), as the Arabs call it.

Nabia Abbott reports that the youthful Aisha had accompanied Muhammad on one of his military expeditions. As they were returning to Medina, they left the last camp at dawn. Aisha went some distance away to attend to a natural need; and on her way back to camp she realized that she was missing her necklace. She retraced her steps, and in so doing was accidentally left behind, as no one noticed that she was not in her litter. She had no choice but to wait on the spot until someone came back to fetch her. It took hours before she was missed. Meanwhile, she was unexpectedly rescued by a handsome young man, Safwan Ibn al–Mu'attal, and when he appeared at the next camp leading his camel mounted by Aisha, it unleashed endless malicious gossip. At first, Muhammad paid no attention to the mischievous talk; in fact, he defended his young wife. But the affair soon took on such scandalous proportions that he himself began to have doubts, and for a month he avoided Aisha's presence, until her innocence was finally revealed to him through divine intervention.

Djebar devotes a whole chapter to this incident, which she orchestrates in seven parts, thus mirroring the architecture of the novel (seven being an important number in Djebar's numerology). The incident is reported through a multiplicity of voices from the past, reflecting diverse points of views on the subject, as well as by the voice of the modern transmitter. These voices can be classified into four groups: the witnesses of the past; the narrator's testimony; Aisha's testimony; God's testimony. The witnesses of the past are numerous, but polarized into two camps: those persuaded of the young woman's innocence, and the enemies or "hypocrites" as they were labeled by the ancient historians. The "hypocrites" represent for the most part the political enemies of Muhammad. However, other dissenting voices are more interesting in that they reveal personal emotions toward "the preferred one," or simply old–fashioned misogyny. Such a voice is that of the poet Hassan Ibn Thabit who wrote a poem "on very young women who pretend to mislay a necklace in the sand"[18] (p. 279). Abbott reports that the poet was forgiven both by Muhammad and Aisha, thus attesting to a great indulgence for the artist on the part of the Prophet. . . . However, Aisha did not forgive nor forget Ali's reply to Muhammad when the latter inquired as to Ali's opinion on the affair. Ali supposedly said: "There are many other women beside her" (p. 281). The grudge she bore Ali lasted decades and had serious political repercussions.

The main difference between the discourses of the witnesses of the past and that of the modern transmitter lies in the vision. Aisha's contemporaries express points of view based on a very subjective vision of the incident. None of them were privy to what happened between Muhammad's wife and the young man. They simply imagined the possibilities given that Aisha was only fourteen, that her husband was in his fifties, and that the young man was very handsome. The scenario was irresistible to a society much prone to sexual gossip and in the midst of establishing a new political and spiritual order embodied by the Prophet. Traditional misogyny is not to be overlooked either with its ever present suspicion concerning women's virtue.

In her turn, the modern transmitter listens attentively to the two protagonists as they tell their version of the event, and her vision is framed by her training as an historian, thus providing her with a certain objectivity. As an artist and as a Muslim woman, Djebar brings her talent to the reconstruction of the feelings that the accused must have felt, in particular in the case of Aisha.

Aisha's protests of innocence are particularly revealing of her personality, but also of the vulnerability of the woman's position in early Islamic society. What was most heartbreaking to Aisha was the doubt she read in her husband's eyes and even in those of her parents. She knew that her only recourse was God:

> By God, I find only one situation comparable to mine in regard to you, and that is the situation of Joseph's father when he declared, "patience alone will protect me. And God alone will succour me against what has been alleged"[19] (p. 285).

The author underlines the anger, the despair, but also the faith of the fourteen-year-old girl, finding herself all at once the object of scandal fueled by political ambitions. She obviously empathizes with Aisha's loneliness and understands her hopes for God's intervention, although Aisha herself confessed later that she had difficulty entertaining the idea that God would intercede in her behalf. But as is so often the case in medieval stories and in theocracies, God intervenes to protect the innocent. The angel Gabriel, Allah's intermediary, speaks to the Messenger of God and reveals to him the Sura of light dealing with the subject of slander and adultery. In Sura 24:11, it is said that terrible punishments will await the slanderers unless they can provide four witnesses to corroborate their accusation. In this case again, as in the question of polygamy, the Qur'an speaks in favor of women since it is not easy to find four individuals to bear witness to adultery. Vindicated by the supreme witness, Aisha, expressing her resentment, refuses to thank the Prophet and reserves her gratitude for God only.

Why, did Djebar re-tell this very well–known story? What does it imply for contemporary Muslim women? For Fatima Mernissi, Aisha's ordeal "is a good illustration of this desire to humiliate women and to put them in their place, as is often the case in periods of history when they have gained access to new rights and scored new gains" (Mernissi 1987, 226) (my translation). In her version, Djebar, as a creative artist, insists rather on the pernicious consequences that the incident had on Muslim women's daily lives then and now. Although Aisha was officially cleared, doubt remains to this day, and Djebar feels that it created, or rather re–enforced, the ambiguity that Islamic society entertains about women's virtue. Consequently, in view of women's alleged moral frailty, the preservation of women's honor becomes the prerogative of the males, thus infantilizing women as well as keeping them under constant suspicion.

> The ordeal of this long month of doubt; after which each woman of the Community of Islam, for fourteen centuries, will have in turn to pay her share: a day, a year, or sometimes the whole of her married life![20] (p. 288).

The Qur'an may in fact protect women against slander, but in order to do so, it recommends that they hide their body, that they disappear from view, so to speak. Public space is forbidden to them, they are no longer free individuals. Muhammad did not wish for this, but had to yield to political pressures and agree to veil his women so they would be protected from abuse. Sura 33:59, the Sura of Light, revealed to vindicate Aisha, again insists on women covering themselves. Mernissi feels in this respect that political Islam has failed the feminist revolution attempted by spiritual Islam. Djebar no doubt agrees with Mernissi, and already in *Ombre sultane* (Djebar, 1987) she denounced the veiling and cloistering of women. Here, she seems to go a step further implying that not even God's word can bend the law of Medina.

Finally, Djebar asks who, the beloved wife or the cherished daughter, is the real heiress: Aisha the transmitter of the truth, setting up her words against so many others, or Fatima the disclaimer, the one who said "No" to Medina. In lieu of an answer, the author allows herself to dream:

> And what if, one day, such a manner of passing along the Word were to encounter the flame of that other Word, the Word of vehemence rhymed in anger? What if one day, by dint of feeding remembrance, Aisha would rise? If Aisha, one day would decide to leave Medina? Ah, far from Medina then, to retrieve the wind, the exaltation, the incorruptible youthfulness of revolt![21] (Djebar 1991, 301).

The Prophet's heritage is yet to be claimed by the daughters and wives of Islam. Like Hagar, they have been abandoned by the law of the Patriarch and left to wander in search of their lives; like Fatima, they have been dispossessed by the law of Medina and left to search for justice; like Aisha, they have been humiliated by male suspicion and robbed of their freedom. The time has come for them to reclaim the true law of God.

Notes

1. "La richesse diaprée du texte d'origine, son rythme, ses nuances et ses ambiguïtés, sa patine elle-même, en un mot sa poésie, seul vrai reflet d'une époque, a éperonné ma volonté *d'Ijtihad*" (my translations throughout).
2. "Il a penché la tête, légèrement, sur le côté, contre la gorge de Aïcha."
3. "Parole donc de la contestation et à l'autre extrême, parole de la transmission: celle de la fille mystique sur un versant nocturne, celle de l'épouse sur le point de devenir femme de pouvoir et de rayonnement, sur le versant d'aube."
4. "Ce fut d'abord le père, le père de la fille–que le salut de Dieu soit sur lui, que sa miséricorde le protège–, ce fut lui qui, le premier, à Médine, a dit "non." Il répéta devant tous "non." . . . Cette dénégation, devant les fidèles, en pleine mosquée. *Sa* mosquée."
5. "'Ali veut se marier': la petite phrase la pénétra lentement, telle un goutte de poison froid."
6. "–ma fille est une partie de moi-même! Ce qui lui fait du mal me fait mal! Ce qui la bouleverse me bouleverse!"
7. "Je crains que Fatima ne se sente troublée dans sa foi . . . !"

8. " . . . Il semble qu'aucun père depuis, du moins dans la communauté de l'Islam, plus aucun père ne se dressa, ne développa une défense aussi ardente pour la quiétude de sa fille."

9. According to Genesis, Hagar was the slave-servant of Abraham with whom she had a son, Ishmael, the ancestor of the Arabs. Sarah became jealous of Hagar's son and saw him as a threat to Isaac's inheritance. She ordered Abraham to take Hagar and her son to the desert and abandon them to their fate. In the Muslim version Abraham escorted Hagar and the child to Mecca. Left alone and almost dying of thirst, Hagar with the grace of God discovered the spring of Zemzem and thus saved herself and her child.

10. "Nous, les prophètes, . . . on n'hérite pas de nous! Ce qui nous est donné nous est donné en don!"

11. "Fatima, la dépouillée de ses droits, la première en tête de toute une interminable procession de filles dont la déshérence de fait, souvent appliquée par les frères, les oncles, les fils eux-mêmes, tentera de s'instaurer pour endiguer peu à peu l'insupportable révolution féministe de l'Islam en ce VIIe siècle chrétien!"

12. "Recherchez le contentement de Fatima car c'est mon contentement! Craignez ce qui met en colère Fatima car cela me met en colère!"

13. "Je sens que je me détache enfin de votre monde et que je vais être débarrassée de tous vos hommes! Car j'ai été tellement témoin de leurs écarts, car j'ai eu tant d'occasions de les sonder que je les repousse enfin tous désormais!"

14. "Des musulmanes de la plus rare espèce: soumises à Dieu et farouchement rebelles au pouvoir. . . . "

15. "La première des rawiyates. . . . Elle, la transmittrice par excellence de la geste. Elle, à la source même de la parole vive. De toute parole féminine sur l'essentiel."

16. "Quand la mémoire va ramasser du bois mort, elle ramène le fagot qui lui plaît."

17. "Elle conte. Elle n'invente jamais: elle recrée."

18. " . . . sur les très jeunes femmes qui font semblant d'oublier un collier dans le sable."

19. "Par Dieu, je ne trouve de situation analogue à la mienne vis-à-vis de vous que celle du père de Joseph quand il a déclaré: 'la patience seule me protégera. Et Dieu seul m'aidera contre ce qui est prétendu!'

20. "L'épreuve de ce long mois de doute; après quoi, chaque femme du Dar el Islam, quatorze siècles durant, aura à payer également sa part: une journée, une année, ou quelquefois toutes ses années de vie conjugale!"

21. "Et si un jour une telle transmission allait rencontrer le feu de l'autre parole, celle de la véhémence rimée en colère? Si un jour, à force de nourrir la mémoire, Aicha, . . . se levait? . . . Si Aicha, un jour, décidait de quitter Médine? Ah, loin de Médine, retrouver alors le vent, le vertige, l'incorruptible jeunesse de la révolte!"

Chapter 5

▼▼▼▼▼▼▼▼

The Re-Racination of Driss Chraïbi:
A Hajj in Search of a New Mecca

JOHN C. HAWLEY

Reading the Qur'an has never made me smile.

THE SIMPLE PAST

In his Introduction to *Faces of Islam*, Kenneth Harrow refers to Clifford Geertz's elaboration of three forms of Islam that he observed in Morocco. The first was based upon a cultic veneration of dead saints and those in a patrilinear descent (the "*siyyid* complex"); the second was centered around individual holy men, marabouts, and their set of practices (the "*zawiya* complex"); and the third was focused on the "royal assumption of sacred power assured through descent in the Prophet's line" (Harrow 1991, 6). This last form Geertz called the "*maxzen* complex" (Geertz 1968, 49–53). While it can be reasonably argued that Driss Chraïbi's many novels focus almost obsessively on characters whose identity as Muslims is foregrounded, the sociological, or even theological, distinctions that Geertz observes are not central to the novelist's concerns. On the other hand, Harrow goes on to observe that

> as concerns Islam in Africa, and its subsequent literary expression, what occurred was a series of adaptations in which Islam came to occupy increasingly important spaces in the lives of various people—psychological spaces, governing first the territory of the mind, at times motivated by economic or other self-interested concerns, and then larger, external spaces of an increasingly political and social nature (Harrow 1991, 7–8).

This chapter will argue that Driss Chraïbi, while no clear exponent of Islamic doctrine, follows Harrow's pattern to a tee. His whole adult life continues to be a journey of self-discovery that centers around his place in the religion of his birth.

Le Passé Simple [*The Simple Past,* 1954], Driss Chraïbi's first novel, is still considered "the most controversial work of the 'Generation of '52'" (Marx-Scouras 1992, 131)—a novel of hatred, anger, and violent departure from all that the young author had associated with his Islamic heritage. It was banned in Morocco until 1977, and is typical of the writing of a turbulent period in which the country struggled for independence and self-sufficiency. As Joan Monego notes, for the most adventuresome writers "the first half of this decade was a time of gestation during which the hero was seen struggling for a personal form of liberation. Rejection of one's own heritage, flight, and assimilation with the Other would be a route elected by many. At this stage the hero had merely begun his anxious quest" (Monego 1984, 22). Certainly, Chraïbi's overstated and adolescent novel was only the beginning of his own journey. He quickly rejected it himself when he saw that it could be used by the French and others to denigrate Morocco's potential for self-rule, though he later regretted having done so. In any case, the novel set an insolent tone that alerted readers to a new breed of writers who readily criticized what they considered to be the injustices and incongruities perpetrated in their societies in the name of Islam. Its impact was strong enough to secure Chraïbi's place as a (if not *the*) "founding father" (Bensmaïn 1986, 15) of Maghrebian fiction.

The dominant figure in *Le Passé Simple* is the protagonist's father, called throughout "the Lord." Chraïbi casts him as a hypocrite and a tyrant. The character of almost equal importance in the book is the protagonist's mother, who is kept tucked away in the back of the house, suffering silently under her husband's infidelity, condescension, and cruelty. If the father is the target of his son's impotent hatred, the mother receives her son's withering insults for remaining so passive. I would like to argue that the parents represent, for Chraïbi, two aspects of Islam with which he continues to struggle. Significantly, whereas the father has, for the most part, dropped out of the later books, the mother has assumed a lasting and recurring metaphorical role as the heart of the Prophet's message—a message Chraïbi has come to embrace almost with a sense of inevitability (since this, and not the French Christianity that surrounds him in Paris, is his heritage) and, finally, of gratitude.

Chraïbi's novels are autobiographical to a degree some would consider remarkable for a Muslim.[1] Yet he is intent on creating a literature of self-affirmation and testimony. This is typical of the aspirations of other writers of his generation. Chraïbi is remarkable, though, in his insistence from the very beginning that women's self-affirmation is as crucial as that of men. His frequent return to the character of "mother," who had apparently committed suicide in the first novel, suggests that he could not, or would not, rid himself of whatever she represented. He resuscitates her in *Succession ouverte [Heirs to the Past*, 1962], though she is not a much happier person there. In fact, with her husband now dead, she faces a crisis of meaning in her own life. She has lived for him and for her children. Chraïbi's focus is still basically upon himself, however, and upon his struggle with both his real and imagined "father." But in the next book, *La Civilisation, ma mère!* . . . *[Mother Comes of Age,* 1972], he has become almost lighthearted, playing with the notion of the mother recreating herself as a feminist activist.[2]

Chraïbi typifies Maghrebian writing of the decade between 1964 and 1975, which focused on the problems educated North Africans faced as a result of their multicultural education. Jean Déjeux calls the writing produced during this period a *"littérature de contestation et de dévoilement"* [literature of struggle and disclosure]. Joan Monego describes the time as "a period of anguish, at the heart of which lay the burning issue of whether to advance along Eastern or Western lines, to follow one's heritage, imbued as it was with Islamic tradition, or to opt for a pagan, capitalist-oriented technological society" (1984, 24).

These psychological and social concerns are certainly important even in Chraïbi's earliest novels; they continue, in fact, to the present day. There now seems to be a much greater sense of resolution, however, than one would ever have imagined possible from the violent writer of the 1950s. Happily, much of that resolution seems based upon Chraïbi's revisionist memories of his mother, who has taken on a symbolism that evades the legalism of Islam (represented by the father) by returning to the source—at least to Muhammed himself, if not obviously to Allah. For Chraïbi, as we shall see, this also means a personal return to his pre-Arabic roots in the Berber people of Morocco.

Chraïbi was born in El Jadida, Morocco, in 1926. His years as a very young boy in a koranic school were, apparently, horrible for him. The corporal punishment, the rote memorization, and his accusations of sexual expectations by the overseers seem to have left a permanent scar on his psyche. Brutal domination, coupled with what he perceived to be hypocrisy among the staff, form the basis for all the problems with Islam as he sees it practiced in the Arabic world, including ritualism, bigotry, and formalism (see Urbani 1986, 30). These are also the characteristics he discerns in the protagonist's father in *Le Passé simple*.

When he was ten, however, Chraïbi became a student in a French school, and later was one of only two Moroccans enrolled among 1500 students in the lycée in Casablanca. He had been chosen to become one of the "évolués," the evolved ones—that is, Muslims who had been educated in French schools in Algeria or Morocco, and gallicanized. In these schools Arab (let alone Berber) culture was denigrated. The hero of Chraïbi's books is told by his family that he is being sent into the camp of the enemy to learn the tricks that he will later be able to turn against them. And "Driss Ferdi" does not come out unscathed. He finds his own culture barbarous, his own religion contradictory.

In 1945 Chraïbi moved to France for further study. He graduated with a diploma in chemical engineering, and then began studying neuropsychiatry. The level of anxiety that this crosscultural experience brought about showed itself on the eve of his completion of his doctorate, when he dropped out of school specifically for religious reasons, upset by the total secularization that his Western education seemed to demand. The implied attack on his faith, coupled with the obvious Parisian prejudice against the "Norafs" (the North Africans), led to a skeptical view of the West. He enthusiastically expressed his enlightenment in his second novel, *Les Boucs* (1955), translated as "The Butts," that is, "the scapegoats." "Le bouc" is a term of derision that the French apply to North Africans working in France. The title, and the very angry book, suggest that the author had begun to move beyond total self-absorption, seeing himself as a spokesman for a whole class of individuals. He writes that the novel is for those persons "in all times and all places . . . and not just North Africans in France— whose fate it was to be sacrificial victims, whether the Negro in America, the Jew in the Middle East, the Moslem in India, the slaves of ancient Rome or Greece, assimilated into a civilization, as though to prove that no creation of man has ever been for everyone or ever been perfect" (p. 5).[3]

While focused principally upon the West, the anger *Les Boucs* directs against authority figures naturally prompts Chraïbi to refer to the first such figure in his own life. In fact, Isaac Yetiv characterizes Chraïbi's obsession with this symbol as setting a standard whereby much other Maghrebian literature can be judged, since, in so much of it, "the Father continues to be their scapegoat and Islam the source of evil" (Yetiv 1977, 860). Like other critics, he notes that the protagonist in *Les Boucs* is named Yalann Waldick, which means "may your father be cursed."

> Against their native society they make use of a different weapon: the profanation of the sacred. They debase and defile the most sacred shrines of Islam and the long venerated pillars of society. Sexuality bordering on pornography, for centuries a taboo in Islamic circles, becomes in their hands an instrument of desacralization and is always accompanied by violence. In revolt against the father and his tyrannical authority, the young writer feels himself castrated, mutilated, and he asserts his virility through eroticism. Chraïbi was the first to combine violence with sexuality as a way to achieve catharsis (1977, 863).

Of course, there is a certain irony in describing Chraïbi as the founding "father" of such literature.

Despite the ongoing anger against *all* authority figures, the movement in this novel—first the attack on the West, and then the identification with underdogs throughout the world—suggests the route whereby Driss Chraïbi could gradually reintegrate much of what he had emotionally dismissed in his rejection of a degraded Islam. This course of recovery seems his conscious intent in writing his next two novels, *L'Ane* ["The Jackass," 1956] and *Succession ouverte* (1962). In the Preface to *L'Ane* he recalls his first novel, *Le Passé Simple*, and offers the following explanation:

> The hero's name is Driss Ferdi. He is perhaps me. In any case his despair is mine. Despair of faith. This Islam in which he believed, which spoke of equality of reigns, of the gift of God in each individual of creation, of tolerance, of liberty, of love, he saw it, ardent adolescent formed in French schools, reduced to Pharisaism, a social system and propaganda arm. Everything considered, he embarked for France: he needed to believe, to love, to respect someone or something (p. 13); translation by Joan Monego.

But the respect he hoped to gain, the object in which he hoped to place his faith, was not to be found in France. Having purged his disappointment by writing *Les Boucs*, he begins a recovery in *L'Ane*. Joan Monego notes the abrupt change:

> Indeed, *L'Ane* retains the full flavor of Chraïbi's North African Muslim heritage. . . . Revolt gives way to bitterness, disappointment, and distress as Chraïbi realizes that nationalist liberation does not automatically make better human beings of its citizens, nor does it morally and spiritually transform a country. *L'Ane*, an extended metaphor in five parts, is a plea for men to interrupt the thoughtless, mechanically performed daily chores that have lulled their brains and to reflect carefully on the meaning of existence, both on the individual and the collective level (1984, 115).

His call to greater awareness is aimed at no particular class, but it is clear that he has lost none of his earlier disdain for the powerful in society. As with many African novelists, *L'Ane* suggests that Driss Chraïbi quickly learned that after the first blush of victory that comes with independence, neocolonialism can simply change the cast but retain the same dehumanizing script.

In *Succession ouverte* the protagonist returns to Morocco from France to attend his father's funeral. This occasion gives the novelist a chance to observe, in his brothers, different sorts of Moroccans, each fairly ordinary and prepared to follow in his father's footsteps. Chraïbi uses their varying perspectives to show different aspects of that father, and he allows himself to admire characteristics that his hatred had blinded him to in the first novel. But he does not withdraw his implied criticism of Islam's apparent failure to open his brothers' eyes to certain inequities in society, like the treatment of the poor and of his mother. The greatest indication that he is prepared to come to terms with his paternal heritage comes in the closing paragraph of the book. Apparently disinherited, he prepares to leave Morocco once again and return to France. At the airport, about to board the plane, a customs official hands him an envelope that the protagonist's father had entrusted to him. From the note inside, Driss reads the following: "Well, Driss. Dig a well, and go down to look for water. The light is not on the surface, but deep down. Wherever you may be, even in the desert, you will always find water. You have only to dig, Driss, dig deep" (p. 107).[4]

The reader may have a difficult time imagining that this philosophical "gift" comes from the same man who brought about the death of one of Driss's brothers in the first novel, and who refused to mourn the consequent suicide of his own wife. Perhaps the wayward son was pleading, with this book of reconciliation, for some way to identify with a world that was now forever beyond him. But his reviewers had long ago made it difficult for Chraïbi to "place" himself, in any case. As Danielle Marx-Scouras observes, in *Succession ouverte*, "he now realizes that he is also a foreigner in Morocco. Caught between two closed doors, forever destined to remain in the gap between civilizations, Driss can only cry out for mutual understanding among peoples" (1992, 138). Thus, he must return to France and continue to dig, but to do so now without the distorting emotionalism that led to the total rejection of Islam in his earliest writing.

Before we see where that search has taken him in his recent novels, it is important that we note where that anger placed him among faithful Muslims, and the extent of the resulting alienation. The most thorough analysis of Chraïbi's relationship to Islam has been that of Houaria Kadra-Hadjadji. Referring to three articles Chraïbi wrote for *Demain* in 1956 and 1957 that deal with contemporary Islam, Kadra-Hadjadji describes his version of Islam as "very personal" and "very largely borrowed from pantheism" (1986, 218). In short, "Driss Chraïbi, like the majority of Maghrebians formed in the French school, does not possess a sufficient knowledge of Arabo-Islamic culture nor, perhaps, of the Arabic language, either" (pp. 218–19). This leads him to misread Islam, and to misdirect his attacks. Kadra-Hadjadji wishes to illustrate these points by following the lead of M. Aouissi Mechri, a professor of Islamic law. These critics discern three degrees of unorthodoxy is Chraïbi's representation of Islam: least offensive are some passages that are inexact expressions of the Qur'an; other passages seem to be naive and childish recollections of the Islam Chraïbi experienced through youthful eyes, and never grew to understand more comprehensively as an adult; and most offensive are those passages that have absolutely no parallel in the Law. Using these rubrics, the critics dissect Chraïbi's references to Islam, his experiences in koranic school, his understanding of the pillars of Islam, Ramadan, the imperative to give alms, and the pilgrimage to Mecca; they note the derision of saints in his novels, the disparagement of Abd el Haï Kettani and of prayer, the destruction of the message of the Qur'an by the those entrusted with its safekeeping, and, yet, his apparent belief in the invincibility of the "Islam of one's heart." In short, Kadra-Hadjadji concludes that "the vision of Islam that reveals itself in the work of Driss Chraïbi is tainted with negativity" (p. 252), because he cannot help associating the religion with the familial power that dominated his youth. This is all the more regrettable, in Kadra-Hadjadji's view, since Chraïbi offers very valuable criticisms of the religious educational system, the maladaptation of the fast to the modern world, the cult of the saints, and other items. In this critic's view, it is the obligation of faithful Muslims to return to their sources, and to show the world that the Qur'an actually teaches tolerance, fraternity, and progress, and is not a system of totalitarian politics (p. 253). These views indicate an appreciation among some believing Muslims for Chraïbi's reformist tendencies, but they also display an understandable concern for orthodoxy—a "setting the record straight." This leaves little leeway for the novelist's gradual and pain-filled accommodation with his own somewhat "protestant" version of Islam, one that, as we shall see, could be characterized as a scripturally centered latitudinarianism with a humanistic, and even "incarnational," emphasis.

The means whereby Chraïbi has returned to Islam suggests the movement in contemporary Christianity known as "liberation theology," since his is also a religion that arises from the lives of practicing Muslims rather than from clearly defined (and imposed) doctrines. Not only does the novelist seek to foreground the aspects of his religion that he sees embodied in his mother, he also seeks to identify Muhammed with the enslaved poor who can hear his message with a purity that leads to spiritual freedom. Thus, in his later books Chraïbi attempts to revive his Berber history and find in it those aspects of Islam that have not been adulterated by the Arabic drive to conquer.

With the semi-comic *La Civilisation, ma mère! . . .* (1972), in an effort to strike a less vitriolic tone, he finds the perfect solution: he transforms his meek mother into a crusader for human rights:

> Nothing, you hear, nothing can compare to the terrible nakedness of a man who has nothing left but his soul stripped bare and who wants his dignity here and now and not tomorrow or later on with promises from

some religion. Do you know what I've done with religion? I've buried it with the other debris of the past under an orange tree. At least the tree will give some fruit some day that can be eaten with pleasure (p. 119).[5]

Danielle Marx-Scouras correctly notes the unusual combination of qualities that Chraïbi projects onto the evolving mother figure: "Chraïbi's mother metaphor is situated at the confines of meaning. In her quest for emancipation and identity, which coincides with the Maghreb's, she carefully blends the ingredients of old and new, past and future, tradition and modernity, progress and backwards, evolution and vestige, in order to prepare an original `pièce de résistance'" (Marx-Scouras 1986, 6). In contrast to an old and powerful order that coalesced behind mercantile interests, the mother is an "ineradicable archaism" (Marx-Scouras 1986, 6). Marx-Scouras contends that Chraïbi typifies two generations of Maghrebian francophone writers who have described their move to France as an abduction from their mothers. Chraïbi, though, does not blame the French as much as "Islamic fathers who acquiesced to colonialism and then colonized women, children, and the underprivileged classes in their own society. The `Seigneur' [Chraïbi's father] and French colonial rule are thus, in Chraïbi's mind, different aspects of the same phenomenon" (1992, 135).

But Chraïbi takes a very interesting additional step, and recognizes the mother as the foundation for *spiritual* and well as political liberation. Chraïbi's journey necessitates both resistance to (and partial incorporation of) the cultures of France and of Arabo-Islamic Morocco, *and* personal sophistication that resists secularization. In silhouetting the archaism of his mother as ineradicable he suggests that this is the real strength that can arise from Islam[6] in the lives of the oppressed—and possibly *only* in such lives. For it is not only to his mother that he looks for a non-manipulative sense of Allah's presence, but also to the Berbers. Thus, he manages to make oppression (experienced by himself as a child, by his mother as a wife, and by Berbers as the conquered) the necessary door to enlightenment.

Joan Monego observes that "the Maghreb's brand of Islam was a blend of the intellectualism and orthodoxy of the ulama and of the superstitious emotionalism of the masses, and so it would remain into the twentieth century" (1984, 5). But Jamil Abun-Nasr is more specific. In his view "the Islamization of the Berbers went further than their Arabization, and in many ways the latter process was the product of the former" (1971, 6). Thus, it is little wonder that the "Islam" to which the Berber Driss Chraïbi finds himself returning in his later works is found somewhat suspect by critics like Houaria Kadra-Hadjadji: it does, in fact, seem to blend a semipantheistic preArabic Berber spirituality with more traditional Islamic theology. Such a blend seems to have a history in

Morocco, where "orthodox Islam and Berber folk religion with its very active marabouts coexisted. The marabouts stressed community solidarity and mutual self-assistance, thus lending psychological support to the masses in a way that the official institutions—mosques and courts—could not" (Monego 1984, 10).

The "archaism" that Chraïbi endorses, therefore, does not imply a return to Islamic fundamentalism, especially in terms of social laws, but rather a return to the simplicity at the heart of Muhammed's message.[7] Marx-Scouras is again helpful in pointing out that Chraïbi,

> by writing about the origins of Islam in the Maghreb, . . . provides a genealogical perspective that restores the complexity of struggles and competing interests to the image of a reality from which oversimplified myths of origin spring. This is the reality that nationalists and fundamentalists often seek to deny, as if the Maghreb were not a site where Africa, Europe, and the Middle East intersect—a potential stage for the interplay of cultural diversity, ethnic pluralism, and multilingualism. Such a cultural perspective, espoused by such writers as Chraïbi, Khatibi, Abdelwahab Meddeb, Nabile Farès, and Tahar Ben Jelloun, denies fundamentalism its basis (Marx-Scouras 1992, 141).

But if Islamic fundamentalism is rejected, a kind of spiritual "foundationalism" is certainly Chraïbi's goal. His recent writings express a religious sense that is not systematic, and far from dogmatic, but based in compassion, fraternity, and, significantly, a rootedness in the earth as the lasting source of all life. In *Une Enquête au pays* (Flutes of Death, 1981) he looks to his fellow Berbers as a long-suffering people, simple and wise and enduring beyond their various conquerors. A chief of police from the city, and his assistant, Inspector Ali, are seeking terrorists among various Berber encampments. The chief is an arrogant racist, in comparison with whom Ali appears reasonable. Their encounter with the Berber worldview offers Chraïbi an opportunity to "convert" the inspector to an enlightened understanding of Allah's demands, at least to some extent. The Berbers themselves seem to think so, and consequently spare Ali's life when they execute the chief. But, at heart, they recognize the two as strangers who are "as aggressive and unhappy as the conquerors of any race or religion who had ever unfurled their banner in the pages of history" (*Flutes*, 42).[8]

The man the authorities are seeking is Raho, who recognizes that his time is passing and that his people will be forced to move yet further into the wilderness. Yet, in the meantime, he resists and prays. He is a Muslim and gives the "five times daily tribute to Islam," though his real strength is from the old ways:

> One after the other, he placed his hands on the ground, the fingers spread. Well before civilization or Islam, beyond the events of History, there was the worship of the earth. From generation to generation, and from one flight to the next before the conquerors of every race, that old religion had perdured right up to him, by the oral route. Raho had done his duty, he had offered sincere hommage to the impersonal god of the monotheists. And now . . . with his hands, and through his pain, he was about to pierce the earth, to gulp down in himself the elemental and prodigious force of the earth. It was really simple: all he had to do was to spread himself out like the roots of a tree. The sap was there, coursing life, right down there (*Flutes*, 26).

Then, he listens for "the voice of the nourishing mother." It was she who endured, and gave birth to human history and all fleeting systems of meaning: "This Islam, this religion which somehow touched him, Raho, wasn't it born way back in time, way back in the arid desert, between the sand and the sun—nothing else? Like Islam, and his own destiny, one was born from the belly of one's mother, naked, and one returned equally so into the entrails of the nourishing mother earth. Your skin and flesh were witness to this truth!" (p. 41).[9]

His appears to be, in fact, the pantheism that Kadra–Hadjadji finds in Chraïbi, circumventing the pretensions of systematic religions: "All religions, whether from the Orient or the Occident, or elsewhere, had only inflicted thought upon him. . . . Raho himself had no notion, no consciousness of what his life had meant" (pp. 41–42).[10] This is about as minimal as a religion can get, and the Islam that Raho's associates practice is more or less that: a practice, a series of rituals that are now part of their tradition. It would be more accurate to speak of this belief system as syncretic rather than as strictly pantheistic, since the monotheism of Islam is arguably dominant, though Allah has been reconceived as feminine.

In any case, the Berbers represented here have learned to be cynical of other alternatives. Hajja, one of the women leaders of the tribe, recalls of the conquerors that "they reinforced themselves with what they called the law, from books which they forced us to read: the book of Hebrews, those of the Christians, the Qur'an of the Islamic ones . . . huge numbers of others which they pretended were holy and sacred" (p. 138).[11] They used these to divide brothers from brothers, terrestrial life into good and evil, the sky a paradise, and the nourishing earth a hell. "And, when they perceived that their books were worn out like old figs and that they couldn't get anything from them or next to nothing, then they invented another strategem: progress, civilization" (p. 138).[12]

The effect this has on Inspector Ali is interesting. He is belittled by his superior, and therefore implicitly identifies with the Berbers he has come to investigate. He shares their cynicism, and recognizes that "elsewhere, in other offices, there were the same types, all chiefs: religious types promoted to magistrates, just because they knew by heart, or almost, two or three chapters of the Qur'an. . . . A plethora of chiefs formed one big giant iron tree, rigid in both directions: horizontal and vertical" (p. 86).[13] Yet he himself has no substance, no guiding principles. At one point he relies on the flip of a coin to determine whether he will continue the investigation, or instead align himself with the Berbers. Ironically, the coin gets lost somewhere in the air. At novel's end, once the chief has been killed and Ali has made his report, he returns to the village as the chief's replacement, now intent on exterminating this troublesome enigma. But the villagers are gone, and little is left: "A void. Not a soul" (p. 146)[14]—which is surely as much a description of Ali as it is of the deserted village. He fails Chraïbi's ultimate test, which is the attempt to live compassionately with one's inner complexities, resistant to the will to power.

Ten years later Chraïbi gives this character his own book, *L'Inspecteur Ali* (1991), or, more clearly, he returns to a semi-autobiographical work about a writer named Brahim who has become world-famous under that pseudonym (Inspector Ali) as a braggart and provocateur, expert in resolving questions having to do with Islam. Brahim is trying unsuccessfully to write a second *Passé simple* (he is starting his fourth draft), but must spend most of his time entertaining his Scottish in-laws who are visiting Morocco for the first time.

The book has some zany twists, and is obviously ripe with occasions for crosscultural ironies. But the real importance of the book, coming late in Chraïbi's career, is the resolution it attempts in the area of his accommodation to Islam. In one passage of the novel that he is writing, Brahim has Muhammed wondering whether, if he were to return to earth, he would undertake the same mission (*L'inspecteur Ali*, 181). In another passage, he has Muhammed seated in the office of a publisher, being told that a book he has offered them for review, called *The Qur'an*, is certainly poetic, and offers a lot of moral precepts, but it couldn't be sold in its present form. After all, this is the twentieth century. Would the author mind very much if they were to submit it to a thorough reworking by the editors? (p. 222). Brahim knows that the effect such writing will have on his Western readers, very lighthearted and mildly cynical toward Islam, will bring him even more fame.

In Brahim's personal life, however, the reader sees that things are far from lighthearted, and by novel's end Brahim implicitly confronts major questions of belief and self-definition. Is he, too, something of a buffoon for the West, like his comic hero? Brahim has become, he says, "the king of the kiosk" (p. 231) and for twenty five years in Europe and America his fans have made him rich; his celebrity has made him a name to be sought for various international causes. Between himself and the common people there have been passionate words, but he has calmly protested: No, not "the Prophet"—do not speak of the one you have constructed over these many centuries. "Speak to me of the man who was there *before* his revelation, flesh and blood like you—illiterate, like you. . . . I want neither myth nor legend. Only the reality, concrete. Some insult me—I was blaspheming, I was a provocateur, an unbeliever, this country's only skeptic in the name of reason—still, one could not return such a being to our level. So how important is their misery!" (p. 232).[15]

Yearning for an impossible encounter with the historical Muhammed, Brahim is suddenly surprised by the miracle of birth, an ordinary event that takes on mystical and hopeful meaning in the book. He ends in a maternity ward, all his worldly cynicism stripped away as he experiences "the joy of creation," which transcends all borders. It is, he says, the first time he has assisted at a birth: it is a boy, with fists clenched and ready to struggle in the world. And then he sees the face of the mother—"And finally I recognized her. She has come to visit me, and calls me by name, and asks for money to go to Mecca and pray for me. There suddenly rises before my memory all my past history, sharp, clear, blinding with tiny details—this past which I have buried so deeply within me" (p. 233).[16] It takes very little imagination to imagine Driss Chraïbi himself in such a maternity ward, seeing in the struggling child *all* struggling humanity, seeing in the face of the exultant—and faith-filled—mother, his own loved mother.

Lionel Dubois points out that Driss Chraïbi has always been a great traveler, and he is perhaps right in concluding that "the voyage does not end with the life of the voyager" (1986, 19). Certainly, Chraïbi's journey has never paused long along the way. Bernard Urbani observes that Chraïbi is fully comfortable in neither France nor Morocco, but he prefers "a royal exile" because "in spite of the injustices and hypocrisy, he remains in the West because it is a world that corresponds to his way of thinking. It allows him to put into practice the message of the Lord [his father]: the maturation of his soul in the reinterpretation of the past" (1986, 34; my translation). That recuperation continues. But in the view of Hugh Harter, one of Chraïbi's English translators, "both *Une Enquête au Pays* (Flutes of Death, 1985) and *La Mère du Printemps* (Mother Spring, 1989) indicate that the Driss Ferdi of *Passé Simple* has come full cycle and made his peace with himself and both worlds he has straddled so long" (1986, 38).

The route he has taken to achieve this tenuous resolution is suggested by Danielle Marx-Scouras, who notes in 1986 that "in his last two novels, *La Mère du Printemps* . . . and *Naissance à l'Aube* (Birth at Dawn, 1986), Chraïbi reinterprets history from the point of view of those whom Memory (as repression moreso than remembrance) has forgotten, and History (as the story of conquerors) has obliterated." He writes now, she notes, "for all the refugees of the world" (1986, 7). Chraïbi says that the most urgent problem that he feels it necessary to treat in his novels now is "the people—the rising generation," and for that reason wishes they were written in Arabic (1986, Interview 24).

Nonetheless, he finds himself perfectly at home in France, where he works, knowing now that he always carries a certain Moroccan appreciation in him, as does anyone who spends some time there:

> The role of the mother is central. One must never forget a very well-known saying, the word of the Prophet, the word of the Qur'an, which has applied to Morocco and to Morocco alone: "Paradise is there at the feet of one's mother." And this, for Morocco, has been true. And moreover: "Respect for uterine bonds increases one's life." And that is something I have rediscovered with a most famous saying of the Prophet. Yes, I am, and we are all—and not only the Maghrebian writers in French, but also the dockworker in Casablanca, the mountain people of Atlas, the poor of Casablanca, the immigrant in Auberville—we are all Muslims (1986, Interview 26).

Which of his readers in 1954 could have predicted the destination of his journey, the "Mecca" his life had found in 1983:

> Well, we, we in the Muslim world, have something phenomenal, I tell you, which is our source, which has not changed at all: it is the Qur'an. I'd like to speak about it at greater length.
>
> One is greatly surprised that the appearance of Islam causes dread. Yet, it grows—it gains more and more. In France alone there are already, officially, 37,000 converts to Islam. It's gaining in North Africa, in Asia, in India, where the colonial powers have failed. Because of its view on women, inheritance, of rights, it is a factor for progress. It is not I who says so, it is journalists opposed to Islam who are obliged to give these reports. This is not at all the foundation. Judaism has evolved over the centuries; Christianity even more so. Marxism has evolved. There is something that has never evolved: Qur'anic law, Islam. It remains as it was; that is, for us in the Arabo-Islamic world, it is newly-born, it is the source. And for me, it is a force: it is my strength (1986, Interview 23–24).

Perhaps Driss Chraïbi can now smile when he reads this book.

Notes

1. Algerian novelist Mohammed Dib notes that "les Algériens élevés dans un milieu musulman considèrent l'introspection comme un peu malsaine. D'un homme plongé dans des reflexions qui paraissent profanes, le proverbe dit: `C'est quelqu'un qui mène paître les vaches d'Iblis'. . . . La psychanalyse est impensable en Algérie pour l'instant." Interview with Claudine Acs, 10. ["Algerians raised in a Muslim milieu consider introspection a little unhealthy. Of a man plunged in reflections which seem profane the proverb says, 'It is someone who leads the cows of Iblis to pasture.' . . . Psychoanalysis is unthinkable in Algeria for the moment (translation Joan Monego)].

2. See Isaac Yetiv, "The Evolution," for a discussion of Chraïbi's development of this character.

3. In a 1976 appendix to the novel Chraïbi writes: "The question has been asked me, and I have asked it of myself, if I am capable now twenty years later of writing such a book, one equally atrocious. It is hard for me to answer, except with another question: does racism still exist in France twenty years later? Are the immigrants who continue to come to work in this `so highly civilized' country still penned up on the edges of society and humankind? Is it still true, as my master Albert Camus stated, that the bacillus of the plague never dies and never disappears?" (*The Butts*, 124).

4. "Le puits, Driss. Creuse un puits et descends à la recherche de l'eau. La lumière n'est pas à la surface, elle est au fond, tout au fond. Partout, où que tu sois, et même dans le désert, tu trouveras toujours de l'eau. Il suffit de creuser. Creuse, Driss, creuse."

5. "Rien, vous entendez, rien ne peut tenir devant cette nudité atroce d'hommes démunis et à l'âme nue et qui veulent leur dignité maintenant et nondemain ou plus tard, comme la leur promet la religion—et savez–vous ce que j'en ai fait, de la religion? Je l'ai enterrée au moins donnera un jour des fruits, de vrais fruits que l'on mangera à belles dents."

6. Chraïbi's obvious valorization of the mother is not shared by other contemporaries. Jean Déjeux notes, for example, that "the use of French allows writers to transgress boundaries they might encounter in Arabic. For example, Ben Jelloun admitted that he could not have written *L'Enfant de sable* in Arabic because the material in the novel is on the order of a heresy against the Koran, religion, and his parents. Only by taking refuge to another language—a form of 'otherness'—could he overcome the constraints of the parental superego, especially its feminine (maternal) component" (Déjeux 1992, 10).

7. Chraïbi, in fact, falls in line with Jean Déjeux's observation that "in addition to the expatriate Maghrebian community, numerous internal exiles feel ill at ease in their own countries, especially after the rise of fundamentalism throughout North Africa" (Déjeux 1992, 9).

8. "L'une après l'autre, il posa ses mains sur le sol, à plat, doigts écartés. Bien avant la civilisation ou l'Islam, derrière les événements de l'Histoire, il y avait eu le culte de la terre. De génération en génération et de fuite devant les conquérants de toute race, il s'était perpétué jusqu'à lui, par voie orale. Raho avait fait son devoir, il avait rendu sincèrement hommage su dieu impersonnel des monothéistes. Et maintenant, par les mains et par son siège il était en train de percevoir la terre, d'avaler en lui la force élémentaire et prodigieuse de la

terre. C'était très simple: il lui suffisait de s'ouvrir, comme les racines d'un arbre. La sève était là, la vie, tout au fond."

9. "Cet Islam qui était parvenu jusqu'a lui, Raho, n'était–il pas né là–bas dans le temps, tout là–bas un désert aride, entre le sable et le soleil—et rien d'autre? Comme l'Islam et sa destinée, on sortait nu du ventre de sa mère et on retournait aussi nu dans les entrailles de la mère nourricière, la terre. La peau en était témoin!"

10. "Toute religion, venue d'Orient ou d'Occident ou d'ailleurs, ne lui avait apporté rien d'autre que la pensée. . . . Raho n'en savait rien, n'en avait nulle connaissance."

11. "Ils ont apporté avec uex ce qu'ils appelaient la loi, des livres qu'ils nous ont obligés à lire: le livre des Youdis, celui des Nazaréens, le Coran des islamiques . . . quantité d'autres qu'ils ont prétendus saints et sacrés."

12. "Et, quand ils se sont aperçus que leurs livres étaient usés comme des figues sèches et qu'ils ne pouvaient plus rien en tirer ou presque rien, alors ils ont inventé un autre sortilège: le progrès, la civilisation."

13. "Ailleurs, dans d'autres bureaux, il y avait ses pareils, tous chefs: religieux promus magistrats parce qu'ils savaient par coeeur ou tout comme deux ou trois chapitres du Coran. . . . Toute une pléthore de chefs composant un arbre de fer, un appareil rigide dans les deux sens: vertical et horizontal . . ."

14. "Il était vide. Pas une âme."

15. "Parlez–moi de l'homme qu'il avait été avant la Révélation, fait de chair et de sang comme vous, illettré comme vous. . . . Je ne veux ni mythe ni légende. Uniquement la réalité, concrète. On m'injuria, je blasphémais, j'étais un provocateur, un mécréant, le seul sceptique de ce pays au nom de la raison, on ne pouvait pas ramener un être aussi exceptionnel à notre niveau. Et peu importait leur misère!"

16. "Je la reconnus enfin. Elle était venue me rendre visite, m'avait appelé par mon nom, m'avait demandé de l'argent pour aller prier sur moi à La Mecque. Remonta soudain dans ma mémoire tout mon vieux passé, net, clair, aveuglant dans les moindres détails—ce passé que j'avais enfoui si profondément en moi.

Chapter 6

▼▼▼▼▼▼▼▼

Piloting Through Turbulence: Griots, Islam, and the French Encounter in Four Epics About Nineteenth-Century West African Heroes

BRETT C. BOWLES AND THOMAS A. HALE

Early written descriptions of *griots* in West Africa, especially the seventeenth-century Arabic-language chronicles from the Timbuktu region, reveal a subtle but clear rivalry between these keepers of the oral tradition and Muslim clerics who recorded information about the Sahelian empires. (Hale 1990, 45–46). That rivalry stemmed in part from an overlap of social functions in a critical area: advice to the ruler. Kings as well as other members of society would seek counsel from some of the many different Muslim officials who were responsible for the maintenance and spread of Islam—jurists (*fuqaha*), scholars (*ulama*), regional or chief clerics (*imams*), local clerics (*marabouts*), teachers (*muallims*), government secretaries (*katibs*), and a more loosely defined group of cleric/teachers known as *alfas*. The divisions between these different categories were not always as clearly demarcated as this listing suggests. But what distingushed all of them from other members of society was their knowledge of Islam and an ability to read and write Arabic.

Griots also provided advice to their patrons, in addition to serving as spokespersons, ambassadors, masters of ceremony, tutors, praise-singers, historians, genealogists, musicians, composers, town criers, and exhorters of troops about to go into battle. Their role as advisors is evident not only in their own narratives about the past, especially epics, but also in written accounts in Arabic and European languages from the fourteenth century to the present. Their counsel was especially important when dealing with other states or with internal rivals of their patrons. In one example from early Songhay history, a *griot* with a clear sense of human motivation saves his patron, a provincial governor, who is also a son of the former ruler Askia Mohammed, from certain death at the hands of his brother, Askia Moussa, by putting a halt to plans for a voyage by the governor to the capital of the empire. Askia Moussa had just deposed his father, Askia Mohammed, in 1528, and was planning to eliminate his rival brothers by any means possible (Hale 1990, 40).

The advisory role of *griots* became somewhat more complex several centuries later as political conditions in the Sahel underwent major changes. In the late nineteenth century, rulers of states in the Western Sahel, especially the Senegambian region, faced extraordinary new challenges as wars erupted among Islamic states, non-Islamic kingdoms, and French colonial forces. The purpose of this study is threefold: to discover how *griots*, in their roles as both advisors and guardians of traditional values, responded to these conflicts and to the social changes that emerged; to learn why West African *griots* have managed to adapt with such apparent ease to the colonial and national eras in Africa today despite the growth of literacy in European languages resulting from the introduction of Western-style systems of education and the invasion of the continent by many new forms of communications technology; finally, to suggest how *griots* are influencing the spread of Islam in West Africa today.

Just as there are many different kinds of Muslim clerics, there are also different varieties of *griots*. In the Mandinka-speaking part of West Africa, the *mansa jali*, and his counterpart among the Bamana, the *jeliba*, are master *griots*, not to be confused with an ordinary *jali* or *jeli*; the *jelimuso*, or female *griot*, who does not normally sing epics (Hale, 1994), has slightly different functions from the *jelike*, or male *griot*, among the Bamana. The little-studied *funé* sings primarily praises about figures in the history of Islam in many parts of the Mande world (Conrad, 1995). It is important, then, to recognize that each people has its own referent to identify these wordsmiths, a difference that will be noted in the use, for example, of *guewel* when referring to Wolof *griots*, *jali* for the Mandinka, *jeli* for the Malinké and Bamana, and *jeseré* for the Songhay.

The rivalry between *griots* and Muslim clerics for the attention of rulers and other patrons alluded to above appears not only in early written accounts but also in modern versions of epics about the past.

In the Songhay *Epic of Askia Mohammad* recounted by the late *jeseré* Nouhou Malio, we discover one reason for the differences between Muslim clerics and *griots*. When the Songhay ruler crossed the Red Sea to make the pilgrimage to Mecca at the end of the fifteenth century, he was accompanied by only two people—his *jeseré*, who, by an unusual accident of history, was also his cousin, and his *marabout*, a man named Modi Baja.

305 All the horsemen, those who died, those who were tired, returned.
 Except for Modi Baja, Modi Baja and the *jeseré*, his cousin, who stayed
   with him.
 It is they alone who remained at his side.
 He made the crossing in their company.
 So they arrived in Mecca (Hale 1990, 203).

At the end of Askia Mohammed's visit to the tomb of the Prophet, he gives his two companions a gift of some green shoots found deep inside the edifice. The *marabout* saves his, brings them home from Mecca, and sells them for profit, resulting in great wealth for his descendants. The *jeseré* eats his on the spot, leaving his descendants nothing but a hard life. The comparison between the two different men of the word, with the pointed reference to the way the *marabout* profited from selling items of sacred origin, offers a clear example of the difference that can mark relations between the *griots* and their Muslim counterparts.

At the time of Askia Mohammed, who ruled from 1493 to 1528, Islam was still spreading across the Sahel. Although the Songhay ruler did much to promote the religion during his lifetime, Islam was still a relatively new faith for many peoples in 1591, the year of the fall of the Songhay empire. In the four centuries since then, the peoples of the Sahel have experienced a much more wide-ranging, yet still scattered, impact from Islam that culminated in the formation of a series of theocratic Islamic states in the nineteenth century.

These states, especially in the Senegambian region (Cayor and Bawol, for example), were often much smaller than the vast Songhay empire of the fifteenth and sixteenth centuries, and not evenly distributed across the region. There were frequent wars, many between rulers who attempted to impose Islam on other kingdoms that had refused to accept the religion. During the nineteenth century, the penetration of European political and military power added another disruptive dimension to the political climate in the region.

The growing French and Islamic influence on African societies in the western Sahel led both to conflict and to collaboration at different times, depending on the circumstances and the actors in power. For example, in the case of Lat Dior, one finds at different times that he warred against the French, collaborated with them, and at a crucial turning point, converted to Islam for what appears to be political reasons, all in order to maintain or reassert the independence of his own people during the period between 1860 and 1886.

In this volatile period of cultural and political ferment, rulers who depended on *griots* and *marabouts* for guidance found themselves faced with a new and increasingly violent world. Rapid-fire weaponry, transportation of armies by rail and by steamship, and communication by telegraph were quickly changing the rules of engagement. If ever there was a time when traditional methods and social structures seemed destined to disappear, the latter part of the nineteenth century was it. But the turbulent events of that period appear to have strengthened, rather than weakened, the *griot* as an advisor to rulers.

Evidence from contemporary documents provides some clues about the situation of *griots* during this critical period. For example, photos brought back by the Borgnis-Desbordes expedition in 1882 show rulers flanked by a *griot* on one side and a marabout on the other side—a visual echo of what we read in *The Epic of Askia Mohammed*. Accounts by French officers who fought against Samory Touré, one of the most militant resisters against colonialism in the region, describe *griots* as intermediaries between that powerful and wily Islamic ruler and the colonial forces who pursued him during the last two decades of the nineteenth century (Galliéni 1891).

These visual and written documents illustrate and confirm what we read about *griots* in modern epics focused on nineteenth-century Islamic heroes. The long poetic narratives recorded during the last two decades offer a revealing portrayal of just how the *griots* helped to parry the shocks produced by some of the conflicts that arose during the late nineteenth century between the three major parties involved: French colonial armies, Islamic leaders, and chiefs who did not embrace the religion.

The evidence that we will draw upon comes from four texts, *The Epic of Fode Kaba*, recorded in 1969 by Gordon Innes, *The Epic of Lat Dior*, recorded in 1985 by Bassirou Dieng, *The Epic of Kelefa Saane*, also recorded by Innes in 1969, and *The Epic of El Hadj Umar*, published in 1993 by Oumarou Watta.

In an earlier study, Hale pointed to the syncretic functions of *griots* who, by the twentieth century, had bridged the gap between Islam and traditional values (Hale 1985). The evidence came from the Timbuktu chronicles and from recent interviews with modern *griots* who sometimes spend the financial rewards of their profession on pilgrimages to Mecca. But the gap between the sixteenth and the twentieth centuries is vast, and Islam during that period underwent many changes as it spread throughout the region. When the theocratic states began to emerge in the nineteenth century, some proponents of Islam began to manifest a more militant tone that occasionally led to conflict between Islamic and non-Islamic peoples.

In this challenging new environment, *griots* did not step back from roles that they had played for many centuries. Epics focusing on nine-teenth-century rulers offer evidence to suggest that *griots* played an important part in softening some of the impact that the rapid advance of Islam was bound to cause. That shock-absorbing effect may be inferred from both the portraits of *griots* in the epics as well as from contemporary *griots*, who are in some cases descendants of those attached to the nineteenth-century rulers.

For example, in the 833-line *Epic of Fode Kaba* recounted by the Gambian *jali* Bamba Susso in 1969 (Innes 1976), the narrator provides a subtle yet incisive critique of a jihad that serves as a pretext for personal gain and violates the traditional political order. Fode Kaba was a well-known Islamic warrior in the region of what is today southern Senegal and The Gambia. Born around 1820, he fought in the "Soninké–Marabout" wars, conflicts between Muslim leaders and non-Islamic peoples who were generically called Soninké, even though they were of diverse ethnic origin and may not always have had a connection with the Soninké-speaking peoples who claim descent from the Ghana empire (Innes, 128). Fode Kaba was killed in 1900 while resisting an attack by a combined French and British military operation.

At the beginning of the epic, Fode Kaba settles at Kerewan Dumbo Kono, thirty miles inland from the mouth of the Gambia River where he builds a stronghold and begins to levy taxes on the ships that moor in the river. The neighboring Soninké are suspicious and demand that Fode Kaba stop. As the dispute between the two begins to grow, Bamba Susso, the *jali* narrator, interjects, "At that time Fode Kaba was serving God/ Until the time when God gave him a gun" (lines 52–53, p. 261). Shortly thereafter, Fode Kaba sends his adversaries a specially-prepared black bull whose meat makes them drowsy. Fode Kaba and his army attack the camp and kill the enemies in their sleep: "Each man stood by the head of his victim/ And put a gun in his ear/ And fired" (lines 105–07, p. 263).

This first episode touches off a rampage through the area by the ruler. He kills and plunders everything in his path under the guise of holy war. When he arrives at Korro, another Soninké center, the town elders greet him and agree to convert without conflict. However, at the head-shaving ceremony, which symbolizes a non-believer's acceptance of Islam, Fode Kaba's men slit the elders' throats and then raze the helpless town (lines 132–37, p. 265).

A second instance where the *griot* reveals Fode's *jihad* as a pretext for personal gain occurs when Fode Kaba's father, Fode Bakari Dumbuya, chastises his son's soldiers as they return from their latest campaign.

214 You say that this leader of yours is a saint;
     Did he see those things which are sent down from heaven?
     Men of the army, let any man who has anything
     In the form of slaves or booty
     Take his share.
     All of you, go!
     God's war has come, which is not like a man's war (p. 269).

In the wake of this advice, an epidemic "sent from above" decimates the army. Here it is important to note that the *griot's* criticism of Fode Kaba's actions, expressed through the warrior's father, is not couched in anti-Islamic terms. On the contrary, God is referred to as "Ala" in line 220, and the very fact that "man's war" is juxtaposed with "God's war" implies belief in legitimate *jihad* and Muslim faith.

Perhaps the most striking example of Fode Kaba's violation of both Islamic and traditional values comes toward the end of the epic during his siege of the Muslim towns of Soma and Seno Ba. On the verge of starvation, the leaders of Soma ask that Fode Kaba meet them in the mosque to negotiate an end to the war. Once inside, the warrior promptly slaughters them all (lines 651–53, p. 289), and proceeds to raze Seno Ba, where the narrator implies that even *griots* were killed.

677 It was terrible—
     Except for those whose fleetness of foot had allowed them to escape
     But those whose fleetness did not so allow
     Were all slaughtered
     Even to this day it is not safe for a kora griot in Kabada (p. 289).

The implication that even *griots* would be killed under such circumstances suggests the depth of Fode Kaba's violation of custom. For many West African peoples, killing a *griot*, in battle or otherwise, was a serious violation of the code of conduct, unless it was done for an exceptionally good reason such as to punish a *griot* who had served as a spy. The death of the *griot* in this context may also indicate that their profession paid a particularly heavy price for the introduction of Islam. In fact, this episode marks the third time in the epic that Fode Kaba kills or appears to be willing to kill a *griot* without provocation. The first victim is a *jali* named Yoro, sent as an envoy to Fode Kaba, who in turn "seized him and murdered him" (line 345, p. 273).

The second occurrence involves a grandfather of Bamba Susso, narrator of the epic. Fode Kaba advances seventy-five miles up river to the Jarra region where he attacks the town of Kani Kunda and declares:

605 . . . I am a Muslim
     And you are Muslims;

I have come here, and you say that I cannot enter the town.
In that case I will burn your town to the ground [. . .]
619 The army assaulted Kani Kunda.
One of my grandfathers was there; he perished there.
He was called Hamadi Banko (p. 287).

That Bamba Susso's ancestor was a Muslim at the time of his death is crucial to understanding the nature of the modern *griot's* message concerning Islam. Bamba Susso's criticism is not of Islam as such, but rather an Islam that refuses integration with traditional social and political structures embodied by the *griot* in his role as advisor, messenger, and spokesman for African rulers.

However, the *jali* modifies his view of Fode Kaba at the very end of the epic when the French and British demand that the ruler hand over a group of his warriors against whom they had fought at Sankandi. Fode Kaba refuses the Europeans' ultimatum by declaring:

831 "I will never hand over a Muslim to an infidel."
It was then that the French rose up and went
and crushed Medina.
That was the end of the career of the great *marabout*;
he himself perished there (p. 297).

In this passage, the *jali's* attitude toward Fode Kaba seems to have changed as the result of the new political context. Fode Kaba is no longer a menace to traditional society, but now "the great *marabout*" who bravely dies rather than submit to the Europeans. The message here appears to be that the brand of Islam that respects certain autochthonous values is the ideal. But this ideal becomes of secondary importance where resistance to colonialism is concerned.

Throughout this epic, the *jali* finds himself constantly in a state of conflict. He is ultimately sacrificed to the whims of a leader who tramples on tradition. In the instance of the first murder, *jali* Yoro plays the role of the point man, the first person who will be sent forward in the attempt to establish negotiations between two peoples. In the context of the fierce passions provoked by the Islamic hero, these artisans of the word who represent tradition appear to be the last best hope, a kind of human cushion for those who send him to deliver their message to the warrior. There are of course many ways Fode Kaba has violated tradition, but the mistreatment of the *griots* seems to be Bamba Susso's greatest concern.

A second epic in which the Islamic and colonial presences play an important role comes from the Cayor region of Senegal. *The Epic of Lat Dior* (Dieng 1993) was recorded from *guewel* Bassirou Mbaye in 1985 by Bassirou Dieng[1] and published in a bilingual Wolof–French format eight years later, along with twelve other Wolof oral texts (the English translations cited below are by the authors). These epic texts take the reader from the sixteenth to the nineteenth centuries, and in particular to the story of Lat Dior (1842–1886). He is without doubt the most famous of these Wolof heroes because he frequently dominated the political and military scene in western Senegal from 1860 to his death in 1886.

In this 1074–line narrative, the *guewel* selectively rearranges events surrounding the 1860 crisis of succession to the throne of Cayor, both to legitimize Lat Dior having resisted the French and to reinforce the traditional primacy of matrilineage in the face of the paternalistic system of inheritance introduced by Islam. When the reigning ruler of Cayor, Lat Dior's half-brother Birima Ngoné Latir, died in January 1860, Lat Dior briefly became a candidate for the position of Damel, but was rejected by the Cayorian freemen in favor of Makodou Kodou Diouf Fal, Birima's father. In the epic, however, the *guewel* replaces Makodou with Madiodio Déguène Kodou Fal, a French puppet who was actually installed as Damel by Governor Faidherbe in May 1861. Although Lat Dior was of Gej matrilineage, one of the traditional requirements for Cayor's rulers, he was not yet circumcised and not of Fal patrilineage, a secondary prerequisite to become Damel. The substitution of Madiodio for Makodou as Lat Dior's rival discredits the Fal line by linking it to collaboration with the French and thus legitimizes Lat Dior's otherwise shaky claim to the throne. In the same way, the *guewel's* privileging of Gej over Fal heritage adapts Islamic beliefs to the local value system, for in Cayor matrilineage had traditionally taken precedence over patrilineage until the rise of militant Islam (Dieng, 13).

The narrator continues to balance Islamic and traditional practices throughout the epic, establishing a relationship between the two that parallels the one already identified in *Fode Kaba*. After Madiodio seizes power, Lat Dior exiles himself to his father's lands to study the Qur'an with Serigne Koki, presumably to gain the wisdom and authority to displace his rival. However, when Madiodio begins to rule cruelly, making the Cayorians "cultivate his fields in the middle of the dry season" (line 38, p. 377) and randomly sacrificing his subjects to his bloodthirsty vulture-spirit Njëbb (lines 55–65, p. 377), Demba War Dior Mbaye Ndéné, eldest of the Gej line, promptly calls back Lat Dior to help overthrow Madiodio. At first, Serigne Koki refuses Demba's request, saying, "I can't, because Lat Dior is a religious leader / And you are still pagan warriors" (lines 78–79, p. 379). But Demba explains the situation, and the teacher yields: "Take him, if that's the way it is" (line 81, p. 379). The obvious implication is that learning the Qur'an and becoming a *marabout* is not as important as righting Madiodio's crimes and violation of traditional rules of succession.

Although he successfully completes the rites of circumcision and horse mastery, Lat Dior is still not strong enough to take power and must seek help to defeat Madiodio. He first goes to the neighboring kingdoms of Bawol and Sine, but is refused aid by their rulers. He finally turns to the Tijani cleric Maba Diakhou, who offers him aid provided that he accept Islam. In fact, it is Maba Diakhou and later Amadou Bamba, both major Islamic figures, who intervene at the crucial moments of this dynastic epic: exile and the final battle.

Upon hearing Maba Diakhou's ultimatum, Lat Dior exclaims, "My fathers, I refuse to abandon my traditions" (line 352, p. 395), but then reconsiders after Demba War tells him that "Converting is like getting a haircut / When the hair grows back, it is as if you never cut it" (lines 354–55, p. 395). Lat Dior promptly converts and joins Maba Diakhou in a combined effort to mount a jihad, resist the French, and reassert control of the throne of Cayor. In this context, traditional values complement Islamic sources of power. For example, when it comes time to select a warrior to lead an expedition to sink a shipload of French soldiers, the candidates are "All elite riflemen / Who have powerful *marabouts*" (lines 435–36, p. 401). But one leader, Galo Déguène, is singled out for leadership of the mission. "But Galo Déguène has the best mother / The virtues of a mother support you in every undertaking (lines 437–38, p. 401).

Needless to say, Galo is chosen and the enterprise succeeds thanks to the strength of his Gej matrilineage, which is recounted by the narrator for the benefit of the listeners (lines 445–53, p. 401).

The *guewel's* narration of these events sheds doubt on the sincerity of Lat Dior's conversion and raises questions about the narrator's own attitude towards Islam and his role as social mediator. Again, as in *The Epic of Fode Kaba*, the intervening factor of colonialism is necessary to evaluate accurately the *griot's* view of Islam vis-à-vis traditional society. Before Lat Dior's final battle against the French, which took place in 1886 at Dékélé, he demonstrates his sincere devotion to Islam while still maintaining the honor of his matrilineage. Lat Dior takes a series of ritual steps to prepare for the battle: he buries all of his magic charms, offers his son as the disciple of the widely respected cleric, Amadou Bamba, and accepts the gift of the holy man's boubou to wear into combat (lines 938–52, p. 433). Moreover, having foreseen his demise in battle, Lat Dior declares that he will pray the "tisbar [early afternoon] prayer today with Maba Diakhou, my guide, in the other world" (line 968, p. 433). However, when Amadou Bamba asks Lat Dior to renounce the fight against the French and come away with him too, the hero replies:

> 946 If people ask me for protection and if I start to look for protection for
> myself
> It will seem like cowardice.
> I don't want to tarnish my lineage.
> A noble must never retreat (p. 433).

Just as in *The Epic of Fode Kaba*, the *griot* has privileged traditional values over Islamic faith until the decisive moment of conflict with the French, when the balance shifts in the opposite direction. *The Epic of Lat Dior* thus demonstrates clearly what the story of Fode Kaba only implies: that Islam and tradition can be mutually complementary in a variety of circumstances, provided that the right mix between the two is struck to fit the context.

The 780-line *Epic of Kelefa Saane*, also recounted by Bamba Susso in 1969 (Innes 1978), shows a different way in which the *griot* acts as cultural mediator. By inspiring and advising, Kelefa Saane's *griots* serve to counter-balance the *marabouts*, who predict and facilitate the hero's demise at the hands of his enemies.

Kelefa Saane was a mid-nineteenth-century prince of the Mandinka confederation in Kaabu, a group of states lying primarily between the Gambia river to the north and Rio Corubal in Guinea-Bissau to the south (Innes 1976, 27–28). The epic focuses on Kelefa Saane's intervention in the war between Niumi and Jokadu, two member states of the confederation located in eastern Gambia just north of the River Gambia (Innes 1978, 1).

During his youth, *jali* Maadi Wuleng is constantly at Kelefa Saane's side, recounting the prince's lineage and encouraging him to live up to his noble heritage. Unfortunately, in an attempt to do something memorable for his *jali* to sing about, Kelefa Saane shoots the headpads off the heads of princesses as they come to draw water at the well, and he is sold into slavery for his actions (lines 115–48, p. 35–36). When he manages to ran-som himself and return to the kingdom, *jali* Maadi warns him that such misconduct will gain him no followers (lines 211–18, p. 40).

However, because of his princely origins, Kelefa Saane refuses to farm. He wants instead to win glory and honor through battle. His restlessness disrupts the community, and the elders summon a *marabout* for advice on how to get rid of him (lines 251–264, p. 43). Shortly after the marabout makes an amulet that is thrown across the river to drive Kelefa Saane away, the warrior departs to help King Demba Sonko of Niumi in his war against the Jokadu (lines 326–35, p. 45–46). Along the way, Kelefa Saane is told by a second marabout that he will be killed if he fights in the war (lines 520–21 p. 55). Upon hearing the prophesy, Kelefa Saane begins to weep and loses heart, but *jali* Maadi inspires his patron with the following words: "If your courage has failed, / Why don't you give me the war spear so that I can go and answer the Fula's call? If you die, I will never play my kora for another prince" (lines 530–32, p. 55).

This appeal to Kelefa Saane's pride and affirmation of loyalty by his *jali* immediately raises the warrior's spirits—he laughs and faces his future with a new sense of honor, saying, "A man who has died because of his love for another has not died in vain" (line 537, p. 55).

Kelefa Saane reaches his destination and joins the battle, inflicting heavy losses on the Jokadu, who solicit advice on how to kill him from their own *marabout*. He reveals that Kelefa Saane can be killed only with a bullet of gold and silver shot by an uncircumcised albino (lines 660–67, p. 61–62). The Jokadu waste no time in executing the plan, and Kelefa Saane is fatally wounded (lines 689–90, p. 63). As the warrior lies dying, a *jali* named Koriyang Musa comforts him by singing his praises and reassuring him that he is acting honorably in the face of death (lines 721–28, p. 65).

As Innes suggests in his introduction, the great popularity of *The Epic of Kelefa Saane* lies not in its historical significance, but rather in its relevance as a model for social conduct. Kelefa Saane influenced very little, if at all, the outcome of the Niumi–Jokadu war, yet he does strongly embody the traditional virtues of courage, pride, honor, and loyalty (Innes, 7–10).

As we have seen, *griots* play a crucial role in shaping these qualities in Kelefa Saane throughout his life, especially when they are tested as a result of marabout intervention. It must be noted that the relationship between *griots* and *marabouts* in the epic is not one of good versus evil or open confrontation. The *marabouts'* actions are never qualified negatively by the *jali* telling the story or portrayed as not legitimate in any other way. *Griots* merely help the hero live up to his reputation as a champion of traditional values and also help celebrate those values. In so doing, Kelefa Saane's *griots* counterbalance indirectly the *marabouts'* potentially harmful influence.

It is important not to overstate the friction between *griots* and Islam, for there are cases in which the former are overtly allied with the religion. One such case appears in *The Epic of Umaru Seku Tal*,[2] where *griots* play a decisive role in the deeds of the famous Muslim cleric-warrior. Born around 1794, he spread Islam across West Africa and opposed the French from 1852 until his death in 1864 (Clark and Phillips 1994, 259–62; see also Robinson 1985).

In this version, Umaru Tal's *jeseré* serves as his constant companion, and is the only one to accompany him on the pilgrimage to Mecca at the outset of the epic (Watta 1993, 6–7). As Umaru Tal stops along the way to lead prayer and teach the Qur'an, his *jeseré* composes songs to honor his knowledge and piety (p. 9). Significantly, when the Arabs ask Umaru Tal what the source of his wisdom is, he tells them it not his patrilineage, but his mother's virtue. "Even better than my father exist in the West," says Umaru Tal (p. 19). However:

> My mother is above women
> Not for her height
> Not for her elegance
> The character God gave my mother
> I doubt there are more than five women
> He gave to in this world (p. 20).

The parallel between the emphasis on the role of the mother in this epic and the privileging of matrilineage in *The Epic of Lat Dior* is striking, especially since here it is presented not in subtle contrast to, but in overt harmony with Islam.

On his way back from Mecca, Umaru Tal performs another act of faith where the *jeseré* plays an important symbolic role. Stopping at Segu to convert its population to Islam, Umaru Tal must face resistance on the part of the Bambara, who blame Umaru Tal for a bad harvest and refuse to give him the annual tithe due secular and religious leaders. When they demand that he leave their land, Umaru Tal responds by making his prayer mat levitate. He climbs on it with his *jeseré* and declares: "Now take your land and show me / That of God so I can sit / Here I am on nobody's land, am I not?" (p. 32).

In contrast to Kelefa Saane, here the *jeseré* is on the side of Islam, tempering the excesses of traditional society exemplified by Segu:

> Segu was the busiest of all
> The cities around, around our neighbors
> For you could see no equal herds
> You could see no equal populations
> You could see no equal fortunes
> You could see no equal valor in war either
> But in misbelieving as well, in those days
> There was no equal to Segu
> Men and women stood up and urinated in disrespect to God (p. 30).

The narrator suggests that it is no longer Islam that needs to be adapted to fit with traditional values, but vice versa. The implication here is that *griots* mediate the relationship between the two in both directions. Indeed, later in the epic when Umaru Tal is blockading a city where a "pagan" adversary is hiding, his *jeseré* advises him to lift the siege, for innocent people are suffering in addition to his enemy:

Alhadji Umaru!
This is not fitting
Children are dying in this city who never
Met you
Let alone fight against you (p. 71).

Umaru Tal promptly takes this advice, and enters the city to confront his enemy directly. In this way, the *griot* moderates the Muslim leader's religious fervor by integrating a traditional sense of honor and fair play into *jihad*, where normally the ends justify all necessary means.

The examples of *griot* functions in these and other texts—advisors, critics, companions, mediators, praise-singers, sources of inspiration, comforters, and cultural historians—suggest several conclusions about the way these wordsmiths cushioned the impact of Islam during the late nineteenth century.

First, the portrayals of *griots* by *griots* reveal that they played a central role in the rapidly occurring social and cultural events of the period. They appear to have a keen awareness of the complexity of the shifts in political power taking place in their lands. Thanks to a professional knowledge of people and their motivations, they seem to have a special talent for piloting their leaders through the social turbulence generated by the changing balance of power between Islam and the growing French influence. The descriptions of them that we read in the epics illustrate Lilyan Kesteloot's point that *griots* are "instruments of power, but they also influence the way it is used" (1991, 21).

Griots in the recent past worked very hard to adapt an increasingly militant form of Islam to traditional political and social structures. In so doing, they appear to have participated directly in the long-term process of reinterpreting the regional identity of their peoples. The syncretism of belief systems that continues to occur in the Sahel region is no less important than the often fluid nature of ethnic identity as peoples interact because of wars, drought, trade, and other factors. With their narratives about family, clan, and state relations, *griots* are intimately involved in both of these processes.

The second conclusion emerging from the texts is that when a contemporary *griot* recounts these stories of late nineteenth-century Islamic heroes, the narrative undergoes a "multiplier" effect based on two factors, one internal to the text, the other external. The internal impact comes from the fact that in their profession *griots* are both the actors in the events of the past and serve today as interpreters of those events. It is not surprising, then, that these wordsmiths reveal in their narratives a high degree of self-referentiality. Often, the *griot* recounting the epic is closely related to counterparts in the epic, as in Bamba Susso's version of *Fode Kaba* discussed above. This relationship, underscored by the modern narrator, gives authority to the epic, and, in turn, prestige to the *griot* who recounts it. The result is that both the heroes of the nineteenth century and the *griots* who served them are remembered in vivid detail. Finally, the names and places cited in the epic are often fresh in the memory of both the *griot* and the audience. When the modern narrator of *The Epic of Lat Dior* refers to the construction of the St. Louis–Dakar railroad, everyone in the audience is familiar with it. The recent nature of the events and the close link with the ancestors in the form of family referentiality cause the narrative to take on an immediacy that epics focusing on earlier centuries cannot match.

The external factor is communications technology. The contemporary narrator of these epics is no longer limited to a local audience—for example, a group of listeners in the courtyard of a noble patron. Radio, television, audio cassettes and video cassettes that are sold on the sidewalks in cities and towns enable the *griot* to recount these epics of Islamic heroes to national and regional audiences. If Lat Dior's fame was probably limited to western Senegambia in the nineteenth century, today, thanks to a larger sense of Senegalese identity cultivated by radio and television, he has become a full-fledged national hero. The epics and their component forms such as praise-songs and genealogies, no less than plays performed in secondary school assembly rooms, contribute constantly to this celebration of a great hero who embraced a form of Islam without giving up his traditional beliefs.

The third and perhaps most significant consequence of the diffusion of epics about these nineteenth-century heroes is to be seen in the narratives' bridging of the gap between the written culture of the Qur'an and the oral tradition of Africa. Kristina Nelson emphasizes that "the transmission of the *Qur'an* and its social existence are essentially oral" (1985, xiv), a trait that contributes significantly to the ease with which Islam has found a receptive audience in much of the Sahel. But the oral epics recounted by *griots* in their own languages to large audiences serve to root the religion even more firmly in societies with limited literacy rates.

Finally, the diffusion of these epics about Islamic heroes, by *griots* in live performances, via cassettes, on the radio, and in television programs, contributes in a direct way to the rising Islamic consciousness that is spreading across West Africa. From Senegal to Niger, local coalitions of groups are pressing for closer adherence to Islamic values. For example, in Niger a group has blocked implementation of a new family code that their members consider to run counter to Islamic values (Vincent 1994).

The contemporary resurgence of Islam in the Sahel, though feared by some as a rising tide of fundamentalism, must be seen as a phenomenon inspired by many sources—the early proponents who led the ancient empires, some later rulers in the seventeenth and eighteenth centuries, and above all a variety of nineteenth-century rulers who gave the religion a powerful boost. The recounting of epics, especially those about recent Islamic rulers, reflects the strong pull of history for people in the Sahel today. No less than the call of the muezzin, many of whom are from *griot* families, the narration of an epic about an Islamic ruler from the recent past perpetuates a system of belief that is many centuries old.

Notes

1. The authors thank Bassirou Dieng for his comments on a draft of this study.
2. This version of the epic was recounted in the Zarma dialect of Songhay by Djeliba Bagué, also known as Djeliba Badié, an extremely popular *jeseré* in Niamey Niger. Several minor anomalies in this text need to be noted. First, the translator, Oumarou Watta, gives no time or place for the recording. Second, he spells the Songhay word for *griot* as *gesere*, though the more common usage is *jeseré*, which we will use here. Finally, there are no line numbers.

Chapter 7

▼▼▼▼▼▼▼▼

Islamic Inscriptions and Motifs and Arab Genealogies in the Epic Tale of the Kingdom of Waalo

SAMBA DIOP

This paper will deal with oral narratives and more specifically, Wolof oral narratives of the Senegambia region. In December 1989 and January 1990, I had the opportunity to record two versions of the Epic of the Waalo Kingdom, as performed by Sèq Ñan and Ancumbu Caam, both prominent Wolof *griots*.[1] The epic is a foundation myth that recounts the origins of the Wolof people and their original ancestor, Njaajaan Njaay. These *griots* are attached to my family and are natives of the Waalo region, along the banks of the River Senegal. Both *griots* are well known genealogists, poets, singers, and oral historians in their community. An extract from the Waalo epic is included below as an example of the oral narratives I am discussing; the full text is available in Diop 1995.

The inclusion of Arab genealogies in the epic tale of the Waalo kingdom indicates how difficult it is to separate Islam in West Africa from Arab and Berber proselytizers, war wagers, and traders. Thus, for the same reasons, West African *griots* (mostly Wolof and Mandinka) tend to link indigenous genealogies to Arab and Berber ones. Since Islam is a prestigious religion and culture, this strategy on the part of the *griot* would give more authority and credibility to his narrative. For instance, Ñan connects Njaajaan to an Arab father named Bubakar Umar. Interestingly enough (and as if intended by the *griot*), Njaajaan's mother was a native local black woman.

This paper will analyze the encounter between Islam and indigenous Wolof beliefs, the incorporation of Islamic and Arab beliefs into Wolof culture. In order to understand contemporary Wolof culture, one has to travel back in time with the *griot* and consider all the Islamic inscriptions as well as the overall Islamic influence over Wolof culture.

The Cultural Syncretism of Islam and Wolof

Since Wolof society is mostly orally based, there is no written text that corresponds to the Qur'an. With the advent of the trans–Saharan trade and the coming of Arab, Almoravid, and Berber merchants, the Qur'an and its commentary were gradually incorporated into Wolof beliefs. As far as the masses and the *griots* were concerned, it was not the original Qur'anic text that really mattered; rather, they were more interested in the derivative tales and anecdotes bearing on the prophets' lives, the wars and battles, and the hadiths (the sayings and deeds of the prophet Muhammad).

The Old Testament, particularly the book of Genesis, forms an integral part of the Waalo epic and of the religious and intellectual formation of the *griot*. Interestingly enough, the Wolof *griot* starts the epic with the Flood myth and the story of Noah and Ham (the latter is considered the ancestor of all black people). The Islamic element and the prophet Muhammad are mentioned much later in the epic.

The Wolof *griot* (and other Senegalese Muslims) travels with ease between the Qur'anic text and its derivative elements on the one hand, and indigenous beliefs and traditions on the other. The line between these two entities is blurred: the Biblical and Islamic historical figures are reconstructed in the epic so that these figures become legitimate agents within Wolof society and culture. The *griot* has obtained most of these figures from the Old Testament and the Qur'an. Conversely, in Wolof and Senegalese society in general, the founders of Muslim sects such as Cheikh Ahmadou Bamba (Mourid), El Hadji Malick Sy (Tijaan), and Seydina Issa Laay (Layène), Baye Niass (Niassène), have acquired a saintly and holy place among the Muslims of Senegal. This is the other side of the coin, namely, the incorporation of local black saints into the mainstream of Islamic thought. Thus, contrary to what one might think, there is a dual reception between the Qur'an and Islam on the one hand and Wolof Muslims on the other.[2]

Throughout the epic the *griots* have transposed major Biblical and Islamic figures from the text (Qur'an) and its derived commentary into local Wolof culture. It is important to emphasize the fact that the *griots* (and the Wolof and Muslim populations of the Sahel at large) tend to confound Arab and Qur'anic saints with Berber and Almoravid proselytizers, military figures, merchants, and marabouts. Physical appearance is certainly relevant, for Arabs from the Arabian peninsula and the Middle East often resemble the North African and Saharan local populations, at least in dress and out-

ward aspect. Moreover, the Almoravid and Berber populations were converted to Islam by the Arab conquerors; the former have borrowed the
Arabic language as well as adopting Islamic values from the latter.

One also finds examples of conflation in the epic. The *griot* mentions
Abu Bakr who traveled from the Middle East to West Africa in order to
convert the local populations to Islam. There is, however, an original Abu
Bakr who lived in the seventh century, at the time of the prophet
Muhammad, and a twelfth–century Abu Bakr who was a Berber or
Almoravid and lived in North Africa. The Abu Bakr mentioned in the
Wolof epic tale is probably a conflation of the seventh–century and the
twelfth–century figures, since he is both a figure of high antiquity and a
leader who came to West Africa.

Another indication of Arab prestige in the epic is the preeminence
given by the *griots* to Arab founders and historical figures. The *griots* of the
West African Sahel often link the founder of their ethnic group to a mythical Arab founder.[3] In the epic, the *griot* repeats that Njaajaan Njaay's original name was Muhammadu Aydara. Muhammadu is from the prophet's
name, Muhammad, and Aydara is a stock name among the Berbers and
Almoravids. (The folk etymological meaning of Njaajaan Njaay is "this is a
calamity.")

Also, in the epic, Bubakar Umar (an Arab hero) fights a local black
king named Hamar–the Scolder–of–Old–People (the pagan villain and
anti–hero). Hamar kills Bubakar Umar. As expected, the latter is avenged
by his son Njaajaan who, later on, kills Hamar–the–Scolder–of–Old–People.
Thus, to this day, and in the foundation myths of most ethnic groups of the
West African Sahel, there is no absolute certainty as to the origin of the
founders of those ethnic groups because of the intrusion of the Arab,
Almoravid, and Berber elements. Was Njaajaan of local stock, or was he of
Arab or Almoravid origin? The only indication the *griot* gives in the epic is
that Njaajaan's father (Bubakar Umar) came from the East, from Arabia,
whereas Njaajaan's mother (Fatumata Sal) was a local black woman (Sal is
a Tukulor name). This is perhaps a borrowing from Qur'anic prescriptions
to the effect that a Muslim man can marry a non–Muslim woman and
later convert her to Islam (a non–Muslim man marrying a Muslim woman
and therefore converting her to any other religion is forbidden by Islam).
Thus, in the epic, the *griot* has a perfect device (Bubakar marrying Fatumata
after converting her father to Islam) to give Islam authority and preeminence over the local Wolof institutions, religious creeds, and customs.

Still, in the epic Bubakar is accompanied and aided by Mbaarik Bô.
The latter is certainly a black man if one takes into account his physical
description (for instance, his nose is pierced and there is a ring dangling at

its end). However, Bubakar is the chief, the one who gives orders and makes plans. Mbaarik follows those orders. Additionally, Bubakar has converted Mbaarik to Islam. This pairing evokes another famous pairing in Islamic history, that of the prophet Muhammad and his muezzin and companion, Bilal. Bilal was reputedly a black slave who was bought by Abu Bakr and then freed. This relationship of Bilal to Muhammad could be taken as a metaphor for the larger relationship between an Arab Islam and an African Wolof tradition.

Before concluding, it is important to point out that the perceptions European Christians and Middle Eastern Muslims had of each other during the crusades affect Muslims throughout the world, including the Wolof. Wolof Muslims shared the Arabs' negative perceptions of Christians in general, extending this to include white persons in particular.

Islam is vibrant and alive in Senegal and among the Wolof. One may argue that we are in the presence of a syncretic religion with the mixing of Islam and indigenous religions, but the important point to remember is that a distinct people, through their oral literature and their *griots*, have inscribed Islamic motifs into their original beliefs, and incorporated Arab, Berber, and Almoravid genealogies into their own. Yet, one can still see that the Wolof have kept some of their customs, beliefs, and mores, and therefore have constructed and retained a distinctive personality.

The Epic Tale of the Waalo Kingdom[4]

God the Most High said to Noah:
"The Great Flood will originate
From that day when your wife is cooking.
It will come from one of the stones
That support the cauldron.
That stone will fall off;
You then must proceed to the ark."
The Great Flood came.
During the Great Flood,
It is said that everybody entered the ark,
Except a man called Iwet.
Iwet was the only one not to enter the ark;
He drowned in the Flood.
Noah's ark landed in a place called Dundogi.
There were eighty people on board.
One of Noah's sons name is Sham.
The other is named Ham.
The last one is Ibn Noah.
Tradition says that,
One day,
Noah fell asleep;

Ham the eldest son was laughing.
Sham asked him:
"Why are you laughing?
Are you laughing about our father?"
Right at that moment,
Noah woke up.
Noah said:
"From today on,
You, Ham!
You will be the precursor of the black race.
You, Sham!
You will beget all white people."
Thus Sham begot two persons called Yajojo and Majojo.
Ham begot a son called Anfésédé.
Anfésédé addressed Ham his father in these terms:
"Noah is my grandfather,
You are my father.
I am asking for your grace to fall upon me."
Anfésédé himself begot a son called Misrae.
Misrae himself is the founder
Of a town called Misrae.
Ham also begot two black children:
One male and one female.
Some of them [Ham's children] created Jordan.
Jordan means the country of the Black people.
The following people belong to Ham's clan:
Saxewil, Bateres, Mayaasin, and Sanaaf.
From there, I want to tell you
About the history of the Empire of Ghana.
Beforehand, I would like to come back
To the region of Jordan.
Jordan is a very old country.
The prophet Muhammad (peace upon him)
Had called upon people to follow him.
He lived to be sixty three years old.
Ababakar Sadex succeeded him.
He ruled for two years.
Umar Ibn Xatab succeeded Ababakar Sadex.
He stayed in power for fifteen years.
Some sources said that
He stayed in power for twelve years.
Bubakar Umar and Ibn Xatab fought a jihad.
They converted people to Islam.
The two of them considered the pagans to be very arrogant.
The jihad is the reason why Bubakar Umar left Jordan
Jordan the country of the Blacks.
He was accompanied by a man called Mbaarik Bô.
Mbaarik Bô was originally from Masaasi.
Mbaarik Bô had his nose pierced.

He wore a big ring in it.
It is said that when it was very hot,
The ring used to fall off.
When it was very hot,
The ring used to expand like rubber;
It would then fall to the ground.
Mbaarik Bô and Bubakar Umar arrived in Ghana.
They fought in Ghana for fourteen months.
Actually, they fought for thirteen months.
In the fourteenth month,
A new king came to power.
His name was Gana Kamara.
The Ghana Empire was named
After that king called Gana Kamara.
But before that,
It wasn't called the Empire of Ghana.
It was called Jordan,
The country of the Blacks.
Mbaarik Bô and Bubakar Umar fought for fourteen years.
They converted many pagans to Islam, namely Mbaarik Bô and Umar,
Mbaarik Bô asked Bubakar Umar:
"Chief, where are you heading now?"
Bubakar Umar replied:
"Me, where am I heading?
I've heard of a king living in a far away country;
A far away country in the West.
I want to make a Muslim of him."
Mbaarik Bô said to Bubakar:
"Chief, I am more than willing to accompany you;
But I want to be king;
I want to be crowned;
Given the fact that you are a wise man,
And that you have a lot of spiritual power,
I would like for you to pray for me.
Pray for me to God so I can become a king.
If I become a king,
That crown will be fruitful.
It will be fruitful because of your prayers."
That's the reason why Mbaarik Bô
Was of very good company to Bubakar Umar, Njaajaan's father.
Mbaarik Bô was very close to Bubakar.
One day, Mbaarik Bô asked Bubakar:
"Where are you leading us?"
Bubakar replied:
"God hasn't told me yet the path
I will take for the remainder of our journey.
But thanks to his grace
I had a dream.
In the dream, I clearly saw that we are going to leave again.

We are going to journey to a far–off land."
Thus, tradition says that
Mbaarik Bô and Bubakar Umar left Ghana.
They journeyed westward for many months
Until they arrived at a village.
That village was called Muderi Jaawara.
There, they found a man called Abraham Sal.
Abraham Sal thought that Bubakar was Bilal.
That's why he didn't fight Bubakar Umar and Mbaarik Bô.
Njaajaan Njaay was the first ruler of the Waalo empire.
Your ancestors, the ancestors of the Diop family,
Were among those who chose Njaajaan,
As a ruler and a chief.
Your ancestors were the jogamaay.
They were the chiefs of the Waalo empire.
Your father Mapaté Diop, sitting next to me,
He knows very well what I am talking about.
He can attest to it.
Njaajaan Njaay was crowned by your ancestors;
The jogomaay were the ones who chose him as a ruler.
In his turn, Njaajaan was under obligations.
He was under obligations to your ancestors the Jogomaay.
I am going to tell you
About the process of the crowning of Njaajaan.
Bubakar Umar, Njaajaan's father left Jordan;
He arrived in Ghana with Mbaarik Bô.
They fought on the way;
They converted people to Islam.
There, they found Hawaat, another chief.
Then they left Ghana.
They arrived in Muderi Jaawara.
Mbaarik Bô was a pagan;
Bubakar converted him to Islam.
Hawaat was given the family name Gaye.
He was given that name by a man called Aali Gaye,
For Hawaat didn't have a family name.
Bubakar too had Aydara as a family name.
He was given the family name Gaye.
Thus, Mbaarik Bô was Bubakar's personal secretary.
After they left Ghana,
They arrived in this region;
They arrived in the River Senegal area.
More precisely, up the river.
There, they found Abraham Sal;
They converted Abraham to Islam.
Abraham thought that Bubakar was Bilal.
Bilal himself was the companion of the prophet Muhammad;
(Peace upon him)
That's why Abraham didn't fight Bubakar

Abraham Sal is the ancestor
Of all the people bearing the name Sal,
Among the Lamtoro, the Tukulor people.
Thus, Bubakar was the one,
Who converted Abraham to Islam.
Abraham begot Fatumata Abraham Sal.
Fatumata was Abraham's daughter.
Her father gave her in marriage to Bubakar.
She became Bubakar's wife.
Thus, Bubakar converted the Sereer people.
He came to Dogo . . .
. . . He came to Godo [Gédé] in the Bakel region,
On the left bank of the river Senegal.
That area was empty;
Only a fortress was there.
Thus, Bubakar converted the Sereer,
Until he came to face a big Sereer chief.
That chief was called Hamar–the Scolder–of Old–People.
Hamar used to scold old people; that's why he was called that name.
Mbaarik Bô was Bubakar's companion.
He went behind the compound.
There, he spread his prayer rug.
He started reciting the Qur'an.
Remember that,
He was converted to Islam by Bubakar.
Bubakar called on Hamar–the Scolder–of–Old–People.
He said to him: "Come here!
I am going to shave your head;
I am going to convert you to Islam."
Hamar–the–Scolder–of–Old–People replied:
"Can you let me go to the outhouse first?"
Bubakar said:
"Yes, you can."
Hamar–the–Scolder–of–Old–People did not enter the outhouse.
He went behind a nearby tree.
His bow and quiver were hanging there,
With many arrows inside.
He took the bow;
He adjusted an arrow;
He then hit Bubakar on the forearm.
The latter quivered, quivered, and quivered;
He was in pain.
He went to his wife Fatumata and told her:
"Let's go inside the room.
I want to talk to you."
Mbaarik Bô was sitting on his raw sheephide prayer rug.
He was outside the room;
Nobody could see him;
He was the only one to hear the conversation;

That conversation that took place
Between Bubakar and his wife Fatumata.
Bubakar said to his wife:
"I want to go back East;
I know that I am going to die,
As a result of the wound
Caused by Hamar–the–Scolder–of–Old–People.
The arrow is poisoned;
I don't want to die here.
I want to die back East where I am from.
I am going back East.
You shouldn't marry a man whose body
You would see when he's washing himself.
You shouldn't marry a man whose body
You would see when he is in the outhouse.
If the man asks you to sleep with him,
The mattress must fall first on the floor,
Before you can sleep with him."
While Bubakar was saying these lofty words
To his wife Fatumata inside the room
Mbaarik Bô heard all the conversation.
At that time, Fatumata was pregnant with Njaajaan Njaay.
His given first name was Muhammadu;
It wasn't Njaajaan.
Fatumata said to her husband:
"These are the things
You want me to do before marrying any man?"
"Yes," replied Bubakar.
A few days later Bubakar left the village.
He headed back East to his native homeland.
He didn't make it back East;
He died halfway through his journey;
He died in a settlement called Singiti.
His grave is in Singiti;
It is near the town of Ataar.
After that happened,
Mbaarik Bô put his shoes on.
He put on a white robe.
He took the jar he used for his ablutions.
He went to the outhouse;
He went very far from the village,
Until nobody could see him anymore.
He then went inside the outhouse.
He came out of the outhouse.
Fatumata erected a high pillar;
She would stand on it;
She would watch the men going to the outhouse.
When the men wanted to go to the outhouse,
They would just go behind the fortress.

Only Mbaarik Bô would go far away,
Until nobody could see him anymore.
There, He would relieve himself.
Fatumata said to herself:
"I am really puzzled. What a shame!"
Muhammadu, Njaajaan was born.
When he was eleven,
He fought Hamar–the–Scolder–of–Old–People
In a very celebrated combat;
Njaajaan smote him with his swift hand behind the ear;
He smashed both jaws killing him instantly.
Fatumata refused to marry all the men
who courted her
For none of them fulfilled the conditions,
Those conditions her late husband dictated to her.[5]

Notes

1. I traveled first to Rosso–Senegal in the heart of Waaloland, 370 kilometers from Dakar, the capital of Senegal; Rosso is also on the riverine border between Senegal and Mauritania. Ñan came over to my father's house and recited (over two days) the epic tale of Njaajaan Njaay while playing the *xalam* (a traditional Wolof guitar). The recording, transcription (in Wolof), translation into English, and publication of this epic is the first of its kind. There was no previous literary version of this epic; however, various historians and anthropologists such as Charles Monteil, Vincent Monteil, Maurice Delafosse, Captain H. Azan, Boubacar Barry, Faidherbe, and Henri Gaden have used oral sources bearing on the person of Njaajaan Njaay.

2. In the interview that I conducted with Ancumbu Caam, he remarked that his ancestor *griots* used to travel from village to village in order to give performances consisting of singing, drum playing, and dancing. Before each performance, however, these ancestors used to retire to a nearby bush area where they would meditate and write in Arabic verses from the Qur'an; they would also do their ablutions and then would perform the five daily prayers prescribed by Islam. Caam does not tell us whether these prayers were performed at once, one immediately after the other, or at the designated times. We can infer that once these ancestors started singing and dancing, they would not have time to perform the Islamic prayers.

   In general, there is a bias against indigenous traditional beliefs in favor of Islam. Yet the majority of Senegalese Muslims have retained some of those traditional beliefs and creeds. In the mind of the people, there is no contradiction between being a Muslim and still wearing charms, amulets, *gris–gris*, following ancestor worship, performing libations for gods and goddesses such as Mame Coumba Bang, seeking traditional therapeutic healing among the Lebu (Ndëpp), and visiting the diviners.

3. Sometimes this attitude does not make sense, since blacks are portrayed negatively in Arab society, as shown by Kole Omotoso (1984, 111–17). Bernard Lewis, however, has shown that there is ample evidence in the Qur'an on the lack of racial prejudice in pre-Islamic and earliest Islamic times in Arab society (Lewis 1971, 7). Lewis also shows the negative portrayal of blacks and dark–skinned people in the Arab popular mind.

4. Sèq Ñan was sixty-one years old at the time of recording. From 1950 to 1952 Ñan had been conscripted into the French army, where he learned to drive; however, he had minimal exposure to French language and culture. Upon leaving the army, he became a truck driver for a sugar mill (Compagnie Sucrière Sénégalaise) located in Waalo. Ñan retired in 1983. While working as a truck driver, Ñan remained a *griot*; he visited patrons like my father in order to praise and sing their genealogies; in return, he received gifts in kind or cash.

    Ñan used an *Ajami* type script in order to transliterate the Wolof language into Arabic. After reciting the epic tale of Njaajaan, Ñan also performed the genealogies of all the rulers of the Waalo kingdom. While reciting, Ñan would glance at his logbook, where he had written down in Arabic the names of the *Braks* (army chiefs and kings) as well as the number of years they stayed in power. There were altogether fifty-two rulers totaling 625 years of rule. The last year of reign was 1854, which coincides with the coming of Faidherbe and French colonization.

    Ancumbu Caam, the second *griot*, was eighty-one years old at the time of recording. Since he lives on the outskirts of Dakar, I recorded him in my family compound in Dakar. To be more precise, I interviewed Caam. Caam is blind; thus he is always accompanied by his son, Magate. Magate serves as a guide, but he is also learning at the same time from his father whenever the latter is performing.

5. Mbaarik Bô ultimately satisfies the conditions set by Bubakar Umar and marries Fatumata.

Chapter 8

▼▼▼▼▼▼▼

The Fusion of Sufi and Nomad Thought in the Poetry of Hawad, Tuareg Mystic

DEBRA BOYD–BUGGS

Literary artists in Niger spring from a land whose history has been impregnated with Islam just as it has been marked by the severe desert dryness. Approximately 95 percent of Niger's population professes the religion of the Prophet Muhammad. However, the syncretism of Islam with traditional religious beliefs is as much a reality in Niger as elsewhere in Africa.

The Kel Tamajak or Tuareg (Touareg, in the French spelling) are Saharian berberphones who were chased from their original homeland by the severe arid conditions in the Sahara, as well as by Muslim Arab invasions starting in the eighth century, and the colonial conquests that began in 1830. Originally the Kel Tamajak formed five large confederations; today they are redistributed between six north and sub–Saharan African nations: Libya, Algeria, Nigeria, Chad, Mali, and Niger.

Nigerien Tuareg belong essentially to two confederations in the southern region: the Aïr Confederation whose sultan resides in the city of Agadez, and the Ouelleminden Confederation that has two subgroups: one from Mali and the other Niger, the latter established in the Niger River valley, northeast of the department of Tahoua. Aïr of long ago was inhabited by Black peoples. Then the Kel Tamajak, still called Kel Tagelmust, arrived in the country in successive waves between the eighth and fourteenth centuries. According to legend, the kingdom of Aïr was created in 1405 by a certain prince of Turkish origin named Younous. While the first century of Aïr's history was marked by a period of great instablility, the sixteenth century was synonymous with calm and prosperity, which allowed Islam to make considerable progress in the country.

Social organization in Tuareg society, very rigid long ago, has today lost its feudal, medieval character. Distinctions between nobles, men of Islam, vassals, free men, craftsmen, and slaves are beginning to disappear. *Tifinar*, the writing system of the Kel Tamajak, formerly the domain of noblewomen, is also in a state of decline. Even the oral literature that flourished long ago and accentuated war and love, the two main areas of nomad life, is in regression. The cultural and linguistic unity of the Kel Tamajak, who have become sedentary, is in full erosion, and its decay marks them as an endangered culture.

Our discussion will focus on the Nigerien writer and calligrapher Hawad, whose origins lie in the desert. In his poems, drought, a natural phenomenon that challenges the nomad's physical survival, becomes a metaphor for the dryness, lack, and deprivation that are hostile to his spiritual and social development:

> I burned my tent
> Drought, a rain of rats and
> a tornado of locusts
> did not even leave a trail of grain
> in my storehouses
> My goats
> I entrust them to the one–eyed vulture
> My writings
> I abandon them to the bald owl
> around whom the lame spotted bitch
> walks in procession
> My reason
> I bequeath it to my humpbacked donkey
> the only survivor of my tribe.
>   ("Drought," Hawad 1985, 26)[1]

Hawad's poetry brings together elements of religion, philosophy, and art, constituting the deepest and finest expression of the mystical spirit. Through his art he undertakes a mystical quest to re–establish and preserve Tuareg identity by merging the Tuareg conception of the universe with Sufi thought.

Hawad's message is directed first of all to his nomad brothers. He is a type of cultural hero in that he transforms *tifinar* into a conceptual and philosophical writing system by creating the necessary elements that are missing. To what is a consonantic writing, Hawad brings modifications like the creation of vowels and the invention of a cursive style of linking and modifying the letters to the thread of the pen. If, today, only the French translation of these texts has been published, it is because no other current method exists to mechanically reproduce the *tifinar* characters and Hawad refuses to transcribe Tuareg into a borrowed alphabet that would remain indecipherable for most nomads. He is thus able to resolve the painful language problem that most African writers face.

Hawad was born in 1950, north of Agadez, to a nomadic family of the Kel Aïr Confederation. Since that time, an aggressive and seemingly insurmountable reality has replaced past poetic images of wars of honor and courtly love:

> Look
> deep into the horizon
> behind the sand dune
> The shadows of nomads
> leaving the campsites
> Overturned cooking pots,
> where the spider, toy of summer whirlwinds,
> now dwells
> They left
> their feet shod with embers
> in search of exhausted dreams
> on the path of exile
> A pillar of the world
> crumbles on the cities
> Each day modern man
> rips off a little of the roof of the universe
> like the child who hollows out the sand
> under his castle.
>   ("Viper–Grief," Hawad 1987a, 72–73).[2]

Together with his people, Hawad has witnessed the shackling of the nomad way of life, the strangling of spaces, the hardening of boundaries that have already slashed Tuareg country into several nations, the halting of caravans, the dissolution of exchanges and solidarities. Hawad is well aware of the brutal imposition of modernism and the logic of sedentary technocrats. But the poet's cry is more than a simple question of lost values; it is the song of exile and pain:

> Exile is eating away at me, a stalk in a storm of
> sand dunes
> ....
> The perfume of nostalgia suffocates me
> ....
> The sun is drying out my heart
> ....
> Today, thousands and thousands of steps,
> valleys of vipers, and cliffs of smoke and darkness
> separate me from the campsites of long ago
> where crows have now devoured the rays of nomadic life

Exile binds me like sailor's ropes
....
Anguish wears at me with its needle of pain
("Exile," Hawad 1985, 13).[3]

With Hawad's writings there are signs of a transition, of a passage between oral and anonymous literature melted in a collective crucible, and individualized creation, fixed in writing and then marked and signed by a single personality (Claudot 1985, 5). At a crossroads between two spiritual worlds, Hawad's works reunite different currents from an inspiration that is both philosophical and poetic. Characteristic of Hawad's poetry is the circular or cyclical movement of the nomad, along with sand dunes, caravans, tents, campfires, remembrance, and the nostalgia for a way of life that is facing extinction. The Hawadian universe is inundated with the litany of melody; each poem is a type of song that is accompanied by metaphorical forms of instrumentation: "because only these chords can sound the howling of your tears."[4] There is burning fire, objects are aflame: "a breath of air ignites into mirages."[5] Images are frequently paradoxical, for example: "a caravan guided by the melody of silence" and "the flute of nothingness."[6] Light and darkness, life and death are juxtaposed and then fused: "being and nothingness suspended/ on its wings/ life death."[7]

Present also in many of his texts are references to the noble women who initiate those who search into the realm of Tuareg cosmogony:

At twilight
an old woman
upright like the reins of eternity
rises among the throng
and stands firmly on the edge of the well
Children my children
Let us go back to our shelters
Let the night come
Only it will bring the answer
to our groanings
And the gangling exhausted crowd
turns it back to the well
("The Lament of Oblivion," Hawad 1987b, 25).[8]

Women played a major role in Hawad's formation. The author states that he received a Tuareg education "in his mother's tent." Tuareg education is based on an apprenticeship of life in the desert, the moving of flocks, knowledge and classification of plants and animals, but also a very elaborate teaching of the five cycles of Tuareg tales. In a family, there are many celibate old women, priestesses who teach Tuareg cosmogony and nomad thought. It is a system of teaching based on space, the architecture

of the tent, and the projection of one's body into space. Hawad was educated in this tradition by his mother's sister. From his grandfather, of whom
he was very fond, he learned to master the art of the spoken word (Penel
1991, 86).

When his grandfather died, Hawad's world was shattered and he began
to question Tuareg cosmogony. Although he had previously despised everything associated with Islam, he found solace in unfamiliar Tuareg chants
that he heard echoing in the desert. Thanks to a maternal uncle, Hawad
met a group of itinerant Sufis and he accompanied them to further his
knowledge of Islam in Sufi monasteries, at the border between Egypt and
Libya and in the nomad camps around Bagdad in Iraq. Through these associations he was introduced to the marvelous world of Arabic characters
that resulted in his fascination with writing. In accordance with the rhythm
of the seasons, he continued to accompany the moving of herds and to
travel with the caravan that went from the desert to the banks of the Medi-
terranean. Eventually this coming and going between two states of flux
brought communion in Hawad's philosophy.

Heir of nomad culture, Hawad transmits to us an experience and a
vision of the world built on mobility:

> I wander, I am mad, naked
> elegant, wincing, smiling
> behind the dust of the caravan
> which goes up from the desert toward the oasis
> where the waters of *Unity* spring up
> ("I Wander," Hawad 1985, 11).[9]

The indispensable and irremoveable pillars around which nomad life is
organized are the well—"aman iman" [water is life] according to the prov-
erb—and shelter, which the tent represents for humans, the nest for the
bird, the burrow for the jerboa, the hearth for flames, the hollow of the
dune for grains of sand. In the poem "Silhouette infinie" it is again the
female that embodies the circular path that leads to the annihilation that is
absolute unity, known as *Inta* in Tuareg cosmogony:

> A thin old woman, tall
> veiled in worn clothes
> a basket on her head
> breaks away from the campsite
> a shadow snatched from her shelter
> she climbs up the cliffs
> her arms dangling, carried off by the wind
> All of the Eternal's melodies
> are engraved in the movement of her arms
> and on the curved laces of the road

that ripple toward the mountainous plateaus of Inta
The shape of this motion contains the dream
of the path that leads to the well
to a life without thirst
What we lack is inscribed
in the melody of each step
the smile of each lip
    ("Infinite Silhouette," Hawad 1985, 18).[10]

According to most Islamologues, "there is no Sufism without Islam. Sufism is the spirituality or mysticism of the religion Islam" (Stoddart 1986, 19). During a lecture he gave at the University of Niamey in February 1992, Hawad said: "I have become an itinerant vagabond in search of myself under the pretext of science." One critic viewed this statement as indicative of Hawad's goal of becoming a mystic without God (Bali 1993, 172). What is clear is that he is kept in a state of perpetual anguish due to the personal drama of his own identity and the collective plight of the Tuareg people:

In the dregs of the city
tents of ripped open rags
accumulate in the Tahaggart sector
where only vermin and vultures reign
under the glare of those
of the Qur'an and of guns
    ("The Lament of Oblivion," Hawad 1987b, 28).[11]

Hawad admits that he became a Sufi without any act of self–repudiation or neglect of Tuareg culture. The result of this fusion is a poetry saturated with images that have double meanings. An illustration of this duality is to be seen in the desert, not just as physical space void of greenery, but as any space characterized by the absence of humanism.

According to Hawad, "thought only exists in treading and singing. But we are no longer in the era of nomadism due to the borders that have fractured our way of life. Today you can no longer nomadize. For me writing is another way to nomadize." (Penel 1991, 89). Such is clear even in the very titles of his four collections of poetry: Caravan of Thirst, Songs of Thirst and Deviation, Nomad Testament, Ring Footpath.[12]

In search of water, the thirsty one departs from the forged pathway; he leaves behind domesticated lands; he moves away from known boundaries and limits; he penetrates the desert; he loses his orientation; he deviates; he rambles, and finally he is ready to forge his own way:

The sun is his turban
clothed in a gown of scorpions

his feet shod with thorns
He rests against the forked viper
He has domesticated the *essuf*
Death strays from his path
Before him mountains of fire collapse
Behind him the carpet of the earth coils
His path is traced by thirst
("The Nomad," Hawad 1985, 20).[13]

At the root of this thirst, flames burn, burning embers consume themselves by the wrenching apart of the nomad world, by the oppression of its breath, by the choking of its dreams, by the extinction of its being. In order to pull itself away from the tangible, in order to support the unbearable burden of present reality, the bridle is placed upon the nomad spirit:

He returns to his moanings while singing
the melody of wandering
("The Nomad," Hawad 1985, 22).[14]

The departure, the trip, and its steps recapitulate the eternal movement that leads from the tent to the well and from the well to the tent. Hawad's poems unwind the thread of this necessary motion that allows each being, each thing, each particle, to exist.

Similar to the pilgrims setting out on the "road that leads to the well," the elements of the universe cross valleys, arid plateaus, travel through peaks and passes until attaining the ultimate place of rest: the point of departure for a new voyage. Life and the after–life are seen as parts of a chain of cycles that lead to this privileged moment of transition and harmony, to that instant of equilibrium that follows the end of one action and precedes the beginning of another.

Far from establishing the disappearance or the blatant destruction of beings, the "annihilation" that characterizes the outcome of the cycle signifies the surmounting of the sufferings of existence, the end of fear and of the anguished search for a refuge from thirst and the perpetual quest for water. In comparision with previous voyages, the cycle of nothingness is a light passage bound up with the currents of the universe, in quest of total fusion with cosmic forces, the ultimate cycle of unity, complete disintegration. This the Tuaregs refer to as *trance*.

The Sufis by *ecstasy*, the Tuaregs by trance, strive to break the bonds that tie creatures to the tangible world, that they might vanish into the oceans of the void of absolute appeasement. Both ecstasy and trance are types of spiritual stations or degrees of ascent, reached through rites usually accompanied by dance, music, and chant:

Dance the music of the world beyond these visions
the music of *Unity*
far from twilight and from dawn
death and life
Only these chords can sound
the howling of your tears
and the laughter of your hopes
Only this melody can carry
the burden and the plumes
of your despicable acts of bravery
Only these chants can reassemble the reins
that guide the caravans of our souls
    ("Misled into Death Country," Hawad 1985, 34).[15]

In Tuareg religious practice, dancing, singing, and chanting are means to project the soul from the cycle of existing things into the realm of rapture. For the Sufis the resistance of the restless pscyhe is gradually worn down by these same practices and the body becomes the temple of God, empty of self and filled with self. Before the creation of human beings the universe had been brought into being, but it was unpolished, unreflective, unconscious of the Divine Presence. The macrocosmic universe came into being so that the manifestation of Self in the form of a Divine Name would have have a "place." Throughout Hawad's poetry, the philosophical principle of structural homology is drawn between notions of macrocosm and microcosm:

Life is only the outburst
of an ancestral memory
where so many travelers have left
their grimacing faces
O smile of birth
Groaning in the lungs of love
that the unfurling streams of the Eternal One
erase
Desert
where other caravans pant from illusion
believing that no shadow of the soul
has ever evaporated
Aridity
Poor Toutankhamon of the Egyptians
his chest bulging
in front of the flattering geometry of the pyramids
oblivious to the palaces of the mason housefly
Before the monkey could stagger on two paws
the termites had already built
temples on the trunks of olive trees
ants were already moving galleries
through the bowels of the earth

Man standing erect
a little kernel
in the waves of sand
        ("Life–Memory," Hawad 1985, 92).[16]

Subtly woven, the symbolic correspondance is drawn, the wandering cycles are formed by the motions of the atoms of the universe and the multiple caravans that are torn by the same thorn and ravaged by the same thirst.

Symbolism is perhaps the most sacred dimension of Sufism, for it is through symbols that one continues to remember, to invoke. In Sufism, universal metaphysical symbols, expressed particularly in architecture, music, and calligraphy, stem from the Qur'an, the Word; and the Word contains names and qualities. Symbols connected to sound, light, and the intellect convey the most profound beliefs of Sufism.

Hawad mixes writing and calligraphy in a unique relationship. All of Hawad's poems are written in *tifinar*, the alphabet of the Tuareg, and accompanied by calligraphic drawings. After several years of wandering in Europe, Hawad returned home to interpret Tuareg writing, the geometry that is found of jewelry, spoons, tent posts, and other items. He also studied the psychology of the trance. Hawad stayed in Aïr for seven years before returning to exile. It was during this period that he came to understand why the Tuareg did not record their history nor their thoughts even though they have a writing system. It's because Tuareg thought expresses itself either by treading, nomadism in space, or by metaphorical writing, a type of geometry. In his evolution he realized the incapacity of words to express thought and the necessity to transcend writing and words; everything that is nomad must be sung or marched. For Hawad the blank page is a space like the desert. He does calligraphy, not for its aesethic possibilities, but because for him the trait or the feature is more self–revealing than the word:

> The trait or feature necessitates gesture. I have managed to seize the spontaneous and fleeting nomadism of gesture and of movement. . . . What is important is to seize the infinitely small by way of the infinitely large. And what I'm looking for can be found neither in the infinitely grand nor in the infinitely small. It is between the two. It's like when you throw a stone into water. It is not the stone that interests me, nor the water, but the ripples, the multiple ripples that the stone projects.[17]

To me, the best calligraphy transcends everthing cultural in order to enter the realm that comes before nomenclature. It is this state that one obtains through *litany*. It is like a word–mill that consumes us, that burns us. One writes, one writes, and after a moment one reaches a state of fusion (Penel 1991, 88–89).

In Sufism, meditation is the passive counterpart of the *dhikr*. Calligraphic symbols manifest characteristics of both the *dhikr* and the *wird*. However, Hawad's desire is not to reproduce the sourates of the Coran or even to use *tifinar* for strictly traditional purposes. Each of his calligraphies contains a message that only the poet is able to decode. Hawad hopes to enter into correspondance with nature by way of his calligraphy. In his personal cosmos, nature not only refers to the human condition, but it is also the blank page that he must occupy at all costs. Calligraphy is another dimension of Hawad's nomadism that propels his writing. "The heart, like a pen is bound to write every calligraphic style, to turn left and right without resistance. One of the qualities required in a pen is that its tongue, or even its head, be cut off: the pen becomes the symbol of the mystic who must not divulge the secret, who `speaks without tongue'" (Schimmel 1975, 415). Calligraphy is also a part of a transition. According to the poet, it is like night in the temporal cycle, the gateway to a potential text and a facet of his search for the infinite.

Proceeding from the same quest for "nothingness" found in his writing, Hawad's calligraphy creates images beyond the mirror outlined by the letters, beyond messages translated by languages, leading to a state of rapture from which meaning is excluded. Through the melody of sounds, the rhythm of syllables, the graphics of letters, Hawad pursues the trance, the state of the mystical that leads to the inexpressable, the unexplainable, to annihilation or dissipation into the flux of the universe, to the state of non–being:

> In my opinion, poetry is the voice behind the feature. It follows the trait. Poetry cannot replace the trait but it becomes asocial, incomprehensible. It is not like the spoken word, made to communicate. The best poetry is given to sound, based uniquely on sound. My writing is a search for myself. I write: it's like walking in the desert, nomadizing in space, in the cosmos. When I nomadize, I do not nomadize so that others will love me. No, I nomadize to find myself, not to become a perfect being, not to assert myself. I do not exist except when marching, walking (Penel 1991, 90).

It may appear that Hawad's texts can be read without knowledge of the referent; however, Hawad is at the same time committed to address the plight of the nomad who has been rejected at the intersection of cities:

> The nomad enters the city
> to buy three measures of wheat
> Those who worship concrete
> spit in his face
> hit him in the back with
> the bones of his sheep

Yelling in the city
Be cursed nomad
fox thief looter traitor
savage companion of the spider
camel's brother
        ("The Nomad," Hawad 1985, 21).[18]

The Tuareg comes from a complex community and has an identity. He is not the blue man of clichés and stereotypes, nor is he a stealing beggar.

Despite invitations to read his poetry and display his calligraphies in various parts of the world, Hawad is still a man of the periphery:

I would like to be a bridge between society and the outside. Tuaregs must not lose their nomadism; I speak of spiritual nomadism (Penel 1991, 91).

The poet still lives in and talks about exile:

Poor poet
carried away by the twisted cramps of metaphor
His passion is annihilated
Pain throws him back into the desert
Bewildered like the dream
that has lost the mirror of consciousness
        ("Silences," Hawad 1985, 47).[19]

To read Hawad is to accept a world of movement, a world of fire and night. The desert and the sky are scored with paths and enigmatic beings in search of themselves, lost to themselves. To read Hawad is to agree to enter into a trance in order to redistribute the symbols in his texts. He will use his multifaceted spiritual formation to reconstruct rather than simply invoke a new identity. The Sufi is always searching to lose the self in the Self. Unable to find his identity in various religions, reason or other sources, Hawad will discover it within himself.

Notes

1. J'ai brulé ma tente/ Sécheresse et pluie de rats/ et tornade de sauterelles/ n'ont pas laissé un grain–fil/ dans mes greniers// Mes chèvres/ je les confie au vautour borgne/ Mes écrits/ je les abandonne au hibou déplumé/ autour duquel processionne/ la chienne boiteuse tachetée/ Ma raison/ je la lègue à mon âne bossu/ seul survivant de ma tribu ("Sécheresse.") All English translations of Hawad's poems are by Debra Boyd-Buggs.
2. Regarde/ au fond de l'horizon/ derrière la dune/ Les ombres des nomades/ désertent les campements/ Marmites renversées/ où loge l'araignée/ jouet des tourbillons/ de l'été/ Ils sont partis// chaussés de braise/ épuisés/ sur le parcours de l'exil/ Un pilier du monde/ s'écroule/ sur les cités/ Chaque jour l'homme/ moderne/ arrache un peu du toit/ de l'univers/ comme l'enfant qui creuse/ le sable/ sous son château ("Vipère-chagrin").

3. L'exil m'érode, tige dans la tempête de dune/ .... / Le parfum de la nostalgie m'étouffe/ .... / Le soleil dessèche mon coeur/ .... / Aujourd'hui, des milliers de milliers d'étapes/ vallées de vipères, falaises de fumées–ténèbres/ me séparent des campements de jadis/ où les corbeaux ont dévoré les rayons de la vie nomade// L'exil me noue comme les cordes des marins/ .... / L'angoisse m'élime en une aiguille de douleur ("Exil").

4. "Car seuls ces accords peuvent accueillir les hurlements de tes pleurs."

5. "Le souffle s'enflamme dans les mirages."

6. "Caravane guidée par la mélodie du silence," and "la flûte du néant."

7. "l'existence et le néant suspendus/ à ses ailes/ la vie la mort."

8. Au crépuscule/ une vieille femme droite/ commes les rênes de l'éternité/ se dresse parmi la foule/ et se campe sur la margelle du puits/ Enfants mes enfants/ revenons à nos abris/ Laissons venir la nuit/ elle seule apportera réponse/ à nos gémissements/ Et la foule dégingandée/ épuisée tourne le dos/ au puits ("La Complainte de l'oubli").

9. J'erre, je suis fou, nu/ élégant, grimaçant, souriant/ derrière la poussière de la caravane/ qui rémonte du désert vers l'oasis/ où jaillissent les sources de *l'Unité* ("J'erre").

10. Une vieille maigre, grande/ voilée de hardes/ un panier sur la tête/ se détache du campement/ Ombre arrachée à son abri/ elle grimpe les falaises/ bras ballants entraînés par le vent/ Toutes les mélodies de l'Eternel/ sont gravées dans le geste de ses bras/ et sur les lacets incurvés de la route/ qui ondule vers les plateaux montagneux/ d'Inta/ La forme de ce geste contient le rêve/ du chemin qui mène au puits/ dans une vie sans soif/ Ce qui nous manque est inscrit/ dans la mélodie de chaque pas/ le sourire de chaque lèvre. . . ("Silhouette Infinie").

11. Dans les bas–fonds de la cité/ s'amoncelle le quartier/ Tahaggart chouméra/ tentes de chiffons éventrés/ où seuls règnent/ vermines et charognards/ sous le regard de ceux/ du Coran et des fusils ("La complainte de l'oubli").

12. *Caravane de la soif, Chants de la soif et de l'égarement, Testament nomade, L'Anneau sentier.*

13. Il est enturbanné de soleil/ vêtu d'une robe de scorpions/ chaussé d'épines/ Il s'appuie sur la vipère fourchue/ Il a domestiqué *l'essuf*/ La mort s'écarte de son sentier// Devant lui les montagnes de feu s'effondrent/ Derrière lui le tapis de la terre s'enroule/ Son chemin est tracé par la soif. . . ("Le nomade").

14. Il retourne à ses plaintes en chantant/ le mélodie de l'errance ("Le nomade").

15. Danse la musique de l'au–delà/ de ces visions/ la musique de *l'Unité*/ loin du crépuscule et de l'aube/ mort et vie/ Car seuls ces accords/ peuvent accueillir/ les hurlements de tes pleurs/ et les rires de tes espoirs/ Seule cette mélodie/ peut porter/ le poids et la plume/ de tes bravoures lâchetés/ Seuls ces chants rassembleront les rênes/ qui dirigent la caravane/ de nos âmes ("Egaré au pays de la mort").

16. La vie n'est que l'éclat/ d'une mémoire –ancêtre/ où tant de voyageurs ont laissé/ leurs grimaces/ O sourire de la naissance/ Gémissent des poumons de l'amour/ que les ruisseaux déferlants/ de l'Eternel/ effacent/ Désert/ où halèteront d'autres caravanes/ d'illusion/ croyant que jamais/ aucune ombre de l'âme/ ne s'est évaporée/ Aridité// Pauvre Toutankhamon des Egyptiens/ poitrine bombée/ devant la géométrie–flatterie des pyramides/ oublieux des palais de la mouche maçonne// Avant que le singe ne titube sur deux pattes/

déjà les termites avaient bâti/ des temples sur le tronc des oliviers/ déjà les fourmis aménagaient/ des galeries/ à travers les entrailles de la terre// Homme dressé/ petit grain/ dans les vagues de sable ("Vie–mémoire").

17. Hawad evokes another synthesis of his own philosophy with Sufism: "the mystic is one who is incomparably more preoccupied with the ebbing wave than by the water it has left behind" (Lings 1975, 12).

18. Le nomade entre dans la cité/ pour acheter trois mesures de blé/ Ceux qui vénèrent le béton/ lui crachent au visage/ lui jettent/ dans le dos/ les os de ses moutons/ Hurlements de la ville/ Sois maudit nomade/ renard voleur pillard traître/ sauvage compagnon de l'araignée/ frère du chameau ("Le Nomade").

19. Pauvre poète/ emporté par les crampes entortillées/ de la métaphore// Sa passion est anéantie/ La douleur le rejette dans le désert/ Egaré comme le rêve/ qui a perdu le miroir des consciences ("Silences").

Chapter 9

▼▼▼▼▼▼▼▼

Muslim Perceptions in a Swahili Oral Genre

FAROUK TOPAN

Religion, language, and cultural elements originally foreign to East Africa have played a distinct and yet interdependent role in the emergence of Swahili poetry as a scripted genre. Islam provided the scripture and the traditions from which the early poets drew deeply and profusely; the Arabic script, modified to take account of Swahili sounds, was used as the vehicle of literary expression; and, Arab customs, manners, and behavior were considered, at least by coastal city dwellers well into this century, as supplying the norms of "proper" behavior emanating from a "high" culture.[1] The subjects and themes of early Swahili poetry (seventeenth to mid–twentieth centuries) reflect this influence. One finds in them a conceptual projection in time to Arabia of the seventh century whence the poets drew their inspiration from aspects related to the life and teaching of the Prophet, his spiritual experience and relationship with the early Muslims, particularly his companions (the *ashab*). Fine examples of such poems have been collected and documented in a number of volumes, and although one might sometimes disagree with the translation or with the thrust of the interpretation given in them, they form, nonetheless, a useful collection for students of this genre (Allen 1971; Knappert 1967, 1970; Nasir 1977; also Shariff 1984). The poets speak for themselves as Muslims.

However, other forms of Swahili poetry have not been as extensively documented or analyzed from such a perspective. The situation is rather acute in the case of Swahili oral literature as, with each passing decade, the elders—those guardians and repositories of this genre—decrease in number; with them departs a knowledge of what was once commonplace. Thus the relationship of Islam to oral texts as literature becomes difficult to analyze in its full spectrum. Even so, the texts and contexts that still exist provide adequate data for a meaningful enquiry. Spirit possession cults comprise one such context, and the songs sung in them constitute the texts. As we shall see in the samples of the songs given below, an appreciation of their semantic fullness entails, on the one hand, an understanding of the function of the spirit cult, and, on the other, an elaboration of the meaning of the songs at various levels of communication between the human and the spirit worlds. Perceptions of being Muslim feature in both.

The songs are sung in a spirit–mediumship and possession cult of Mombasa, Kenya, called Ki–Pemba.[2] It is named after the island of Pemba off the coast of Tanzania, not distant from Mombasa. The origins of the Ki–Pemba and of the other spirits in Mombasa are explained in a narrative concerned with the prophet Solomon. According to the narrative, spirits were created by God and put on earth since the beginning of creation. They served different masters at different times, but were brought together during the life of Solomon and placed in his custody as their sole master. They worked for him night and day, and longed to free themselves from the toil. Then, one day, Solomon died while he was supervising the spirits at work, but was prevented from falling to the ground by the staff on which he was leaning. Deceived, the spirits continued to labor for him until a woodworm got into the staff and weakened it. Solomon fell, and the spirits realized that they were free. They scattered themselves throughout the world; the most powerful among them settled on the island of Pemba.

The narrative is based on an interpretation of three verses of the Qur'an which state (34:12–14):

> 12. And (We made) the wind (subservient) to Solomon; it made a month's journey in the morning and a month's journey in the evening; and We made fountain of molten brass to flow for him. And of the *jinn* were those who worked in front of him by the command of his Lord. And whoever turned aside from Our command from among them, We made him taste of the chastisement of burning.

> 13. They (the *jinn*) made for him (Solomon) what he pleased, of arches and images, and bowls (large) as watering–troughs and cooking–pots. Give thanks, O people of David, and very few of my servants are grateful.

> 14. But when we decreed death for him (Solomon), naught showed them his death but a creature of the earth that kept (slowly) gnawing away at his staff: so when he fell down, the *jinn* saw plainly that, if they had known the unseen, they would not have tarried in humiliating torment.

The verses provide a "charter" upon which members of the cult—all Muslims—build the cosmology of interaction between humans and spirits. Such interaction is subsumed under the generic term, *uganga*, which is employed to describe the concept underlying spirit possession and mediumship as well as the practices arising from them. The term lacks a one–word equivalent in English; it refers to medicine, healing, and initiation (into the cult). An important derivative of the term is *mganga* (pl. *waganga*), the agent who is actively involved in "doing" *uganga*; he is thus a healer, herbalist, "medicine–man," the official presiding in an initiation ceremony, and a leader of a group of followers (i.e. those initiated into the cult by him).

Spirit Songs

The songs are sung in an initiation and healing ceremony (called *p'ungwa* in Swahili) which is normally held for a period of eight days. (It is sometimes shortened to three days for economic reasons.) The aim of the ceremony is two–fold: to fulfill the wishes of the spirit possessing the medium (usually a woman) by initiating both of them into the hierarchy of the cult; and, thereby, to bring about a cure and relief for the illness afflicting the woman. Initiation into the cult is effected by the movement of the spirit from the medium's stomach to her head from whence he publicly "declares" his name. And although the "name–declaration" ceremony does not take place until the early morning of the eighth day, the ceremonies and rituals of the preceding days lead up to it. Each of the latter is made to relate to the "name–declaration" ceremony in a way that contributes to its success. And, in so doing, various aspects of Swahili beliefs find expression in action and songs. The songs presented here express the interrelationship between Islamic and indigenous beliefs.

Song one is sung on the first day of the *p'ungwa* ceremony when the initiand inhales from a steaming pot of herbs, leaves, and other medicines. The purpose is to "ripen" the spirit within her and to make it easier for it to move up to her head. As this marks the first ritual that interacts directly with the initiand's spirit—the preceding ones being preparatory—it is appropriate that the action should commence with a plea to God. The plea in the first song is cast in the form of a statement about God's status.

> God is indeed the One to pray to
> (O) people all
> And the Prophet
> God is indeed the One to pray to.[3]

The omnipotence of God is implied in the song; hence the necessity of praying only to Him. Similarly, the status of the Prophet as an intermediary and intercessor is also implied. Thus, the text of the song indicates the two most important spiritual beings in the Swahili Muslim cosmology. But it should be noted that the term *Allah* is not used for "God" in the text nor, as I have mentioned elsewhere (Topan 1992), is it employed in ordinary speech, though it occurs in the usage of Islamic formulas (e.g. *Wallahi*, by God, *Allahu ya'lam*, God knows, etc); instead, the Bantu term *Mngu* (*Mungu*) is retained, as also in the following song as:

> You (pl.) pray to God
> until she gets cured.
> You (pl.) pray to God
> until she gets cured.[4]

The "communication" in the song is from the *mganga* to his followers to pray to God for the cure of their companion's illness. They are asked to be persistent in their prayers until their goal is achieved. In the next song, however, it is the initiand who does the "speaking" and mentions the *waganga* also.

> Let me pray to the Prophet
> And to God, the good
> And you, waganga, pray to them for me
> or (as a variant)
> And pray for the waganga as well.[5]

The *waganga* are here asked to act as intermediaries between the initiand and God (with the Prophet). The status accorded to the *waganga* brings to the fore an intermingling of the beliefs of the cult with those of Islam. This intermixture, called "parallelism" and "dualism" by Trimingham and Lewis respectively (Trimingham 1964; Lewis 1966),[6] is expressed by members of the cult through belief in a hierarchy of beings who wield, or are able to influence, supernatural power. God is at the top of the hierarchy and is omnipotent; next is the Prophet who may act as an intermediary between God and human beings. In popular Swahili Muslim thought, there are beings under the Prophet who occupy positions of varying proximity to him. The closer they are to him, the more efficacious is their ability to intercede. Views differ as to who occupies the position closest to the Prophet, and it is not surprising that different groups designate their own candidate for that status. Thus, the view among the theologians and the orthodox sheikhs is that a pure and pious member of the *'ulama* (Muslim clerics) would be closest to the Prophet; while the Sufi consider that a mystic who has been graced with divine love and light would be granted that proximity. Similarly, among members of the Ki–Pemba and other spirit possession cults, it does not seem the least unusual that spirits should also have that status, and, further, that the *waganga* possessed by those spirits should also be so favored (as mediums).

As Muslims, members of the cult are aware of the critical views and attitudes of the more "orthodox" theologians who condemn the practices of spirit possession and who occasionally rail against them in public, especially in sermons prior to the Friday prayers. However, the members themselves do not see the two sets of beliefs—the Islamic and the cultic—as being in conflict. On the contrary, quite a number of Islamic practices are integrated within the cult's main ceremony of *p'ungwa*. The ceremony commences, for instance, with the recitation of the *fatiha*, the first chapter of the Qur'an. And some verses of the Qur'an are also recited at a ritual described below at which the patient first seeks to learn the cause of her illness.

The ability to inflict illness is attributed both to God and to the spirits; accordingly, its removal is effected through an appeal to the appropriate being. In the case of a spirit inflicted illness, the cure also entails the fulfillment of the wishes of the particular spirit who has "sent" it. But it is recognized that God, being omnipotent, could potentially remove the affliction caused by the spirit, but chooses not to. This was explained at length by a woman *mganga* in the context of a ritual performed at a spirit dwelling when the patient attempts to find out if it is indeed a spirit who is causing the illness. After performing the commencement rituals—reciting verses from the Qur'an, and making an appropriate offering—the "patient" will say (and I quote here part of the explanation in words as spoken by her):

> I have come to this place [because] I have such–and–such thing troubling me. I am ill, or I am afflicted, or that someone [close to me] is ill. And I have tried ordinary medicines for this illness. And I have tried all sorts of medicines for this illness. Now I am told that this is a matter to do with spirits. I have come here, I pray to God and to the Prophet and also to you, spirits. If this matter be of God and the Prophet, I pray to the All–reigning God to remove this illness. But if it is not so, and it is a matter which is in your hands, you spirits, then I have come here to make a request, may God remove it from me. So he/she will then burn incense and depart.

The boundary between the authority of God and that of spirits is rather subtle. On the one hand, God is acknowledged as omnipotent, and yet spirits are also believed to possess the ability to operate within that domain with some authority. An important aspect to note here is that the power of these spirits, and the authority that they wield, is not perceived to be in conflict with the power and authority of God. However, such incongruency emerges obliquely in the exegesis of the fourth song.

Let me appease the spirits of the dead, and
let me appease God;
Let me appease the spirits of the Atate
dwelling, and you appease them as well.
Appease the spirits of the dead, and appease God.[7]

Two more categories of beings are mentioned in the song who are also capable of affecting the outcome of the *p'ungwa* ceremony, and thus, the course of the patient's affliction. Spirits of the dead—*koma*—comprise the first category, and the second consists of spirits who reside at the spirit-dwelling of Atate.

It is believed that the spirits of the dead—and the term is not restricted to spirits of the ancestors—can, and do, influence the lives of the living. Krapf (1882) gives a revealing, though subjective, description in his dictionary of the way *koma* were perceived over a century ago: "[*Koma* is] A man who died and who is believed to exist in the grave, whence he sometimes appears to a relative in a dream in which the *koma* gives his orders with regard to sacrifices and offerings in order to avoid public calamities. The Swahili are almost as superstitious as the pagans on this point. They believe that the dead care for the living wherefore the latter must honour the graves of the dead every year" (p. 168).

Koma (sing.) is regarded as a "soul" or an animate part of a human being that lives on after his physical death. It cares for the living and manifests this caring by giving warning of an approaching danger or by mediating between humans and God. *Koma* (pl.) do not possess humans or use them as mediums, but, as Krapf states, they appear in dreams or they make known their wishes or warnings to people intuitively. Such "souls," like spirits, may stay together at one dwelling, sometimes called *mzimu*.

An interesting characteristic common to spirits who reside at Atate is their affiliation with sorcery, *uchawi*, an antithesis to *uganga*. Sorcerers' activities are underlined by evil and malice in contradistinction to those of *uganga*, which are directed towards doing good, e.g., curing, healing, and participating in the cults for the betterment of their members. Consequently, the relationship of the sorcerers—who are themselves Muslims—to God poses a prima facie problem of theological conflict. The problem is rationalized by *waganga*, if not explained, by invoking a fundamental theological principle of choice granted to man by God. While residing within the universe created and upheld by God, a human being has the choice of either submitting to God's will totally, or of straying now and again into areas that are considered "un–Islamic" for the purpose of indulging one's whims and desires. This does not imply a rejection of Islam per se; rather, the focus is placed, at those times, on matters in life that are considered of prime importance and immediacy, and whose fulfilment lies in the domain of *uganga*. It is thus conceivable for a sorcerer to be regular in prayers, in fasting, and in the fulfilment of his other obligations as a Muslim, and yet be a member of his coven. Perhaps the two represent different types of reality. Whereas God is the ultimate reality, whose attainment lies in the life hereafter, sorcery deals with a reality that confronts one in the here and now. Its promise of power and reward for the sorcerer is too great a temptation to be resisted.

The communication in the song is directed from the *mganga* to his followers to appease (through prayers, offerings, etc) the two categories of beings who are also in a position to influence the outcome of the ceremony.

A salient characteristic of Islam in its interface with pre–established cultures is its capacity to accommodate significant traits of local cultures in a way deemed desirable by the people or particular groups of people. But accommodation can and is also perceived as a reciprocal phenomenon. At one level, Islam is seen as accommodating the traits and creating spaces for their existence and growth; through that act, Islam is also perceived as being "popularized" or, in our instance, "Africanized" or "Swahilized." Either perception has its critics, both academic and theological.

The Swahili themselves make a distinction between *dini* (religion) and *mila* (custom). And the two—to quote from a Swahili saying cited by Middleton (1992, 162)—"are as a rule not incompatible." That would indeed be the sentiments of the members of the spirit cults whose sample of songs have been discussed above. Although the texts mention *waganga* and spirits (both good and evil) as operating in the supernatural domain, the exegeses of the songs make it clear that they do so under the omnipotence of God to whom only the Prophet is the most near.

Such a representation is significant within the context of the society in which the songs exist. For their role is two–fold. Within the cult, they form vehicles of communication between the human and spiritual worlds. But, transcending the cult, the role of the songs relates to the Muslim society within which the texts are created and performed. Here, they reflect attempts on the part of the members of the cult to define and project their worldview in a way that does not exclude them from what they perceive as "orthodox" Islam. The texts thus create, sustain, and reinforce a Muslim identity that is meaningful and dear to the people.

Notes

1. A lexical residue of such a "borrowing" is the word *mstaarabu*, "to be like an Arab," applied to a person who behaves "properly" and in a "civilized" manner.

2. The songs were collected during fieldwork in Kenya in the 1960s and early 1970s. For more details of the cult, see Topan (1972); see also Giles (1987) for analysis of possession cults among other Swahili communities along the East African coast.
3. Muombwa ndile Mngu/ Watu wote/ Na Mtume/ Muombwa ndile Mngu.
4. Muombeleni Mngu/ Hata apoe./ Muombeleni Mngu/ Hata apoe.
5. Niombe t'umwa/ Na Mngu mwema/ Niombeleni waganga nao/ Waombeleni waganga nao.
6. Although the term "dualism" is understandable within this context, "parallelism" is rather misleading; it tends to imply that the two do not meet, but run parallel to each other without interacting.
7. Nigonye koma nigonye / na Mlungu/ Oya ee/ Mzimu Atate na ugonye/ Ugonyere koma na Mlungu.

Chapter 10

▼▼▼▼▼▼▼▼▼

Sittaat: *Somali Women's Songs for the "Mothers of the Believers"*[1]

Lidwien Kapteijns with Mariam Omar Ali

> That you take and welcome us,
> daughter of the Prophet, for that we clamor,
> that you come and teach us how to walk,
> daughter of the Prophet, for that we clamor.
> You, child of the Prophet, most obedient of women,
> give us that for which we call upon you.[2]

It was 4:00 p.m. on Monday afternoon when Omar stopped by to take Mariam and me to something new to both of us, a *sittaat* session.[3] The Djibouti sun was still beating down, as we entered the densely populated area of low-level housing still clearly recognizable as the *quartiers indigènes* of the only recently ended colonial period.[4] Djibouti's "uptown," or former European quarter, with its colonial architecture and (at night) gaudily lit bars and discos frequented by French and Foreign Legion soldiers, lay behind us at about a mile distance. Our way this afternoon led from the house of my host family on the edge of the *quartiers* further into the warren of narrow, unpaved and sun-drenched alleys towards the house of Luula Saalix, the elderly leader of the *sittaat* sessions in Quartier Quatre. As only women attend *sittaat*, Omar took us only as far as the house of a middle-aged acquaintance. Aamina was expecting us and took us the rest of the way. A charcoal burner with incense marked the entrance to the premises where the *sittaat* were held. Inside we found about ten other women, many of them in their fifties or early sixties, sitting on mats and pillows in a circle on the ground. Aamina introduced us to the group that, as I understood later, consisted of regular attenders and experts in *sittaat*, who gathered weekly between the afternoon and evening prayers. Compared to the more formal performances of *sittaat* on religious holidays such as the Prophet's birthday, these short, informal devotional gatherings took place with a minimum of ritual and emotional intensity. Yet the repertoire of songs, and the purpose of singing to the distinguished women of early Islam and of asking for their help in this world and the next, were the same in both contexts. Aamina introduced me as a teacher from the United States who wanted to inform her students about Islam. The women approved of this and made room for us in the circle. Luula Saalix, usually referred to as *ina* Saalix (Saalix's daughter), was quietly but undisputedly in charge. She was seated on the ground behind a round, low and wide drum, typical of the *sittaat*, surrounded with various kinds of eau de cologne, perfume, *cadar* (a dark and sweet Somali-Arab perfume), incense and incense burners. A small heap of money (each participant contributed one hundred Djibouti francs for expenses) lay next to her. Luula's female assistants served in rapid succession *qudhi* (an herbal tea, drunk with milk and sugar), orange syrup, coffee, *salool* (popcorn), and *xalwad* (Turkish delight). *Qaat* (or *chaat*), the leaf stimulant commonly associated with male devotional practice in the area, was not chewed during the half dozen or so *sittaat* sessions I attended; but it was sometimes chewed after the sessions and commonly consumed during all-night sessions such as on the Prophet's birthday, when many men and women spend the whole night, from late afternoon until the call to the early morning prayer, singing the praises of the Prophet and the *awliyo*.[5] The various bottles of perfume were passed on to us, for the religion encourages cleanliness and the Prophet and the *awliyo* love sweet fragrances. *Udgoon*, "fragrant one," is a constant attribute of the Prophet in the songs sung in his praise. Later, as they got to know me better, several older women expressed surprise at the fact that I was not foul-smelling as they believed all non-Muslims to be; they ascribed this to my heart's leanings toward the *sittaat*. During rituals, many Somali Muslims act upon their belief that feasting the senses on beautiful clothes, good food, sweet fragrances, pleasing music, dancing, and stimulating substances such as coffee, tobacco, and *qaat* not only promotes and enhances deeply religious experiences, but also helps to attract the spiritual presence of the saintly individual invoked in prayer and song. We perfumed ourselves. Then Luula asked us to cover our heads and the singing started.

> God, we begin with *bissinka* [the phrase "in the name of God, the Merciful, the Compassionate"]
> God, we begin with my heart loving you
> God, we begin with the blessing of Prophet Muhammad
> God, through the merit of Fatima, daughter of the Prophet, we seek succor
> God, the Day of Questioning is a wonder revealed to us
> Wood was carved [into tablets] for the valuable Qur'an

May they say the quickly pronounced *qulwalla* [the phrase "there is no
  power and no strength save in God"] with pure intention
for it is the [votive] sign which will cool [the Prophet's] grave
and will give peace to the Muslims who are in their tombs
May they say the quickly pronounced *qulwalla* with pure intention
May everyone prepare his soul for the Day of Judgment
The Friday sermon has made my heart rejoice
For our hearts which are with you [Muhammad],
ask the Lord for forgiveness on the Day of Judgment
For our hearts which are with you, Muhammad,
ask the Lord for forgiveness
And for [our] parents' parents and their siblings
Oh God, the One and Only, give us to drink in paradise
and our parents' parents and our siblings
Oh God, let them drink from the rivers of paradise
In the name of God, he [the Prophet] was the first
In the name of God, he was the last
Muhammad was God's creation, but the luckiest of all humans
  (RTD1).

In the next song the women greeted and asked God's blessings for the
Prophet. Songs of praise for him always come first in Luula's *sittaat* group,
followed by a set of songs for 'Abd al-Qadir al-Jilani, the twelfth-century
founder of the Sufi brotherhood called the Qadiriyya. A third set of introductory songs is sung for the other *awliyo Allaah*, the saintly individuals of
Islamic history who continue to inspire and provide guidance to many
Muslims today. They are addressed both collectively and individually. The
songs associate some of these with the introduction of coffee (Somali *bun*)
into religious ritual, using the epithet of *rabb al-bun* ("lord of coffee"), and
implying that the *awliyo* come to earth attracted by the fragrance and taste
of coffee.[6] It is only then that the *sittaat* proper, the songs sung to the
distinguished women of early Islam, can begin:

The honored women [of Islam] are coming
they are coming from heaven
God, our musk has come down to us. . . .
Let us get up and greet the light (Interview 1).

Although Luula's *sittaat* group has some Arabic songs in its repertoire,
most *sittaat* are in Somali, even if with many Somalicized Arabic idioms.
Already during our first session Mariam and I caught on to some of the
refrains and were encouraged to sing along.

On this Monday the *sittaat* proper began, as always, with songs for
Xaawo (or Eve), whose status as "mother of the believers" and exemplary
Muslim goes unquestioned and is likened to that of Ibraahiim (the Biblical
Abraham) and other individuals of religious significance who figure in the

sacred texts of Judaism, Christianity, and Islam alike. After greeting Aadan (Adam), the song addresses Eve, praising her specifically as the first mother of humankind:

> Peace be upon you, grandmother Eve
> Peace be upon you, she is [Adam's] rib
> Peace be upon you, she is his wife
> Peace be upon you, a gift to him
> Peace be upon you, his light
> Peace be upon you, God loved her
> Peace be upon you, God was good to her
> Peace be upon you, God elevated her
> Peace be upon you, God was good to her
> Peace be upon you, and gave her to Adam (Interview 1).
> Before you, [the name of] "mother" did not exist
> Before you, "mama" did not exist
> Before you, respected one, before you
> People did not call each other mother
> Mother Eve, silken beauty, paradise is her shelter
> Before you, "mother" did not exist; before you, "mama" did not exist
> Mother Eve, don't sleep, spread a bed of silk for us
> Before you, "mother" did not exist; before you, "mama" did not exist
> Mother Eve, don't sleep, weave your ropes for us
> Before you, "mother" did not exist, before you, "mama" did not
>   exist. . . .
> Her ancient grave, lies on the beach of Jidda
> Before you, "mother" did not exist; before you, "mama" did not exist
> You, mother of Habiil and Qabiil, I am longing for you. . . .
>   (Interview 1).

After Eve, the *sittaat* address and honor Aamina (Amina), the Prophet's mother, Xaliimo Sacdiyya (Halima Sa'diyya), his foster-mother, and, on some occasions, Xaajra (Hagar), mother of Ismaaciil (Ishmael) and Maryam bint Cimraan (Mary, mother of Jesus), asking them for their guidance and intercession in this world and the next. Next come the Prophet's wives, with preference given to Khadiija (Khadija), his first wife, and Casha ('A'isha), his favourite spouse. This is one of the texts:

> Great Khadija, most blessed among women
> When he [the Prophet] was called a liar
> she spoke the truth about him
> Then he married her and a house was prepared for her
> The Prophet thanked her; she was of high class
> When she passed away, his heart hurt
> He professed that she had gone home to the garden of paradise
> The Prophet cherished her memory and her bond with him
> God, she was lucky, this servant of God
> God, give us free access to her blessing (RTD1).

'Asha [daughter of] Abubakr Siddiq, you were lucky
'Asha Abubakr Siddiq, you had knowledge
'Asha Abubakr Siddiq, you were respected
The Prophet Muhammad built a family with her
The Prophet's love was completed in you
You have reached a safe haven and the light of God
You, paradisical beauty, evil was barred [from being part] from you
You, lucky one among God's servants
God, give us free access to their [the women's] blessing
Mother, remember us, we are holding the hem of your skirt (RTD1).

After the Prophet's wives, the daughters of the Prophet form the next focus of devotion, in particular Faduumo (Arabic: Fatima), wife of the fourth Caliph 'Ali, in whose songs the *sittaat* sessions find their climax. The following song is known by its refrain: "I want the good Fatima."

Taha,[7] the Prophet, gave birth to her—I want the good Fatima
The Lord gave her high honors—I want the good Fatima
She was created from Khadija's womb—I want the good Fatima
She was mentioned in the lines of the Qur'an—I want the good
    Fatima
Blessed paradise was opened for her—I want the good Fatima
She is relaxing in the lofty premises of heaven—I want the good
    Fatima
She is a gift God bestowed on us—I want the good Fatima. . . .
She gave birth to Hasan and Husayn for us—I want the good Fatima
She loves women and children—I want the good Fatima
He [the Prophet] preferred her among all his children—
I want the good Fatima. . . .
May God kindly allow—I want the good Fatima
that she gives us access to her favors—I want the good Fatima
In order to be successful, we will follow your example—
I want the good Fatima
May God kindly allow—I want the good Fatima
that You [Lord] forgive us because of her good deeds—
I want the good Fatima
Sweet lady, God-serving lady, beg the Great God on our behalf
    (RTD1).

In the next hymn to the women of the *sittaat* group urgently call upon Fatima for help:

Madaad madaad,[8] Fatima, daughter of the Prophet
Give us that for which we call upon you. . . .
That you take and welcome us
daughter of the Prophet, for that we clamor
That you come and teach us how to walk
daughter of the Prophet, for that we clamor. . . .
You are the one who opens the Firduus paradise[9]

give us that for which we call upon you
You have carried Hasan and Husayn in your arms
give us that for which we call upon you
Through your good deeds God's light has overflown
give us that for which we call upon you
You, child of the Prophet, most obedient of women
give us that for which we call upon you
The person you love will enter paradise
give us that for which we call upon you (RTD1).

This is a third hymn for Fatima that urgently asks her to help the women singing the *sittaat* gain paradise.

Oh God, you, Fatima, best of women, aren't you residing in the light
and won't you quickly take us there?
Oh God, you, Fatima, best of women,
will you not be there on the Day of Reckoning
and won't you quickly bring us on your side?
Oh God, you, Fatima, best of women
will you not receive us at the Prophet's shrine?
Oh God, you, Fatima, best of women
won't you bring us in the presence of the beloved [Prophet]?
Oh God, you, Fatima, best of women
won't you, who are blessed by God, give us to drink from the well?
Oh God, you, Fatima, best of women
will you not open for us, mother, the gate of paradise. . . . [10]

In the following praise song to Fatima, she is addressed as Sahra Nuuray. The epithet Nuuray is the Somali parallel of the Arabic *al-Zahra'* ("the Shining One"), a praise-name given to Fatima throughout the Islamic world.

Shining One, who were made a gift to heaven, greet the Prophet for
us
Shining One, mother of Hasan and Husayn, greet the Prophet for us
Shining One, ladder for the believers, greet the Prophet for us
Shining One, most fragrant of the *sittaat*, greet the Prophet for us
Shining One, Lady Fatima, daughter of the Prophet,
greet the Prophet for us
Shining One, the great pillar of heaven, greet the Prophet for us
Shining One, for whom all of heaven was prepared as a home,
greet the Prophet for us
Shining One, [all] God's *sittaat* were called for you,
greet the Prophet for us
Shining One, whose party [we hope to join] on the Day of Judgment,
greet the Prophet for us
Shining One, obtain forgiveness for us on the Day of Judgment,
greet the Prophet for us
Shining One, who is suspended in my heart, greet the Prophet for us

Shining One, who is residing in my chest, greet the Prophet for us
Shining One, who is compared to Safa and Marwa,[11]
greet the Prophet for us
Shining One, next to whom people sit down, greet the Prophet for us
All women gather to be in your presence (Interview 1).

Sittaat, also known as *Xaawiyo Faduumo* ("Eve and Fatima"), *madaxshub* ("the anointment of the head") and, particularly in the south, as *Abbaay Sittidey*, *Abbaay Nabiyey*, and even *Kur* (after the wooden bowl used in the ritual) are sung throughout Somalia. Little is known about their history, although oral sources generally point to a southern or southwestern rather than a northern (Djibouti, Somaliland) origin. The *sittaat* form part of a rich and varied range of cultural expressions of Islamic devotion in the Horn of Africa, forms of worship (in Arabic and Somali) that often are directly linked to the Sufi brotherhoods. This is the case with the men's *xadra* or *dhikr* (the ritual "mentioning" of God's name in accordance with ritual prescriptions specific to each brotherhood), the recited or chanted *qasaayid* (poems by and for the saintly individuals of the local and global Islamic past), and the *mawlid an-nabi*, a special ritual prayer about the life of the Prophet, which is performed with great religious zeal and emotion on the birthday of the Prophet, at weddings, funerals, and so forth.[12] While the *sittaat* group of Luula Saalix has no formal connection to a brotherhood, the prominent place given in the hymns to 'Abd al-Qadir al-Jilani and the typically Sufi references (such as to the Prophet's and God's overflowing light and to chains of blessing) give them a strong Sufi and Qadiri flavor. It is possible that the *sittaat* originated during the period of great intensification of Sufi brotherhood activity in the first half of the nineteenth century, but neither this nor casual oral references to a pre-Islamic origin can currently be corroborated.[13]

In contemporary Djibouti, women perform *sittaat* on three kinds of occasions. The first type of occasion is the informal and low-key weekly devotional sessions described above. The objective here is to honor the first ladies of Islam and ask for their guidance. On the second type of occasion women gather to call upon the *sittaat* to come to the aid of a pregnant woman about to give birth. This performance of the *sittaat* is often called *madaxshub*, "the anointment of the head." The *madaxshub* I attended was held for the daughter-in-law of one of the women of Luula Saalix's *sittaat* group in October 1989. While the group of women gathered was much larger and the refreshments and food served much richer than on the Monday sessions, the sequence of the songs was as usual. However, this time the anointment of the mother-to-be's head formed both the climax and the conclusion of the ceremony. The pregnant woman (who was expecting her first child) was put on two pillows. While Luula passed the incense burner over the young woman's head, and touched her belly and head, she recited special prayers (*duco*), calling on the *sittaat* to support the girl during her upcoming ordeal and to help obtain God's blessing for a safe delivery:

> *Maano maano,*[14] my right hand on our Day of Judgment
> Lady Eve, Lady Eve, my right hand on our Day of Judgment
> Lady Amina, mother of the Prophet, my right hand on our Day of Judgement
> Halima Sa'diyya, [foster-] mother of the Prophet, my right hand on our Day of Judgement
> Lady Khadija, wife of the Prophet, my right hand on our Day of Judgment
> Lady 'Asha, wife of the Prophet, my right hand on our Day of Judgment
> Lady Maymuna, wife of the Prophet, my right hand on our Day of Judgment
> Lady Fatima, daughter of the Beloved, my right hand on our Day of Judgment
> Lady Ruqiyya, daughter of the Prophet, my right hand on our Day of Judgement
> It is her *madaxshub*, you who are the one who will not reject our right hand on our Day of Judgment. . . .
> May God make it easy for her, amen
> May He make her the mother of a new-born child, amen. . . .
> Lady Fatima, make it easy for anyone giving birth
> Today make my labor easy. . . .
> May God make her the daughter of goodness, the daughter of blessing, the daughter of health (Interview 2).

After the evening prayer the group dispersed.

The third type of context of the *sittaat* in Djibouti is their full-fledged, formal performance in a public space open to all women of the adjoining neighborhoods who may want to attend. Such *sittaat* sessions may be held during religious holidays or whenever a group of women combines its forces and resources to organize them. The public session I attended was held on 23 October 1989 in the community center of Quartier Six. It was a festive and formal occasion, attended by the wife of a minister and the wives of other members of Djibouti's high society. As Luula Saalix and her *sittaat* singers by now knew me well, my presence in this teeming crowd of women attracted little attention. Although unmarried women are welcome, most women present were of middle age and mothers. When I arrived, scores of women were preparing lunch in the court yard outside. To their great credit, all of us ate like queens, in spite of the crowd, the cramped quarters and our awkward position on the floor, closely sandwiched in between other women. After lunch, many women performed their prayers, individually or led in prayer by one of their number. More carpets were spread. It was not until 4:00 p.m. that the drumming and singing began. From then until almost 6:00 p.m., we sang in praise of the Prophet, 'Abd al-Qadir al-Jilani, and the other *awliyo*.

As the shadows grew longer, the atmosphere in the large room grew more excited and emotional. We had not yet reached the *sittaat* proper when a television crew of the RTD (Radio and Television Djibouti) entered the room, announcing their intent to videotape part of the session. Television was not new to Ina Saalix and her group; she had been videotaped on the preceding Prophet's Birthday as well as on other special occasions—occasions that had yielded clean and clear recordings of the song texts, as she had been asked not to play the drum.[15] The camera- and soundmen, cheeks bulging with *qaat*, impatiently demanded that Luula immediately perform the best-known *sittaat* for Faduumo. Ina Saalix's sudden outburst of anger and the moral indignation of the other singers clarified for me much about the objectives of the *sittaat*. The women's anger expressed that they were not just performing for entertainment but were engaged in a purposeful ritual communication with the saintly individuals of the Islamic tradition, in particular the first ladies of Islam. Botching the sequence, jumping ahead to the climax, these were unthinkable to them. Luula swallowed her anger, stoically ignored the instrument-toting men, and continued the regular sequence. Soon the crew departed. It was almost 6:00 p.m. when we started the actual *sittaat*, singing and clapping for Eve, Amina, Halima, Khadija, 'Asha ('A'isha), and finally Fatima. By then we were enveloped in a cloud of incense and perfume. The atmosphere became frenzied, as scores of women reached a form of religious trance or absorption called *muraaqo*. Some women, individually or in pairs, covering their heads and shoulders with a scarf, got up to dance, a powerful, not very elegant set of movements, not unlike a march. Some women screamed. One woman fell down and rhythmically sobbed "mama, mama, mama," while her companions and neighbors tried to soothe her, covering her face with her *shalmad* (shawl) and perfuming her with incense and cologne. Two women, in trance, began to dance carrying incense burners with live coal on their heads. One of the singers began to shiver and weep; she was comforted and covered with a shawl by her neighbors. Perfume was poured wildly in all directions. Yet another woman began to yell angrily that they should do the *sittaat* right and not botch them up. These are some of the texts sung during these emotional moments:

Madaad madaad, Fatima, daughter of the Chosen One
Madaad madaad, Fatima, daughter of the Prophet
Give us that for which we call upon you
Ecstasy has me in its grip, my body is burning
Madaad madaad, Fatima, daughter of the Prophet
Give us that for which we call upon you
We wandered and wandered, we cannot do without you
Madaad madaad, Fatima, daughter of the Prophet
Give us that for which we call upon you.[16]
You, new moon, mother, lightning that reached the earth
shining Fatima, we need you urgently
You, new moon, mother, the mother whom we love best
You, new moon, mother, I am disoriented for [love of] you
You, new moon, mother, I am yearning for you. . . .
You, new moon, mother, leader who is looking after our interests
You, new moon, mother, fragrant plant, daughter of the Chosen One
You, new moon, mother, noble lady, daughter of the Prophet. . . .
You, new moon, mother, fragrant plant, inhabitant of paradise
You, new moon, mother, the chain that will never be loosened from us
You, new moon, mother, the light that will never be extinguished
  amongst us. . . .
You, new moon, mother, mother of Hasan and Husayn
You, new moon, mother, wife of *Imam* 'Ali
You, new moon, mother, who supported the party of Nur, the
  Prophet. . . .
You, new moon, mother, a ladder for us that does not fall down
You, new moon, mother, light that will never be extinguished among
  us (Interview 3).

It was clear that the women sensed the spiritual presence of Fatima amongst us. Amidst shouts of *way joogtaa, way joogtaa* ("she is present, she is present") and mutual reminders of keeping the head covered (implying her presence), the emotional intensity of the session reached its height. Around 8:00 p.m. the women began to disperse.

The *sittaat* sung by Somali women for the distinguished women of early Islam form part of a wider orature of popular, often Sufi, Islamic expression. Some aspects of this Islamic literature and orature have been described by scholars such as Andrzejewski, Lewis, and Abdisalam Yassin Mohamed. The history of the brotherhoods and the lives of specific Somali religious teachers have received attention as well.[17] However, many aspects and most texts of Somali Islamic orature remain undocumented. Apart from Abdisalam Yassin Mohammed's "Sufi Poetry in Somali," this is true for the beautiful genre of *nabi ammaan* (Arabic *madih*), praise songs for the Prophet, which are sung by young and old, men and women. The following is a widely known (undated) example:

Peace be upon you, moon of Mecca
You, fragrant Prophet
chosen by God
we belong to his community
Oh Prophet of God
every person
Oh Light of God
praises you in his own tongue.

Peace be upon you, moon of Mecca
You, fragrant Prophet
who used to gather
the orphans and needy
Oh Prophet of God
every person
Oh Light of God
praises you in his own tongue.

Peace be upon you, moon of Mecca
You, fragrant Prophet
who lit up with [his] light
the land which lay in darkness
Oh Prophet of God
every person
Oh Light of God
praises you in his own tongue.
Peace be upon you, moon of Mecca[18]

The following *nabi ammaan* song is sung on the Prophet's birthday:

The Prophet's birth
set the unbelievers on fire
and brought the Muslims into being
Thanks be to God
and honor to Muhammad
for lighting up the darkness
When the Prophet was born
the trees put forth blossoms and
the birds sung his praise
Thanks be to God
and honor to Muhammad
for lighting up the darkness
When the Prophet was born
angels led him in procession
Thus he traveled over the world
Thanks be to God
and honor to Muhammad
for lighting up the darkness
When the Prophet was born
we learned to ululate and

experienced the *mawlid*
Thanks be to God
and honor to Muhammad
for lighting up the darkness
When the Prophet was born
he intervened on behalf of the Muslims
and obtained high rank for them.[19]

This genre of *nabi ammaan* shows parallels in content with the *sittaat*. One might even argue that the latter are just a part of the former, as the *sittaat* songs are mostly in praise of those women who are closely related to the Prophet.[20] In contrast to the *nabi ammaan*, however, *sittaat* are only sung by women, following the rules of composition typical of the most prestigous women's poetic genre, that of the *buraanbur*.[21] With the *dhikr* and *xadra* the *sittaat* share the objective of attaining spiritual ecstasy (*muraaqo*), and with the religious recital called the *mawlid an-nabi* it has in common its intent of bringing about the spiritual presence of the saintly individual invoked.[22] The *mawlid* (in Arabic) is recited by men, with great emotional intensity and at high speed, accompanied by energetic handclapping and (sometimes) dancing. When the reciter reaches the passage *marxaba ya rasuul, marxaba* ("welcome Prophet, welcome"), everyone, even women sitting with covered heads at the periphery of the performance, gets up and greets the Prophet, believed to be actually present.[23] This is similar to the *sittaat*'s objective of bringing about Fatima's presence amongst the group.

If the Somali *sittaat* are, on the one hand, part of a wider Islamic orature, they belong, on the other hand, to a wider context of women's culture and orature. In Somali society age and gender have always been strong determinants of the social roles, obligations, opportunities and status of its members.[24] Married women are (and have been) a distinct social group with many common duties, rights, and challenges related to their wife- and motherhood. As a social and cultural activity by women and for women, the *sittaat* sessions are not unique in Somali society, where women have commonly worked, socialized and prayed together, separate (though not secluded) from men. The *sittaat* represent an explicit assertion of the common bond and plight of women in two ways. First, the singers of *sittaat* in Djibouti explicitly emphasize their common problems as wives, mothers and providers in the urban slums of underdeveloped, French dominated Djibouti. Secondly, they appeal to their common bond of womanhood with the famous women (mothers, wives, and daughters) of early Islam. In doing so they explicitly assert the values central to their own lives. They sing in praise of Eve as humankind's first wife and mother. They celebrate the loyal wifehood of Khadija, so beloved by the Prophet, with the lines "when she passed away, his heart hurt." In Fatima they praise the significance of daughterhood (to the Prophet, who "preferred her among all his children"), her wifehood (to `Ali, the fourth Caliph), and her motherhood (to Hasan and Husayn). The imagery used in the *sittaat* concretely links the singers to the heavenly ladies by way of "chains" (of blessing), "ropes," "ladders," and "lights" (concepts typical of Sufism), and by way of the "skirt hems" of the *sittaat* (a concept typical of women's culture).

This assertion of their separate and significant identity as mothers and wives is in accordance with the dominant cultural and religious definitions of (and prescriptions for) these roles. Somali women call upon the "Mothers of the Believers" as women, hoping to learn from them how to become better Muslim wives and mothers so that they may gain paradise. Thus in the prayers (*duco*) interspersed among the *songs*, the women ask God, through the Prophet and the *sittaat*, for help in their relations with husbands, in improving the behavior of their children, in being able to get pregnant and to give birth safely, and in obtaining intercession on the Day of Judgment. The following are two such *ducos*. The first warns the soul that it should prepare for death and has no contents specific to women's conditions:

> You, unaware soul, are you not aware that you will be asked on the day of Judgment about the debt that you owe the Lord? Are you unaware of the lies you used to like? Are you unaware of the evil you like? Are you unaware of the *qasil* [plant used to wash the dead], the bed [on which the body is washed], and the cold water?. . . Are you unaware of the grave, the ants, and so forth, of the day of Judgment, the Hidden Day, that you will not live forever? That the sun will be near when you stand in line on the Day of Judgement? Are you unaware of the difference between good and bad, that you took what was not yours?" (Interview 2)

The second one specifically addresses women's concerns:

> May God bestow on us the blessing of our Prophet Muhammad. God, bestow good things on our children. May they not make their parents, who gave birth to them, go without their just reward. May they festively parade for the religion, may they pray and fast. We are concerned about them; God, put them straight. Against the world which leads them astray, Lord, please protect them. . . (Interview 2).

That women reinforce the dominant cultural values of mother-and wifehood is also evident in the folk *xadiith* (Arabic: *Hadith*) they tell each other, not during the *sittaat* sessions but in conversations relating to them. Many folk *xadiith* do not figure in the prestigeous *Hadith* collections of Islam; however, most have a strong moral lesson, as in the saying ascribed to Abu Hureira, one of the Prophet's Companions: "A woman is as close to heaven as her skirt hem is to the ground" (Interview 2). Wifely obedience figures prominently in the *xadiith* involving Fatima, to whom the *sittaat* refer as *raalliya haween,* "the most obedient of women." Somali women relate that Fatima was initially not keen on marrying `Ali, as he had bad breath, was balding, and had crooked legs. But she had to accept, when her father (the Prophet) explained, that `Ali had bad breath because of having fasted for three months; that he was balding because hard work had made him sweat under his head cover; and that he had crooked legs because he was a great warrior on horseback (Interview 2). Fatima had to be taught to be *raalliya* by her father, who advised her, Somali women relate to each other, that she should prepare in three ways for her husband's return home at the end of the day. She should have a jug of water ready for him, so that he could drink; she should have a stick ready for him, so that he could beat her if he were angry; and she should undo her waist belt, so he could sleep with her if he had that desire.[25] Many younger women take these stories with a grain of salt, but the point that dominant culture makes through them about wifehood and obedience is nevertheless unambiguous.

There is one way, however, in which the hymns called *sittaat* make a strong statement that is somewhat incongruous with dominant societal values and expectations. In spite of the fact that in Djibouti many of the regular participants in the *sittaat* are women who are middle-aged or older, who are divorcees, widows and mothers of grown (often unemployed) children, who belong to the urban lower class and often have to provide for their own living. They nevertheless insist upon their daughterhood in relation to the *sittaat* in heaven. As daughters, they appeal to them for the love, help, care and teaching that mothers give their daughters. In expressing their expectations that the heavenly ladies will take care of them in infinite and intimate detail, in this life, on the Day of Judgment and in paradise, Somali women challenge in song the harsh age- and gender-based realities of their daily lives:

Lady Fatima, take us along with your chain
Lady Fatima, lead us with your light
Lady Fatima, make us as you are
Lady Fatima, give us your raisins to eat
Lady Fatima, make us as you are
Lady Fatima, give us your musk to smell
Lady Fatima, spread your bed for us
Lady Fatima, bring us in the presence of the good Muhammad
Lady Fatima, help us climb your ladder
Lady Fatima, spread your wrap as our bedding
Lady Fatima, wrap us in your silk (Interview 3).

Shining Eve and her good companions
Amina and Asiya and the whole community of the *sittaat*
and you, Maryam, daughter of 'Imran, mother of 'Isa
and Fatima and her highly favored mother
and the wives of the Prophet, mother[s] of the believers
who are the Prophet's family, praised by God
well brought up girls and their companions
May God make us whole [by allowing us to follow]
the road along which you passed
Teach us how to walk, look upon us as your children
 Merciful God, don't keep Fatima away from us
May she take us by the right hand on the Day On Which One Is
 Sorrowful
Make us their companions, Compassionate God
May we all live in one home with their mothers and daughters
May we all eat together with the *sittaat* and [the Prophet's] family
May we come to live in paradise. . . .
May we go to the shrine of Prophet Muhammad
Oh Great God, always bring us in your presence (RTD1).

The *sittaat* represent an authentically Somali poetic genre in which
women express and experience their spirituality and their emotional involvement in Islam. However, like many other forms of women's orature,
the *sittaat* have remained marginal to Somali cultural production as a
whole. This marginality is partly due to the age and gender of those
who commmonly perform and frequent *sittaat* sessions, that is to say,
older women, who have access neither to the religious authority of Islamic tradition nor to the cultural prestige of a western education. Both
culturally and economically, the status of the women who perform *sittaat*
lacks power and authority. The *sittaat* are marginal also because, in the
colonial period, Somali popular expressions of Islam came to be defined
as backward in relation to the power structures of the colonial state.
Although in northern Somalia the colonial encounter produced a definition of "authentic tradition" that gave more emphasis to a newly
hierarchized, formalized and newly defined kinship identity than to Islam,[26] the colonizers nevertheless attempted to formalize and "upgrade"
Somali Islam, thus to some extent marginalizing those local practices
that lacked the foreign, formal stamp of approval. This onus of back-
wardness persisted after independence, when the then ex-colonial middle
class, with its western education and aspirations, set the tone. Some Somali intellectuals (such as Maxammed Cabdillaahi Riraash and Cumar
Macallin, who introduced me to the *sittaat*) have acknowledged and as-
serted the aesthetic, literary and social value of the *sittaat*. They have
begun to record and preserve them as part of the Somali cultural heritage, and have given the *sittaat* performers such as Luula Saalix a small

moral boost through their interest. Yet most other middle-class men (merchants, shop keepers, teachers and professionals rather than writers, literary analysts and intellectuals) at best regard the *sittaat* as backward, ignorant and unnecessary expressions of Islamic piety. A substantial number of these men have become attracted to a lifestyle of intensified personal piety, as advocated (largely by audio-visual means) by religious teachers from the Arab Middle East and Iran. While so far not actually hostile to the *sittaat* groups, these men have their eyes and aspirations fixed on the cultural examples of the so-called Islamic heartlands and have firmly turned their backs on Somali Islamic culture. The growing impact of explicitly politicized Islamist groups is, for the moment at least, intensifing the marginalization of Somali Sufi ritual and orature.

Many young middle-class women too have embraced a more pious Islamic lifestyle in place of the secular, neo-colonial, consumer-oriented culture imported from France. These women have begun to take lessons in Qur'an exegesis and recitation and organize their own study and prayer circles. Whether these women will retrieve the *sittaat* from the persisting cultural marginality and the possible extinction to which they seem presently doomed is yet unclear.[27] The depth of the spiritual, emotional, and aesthetic appeal of the *sittaat*, and the shallowness (both in substance and in chronological depth) of the class gap separating most Somali women from their mothers and grandmothers may yet contribute to the preservation of this unique genre of women's Islamic orature in Somali.

Notes

1. *Sittaat*, derived from the Arabic *sitt*, "lady," plural, *sittaat*, refers here to the songs Somali women sing for the distinguished women of early Islamic history and to those "first ladies" themselves.

2. The format of this book did not allow for the inclusion of most of the Somali texts; for these, see my Occasional Paper of the African Studies Center of Boston University of the same title. This text was transcribed and translated from audio-visual recordings of Luula Saalix's *sittaat* by Radio and Television Djibouti, 1988 (hereafter referred to as RTD 1).

3. This article is based on fieldwork in Djibouti in July-August 1987 and September-December 1989. The session described here took place on 2 October 1989. I gratefully acknowledge the financial support of the National Endowment for the Humanities, the Social Science Research Council, the American Philosophical Society and Wellesley College. In Djibouti Maxammad Cabdillaahi Riraash, Cumar Macallin, Cali Muuse Ciye, and the Honorable Ismaaciil Taani guided me and generously shared their intellectual and audio-visual resources. Thanks also to Luula Saalix and her *sittaat* group, to Yasmiin Muuse and the late Mariam Haibe, who attended the *sittaat* with me, and their families. Louise Marlow kindly commented upon the manuscript.

4. *Quartiers indigènes*, the French term for "indigenous quarters" or "native town." Djibouti, inhabited by two national groups, the Somalis and the Afar (Danakil), was colonized by the French from the 1880s to 1977, when it gained independence as the Republic of Djibouti.

5. Compare the Somali *awliyo* with the Arabic *awliya* (glossary).

6. *Sittaat* session led by Luula Saalix, Djibouti, 2 October 1989. The recorded, transcribed, and translated song texts of this session are hereafter referred to as Interview 1. In this context the women refer to Sheekh Caydaruus, perhaps the Abu Bakr ibn 'Abd Allah al-'Aydarus who is believed to have introduced the Qadiriyya into Harar around 1500 C.E. (Trimingham 1965, 240).

7. In Somali Islamic praise poetry, the Prophet is given many different names. "Taha" also echoes the mystical letters/sounds at the beginning of certain chapters of the Qur'an.

8. The exact meaning of this word is uncertain. It may relate to the Arabic *madad*, plural *amdad*, meaning "assistance, support," or to the term *al-maddad*, which in Somali Sufi brotherhoods refers to the third and highest state of mystical attainment (Trimingham 1965, 238). Compare McPherson (1941, 62), and Waugh (1989, 44, 164).

9. *Firduus* or *Firdaws* is the highest level of paradise either in the seventh heaven or beyond it.

10. *Sittaat* session led by Luula Saalix, Djibouti, 27 October 1989. The recorded, transcribed, and translated song texts of this session are hereafter referred to as Interview 2.

11. Al-Safa and al-Marwa are places near the well of Zemzem, where Hagar is believed to have run back and forth searching for water for her son. This event is symbolically reenacted during the ritual pilgrimage to Mecca.

12. For *mawlid an-nabi*, see *Encyclopaedia of Islam*, "mawlid," and Trimingham 1964, 94-95. In Djibouti, as elsewhere in East Africa, the most common text is that of al-Barzanji.

13. For the Qadiriyya and other brotherhoods in Somalia, see Ali Abdirahman Hersi 1977, 244-80; Trimingham 1965, 239-42, 249; Trimingham 1964, 99-101; and Martin 1976, 152-76. For a hypothesis about relationships between the veneration of Sufi saints and pre-Islamic religion, see Braukämper 1992, 145-66.

14. The meaning of *maano* is said to be similar to *sitt* ("lady"). Notice the name Maanafaay (consisting of *maano* and Faay or Fatima) in use among the descendants of the original inhabitants of Mogadishu (the Reer Xamar).

15. The song texts referred to as RTD1 were transcribed from such clean recordings, which M.A. Riraash kindly shared with me.

16. *Sittaat* session led by Casha Maxammad (from Hargeisa), Djibouti, 13 November 1989. The recorded, transcribed and translated song texts of this session are hereafter referred to as Interview 3.

17. See Abdisalam Yassin Mohammed 1977; Ali Abdirahman Hersi 1977, 244 ff.; Andrzejewski 1974; Lewis 1955 and 1969, 75-81; Martin 1976,152-237; Ali Abdirahman Hersi 1977, 244 ff., and Samatar 1992.

18. As-salaam calayka/ ya qamar al-Makka/ Udgoonow rasuulkow/ kii Ilaahay doortee/ ummaddiisaan nahayoo/ Nabi Allow/ ninba afkii/ Nuur Allow/ kugu ammaan/ As-salaam calayka/ ya qamar al-Makka/ Udgoonow rasuulkow/ agoontiyo maatida/ kii ururin jirayoo/ Nabi Allow/ ninba afkii/

Nuur Allow/ kugu ammaan/ As-salaam calayka/ ya qamar al-Makka/ Udgoonow rasuulkow/ arliga mugdi ahaa/ ku iftiinshay nuurkoo/ Nabi Allow/ ninba afkii/ Nuur Allow/ kugu ammaan/ As-salaam calayka/ ya qamar al-Makka. From the audio collection of Mariam Omar Ali and Lidwien Kapteijns.

19. Markuu dhashay rasuulku/ munaafiq wuu ku oogay/ Muslinkii wuu ahaatay/ Ilaahay baa mahadleh/ Maxammad baa sharafleh/ mugdigii buu iftiinshay/ Markuu dhashay rasuulku/ dhirtiina way magooshay/ shimbirahaa madiixay/ Ilaahay baa mahadleh/ Maxammad baa sharafleh/ mugdigii buu iftiinshay/ Markuu dhashay rasuulku/ malaa'ik baa gelbisay/ adduunyaduu ku meeray/ Ilaahay baa mahadleh/ Maxammad baa sharafleh/ mugdigii buu iftiinshay/ Markuu dhashay rasuulku/ mashxaarad baan aloosnay/ mawlidkii waan kulannay/ Ilaahay baa mahadleh/ Maxammad baa sharafleh/ mugdigii buu iftiinshay/ Markuu dhashay rasuulku/ Muslinkii wuu shafeecay/ maqaam saraa la geyay. From the audio collection of Mariam Omar Ali and Lidwien Kapteijns.

20. As discussed above, this is not quite true, as women such as Eve, Mary, Hagar and the mother of 'Abd al-Qadir al-Jilani also figure in the *sittaat.*

21. The *buraanbur* is similar to, but somewhat longer than the *gabay*, the most prestigous poetic genre composed by men. See Andrzejewski and Lewis 1964.

22. Trimingham (1965, 238) notes about Somalia: "Women, who are generally old, are often affiliated to an order and take part in its exercises. They are called by the Somali term *abbayal* (sing. *abbaya*) which means 'eldest sister'." Women indeed sometimes attend *dhikr* meetings or recitals of the *mawlid*, but do not participate. See also Trimingham 1964, 87, and Mukhtar 1995, 6.

23. Fieldwork Djibouti, 1989. Compare Trimingham 1964, 95-96.

24. Kapteijns 1994 and 1995.

25. Fieldwork Djibouti, 1989. There is a reference to the stick in the *sittaat* recorded in Interview 2.

26. Kapteijns 1994.

27. As wedding parties are frowned upon by the current regime in Sudan, women have begun to attend *madih* parties, at which praise songs for the Prophet take the place of Sudanese pop songs. These are not, however, exclusively sung for and by women. The Sudanese social reform movement called the Republican Brothers represents a unique case of modern Sufism, as among them men and women together compose and sing praise-songs for Fatima (personal information W. Stephen Howard and Ahmad Dali).

Chapter 11

▼▼▼▼▼▼▼▼▼

Women's Islamic Literature in Northern Nigeria: 150 Years of Tradition, 1820–1970[1]

JEAN BOYD AND BEVERLY B. MACK

Muslim women are expected to be rooted solidly in the world, attending to home and family, consumed by daily concerns. However, in what is now known as Northern Nigeria, Muslim women have been active as scholars for at least two centuries. What is surprising is the extent to which their voice has been heard and found acceptable. There are two reasons for this. First, the women literati have been respectable and responsible people. Second, their voices have blended with the main themes expressed by the leaders of the day. In the last century these themes were centered on the nurture, admonishment, education, and protection of the peoples of the nascent Islamic Caliphate. In this century, particularly in the postcolonial era, the theme has been the defense of a distinctive northern Islamic identity in a multiracial secular Nigeria. This study provides representative examples of their writings from the past hundred and fifty years, from a period beginning well before the colonial occupation and continuing through to contemporary times.

Perhaps the best known woman scholar and author of the region is Nana Asma'u (1793–1865), a daughter of jihad leader Shehu Usman 'dan Fodio. She was an important figure in the unfolding of jihad plans and reconstruction following its battles. In contemporary times she remains an influential figure, whose example is cited frequently by women in response to patriarchal voices that challenge their freedom to pursue education and authorship.[2] Nana Asma'u's status and accomplishments belie the stereotype of the restricted Muslim woman. Indeed, her written works attest to collaboration throughout her lifetime with her father, the Shehu, and her brother the Caliph, and to the high esteem with which she was regarded by scholars of the period.

But Asma'u was not the first woman intellectual of her family. Her grandmother Hauwa and great grandmother Rukayya were "also learned and were among the teachers of the community" (Boyd 1989, 4). Within this religious context of community, education was assumed to be a means of improving the spirit; everything that was written—whether focused directly on God or not—served to promote the Islamic context that produced it.

The women discussed here, beginning with some from the Fodio family in Sokoto and continuing to the present time in Kano, represent a continuing tradition of Muslim women writers in northern Nigeria. Their topics range from Islam and its leaders to issues of importance for the community as a whole. They write to inform, admonish, commemorate, and instruct. In each case they speak to Islamic audiences, confident that the message they convey through their works will be understood as one of importance to the betterment of the community of Muslims as a whole.

Hadiza Fodio (1782–1846?)[3]

The Mahdi, "the Guided One," is the subject of an undated poem by Hadiza, eldest daughter of Shehu Usman 'dan Fodio. She grew up in Degel (near Sokoto), a community of Qadiri sufis where reliance on texts and prophecies led scholars to believe in the coming of the Mahdi and the conviction that the end of the world was imminent.

The idea of the expected Mahdi is well known in the history of Islam although there is no reference to the Mahdi in either the Qur'an or the two most authoritative collections of the Hadith.[4] Describing the difficulties facing those who tried to predict the time of the Mahdi's coming, Ibn Khaldun (b.1332), said:

> More recent sufis have other theories concerning the Mahdi. The time, the man, and the place are clearly indicated in them. But the predicted time passes and there is not the slightest trace of the prediction coming true (Ibn Khaldun 1967, 258).

The Shehu, Hadiza's father, had himself fixed the date of the Coming at 1785–89, basing his prediction on the assumption of al–Sayuti, a fifteenth–century scholar. He later revised his views: "after investigation we admit we do not know the time with any degree of certainty" (quoted in Albasu 1985, 11). Furthermore the Shehu refuted the idea that he himself was the expected Mahdi: "Know, O my brethren that I am not the Mahdi" (cited in Albasu 1985, 13), and in a Fulfulde poem he described himself thus: "I am a precursor, like the wind before a storm/That is how I am to the Mahdi" (*Munasaba* v.62, quoted in Said 1973, 91–96).

On the Shehu's death in 1817 his son Caliph Muhammad Bello inherited responsibility for the deep concerns felt in the Community for the Precursor of the Day of Judgment, the Mahdi, a responsibility shared by his contemporaries including Hadiza. Writing many centuries after Ibn Khaldun and probably after the death of her father, she appeared to be answering three questions put to her by a person unnamed. To the first question, "Will the Mahdi be the son of Askiya'u?" she said, after a brief doxology[5]: "It is my intention to speak on the Mahdi/ And to set out what is known.[v.3]/ The consensus is that/ He is not the son of Askiya'u (Askar [F.] soldier) [v.4][6]/ I repeat, this is false/ And does not accord with the correct view [v.5]/ Which has been stated in a tradition/ Where the conditions of his coming are made clear" [v.6]. We presume here that the second question was, "When will he come?" for in verses 8–20 Hadiza made calculation based on prophecies all of which pointed to the fact that while there was no absolute agreement on the precise date, his coming would be round about the year 1300 A.H. (1979 A.D.).

Finally she tackled the problem, "What are the signs of his coming?" and her answer was very explicit: "There will widespread disturbances . . . [v.21], the people of Syria will be crushed . . . [v.22], there will be an eclipse of the sun and moon during Ramadan . . . [v.23], a comet will appear . . . [v.25], and a meteor will fall . . . [v.26], Turkey will be overthrown by Egypt . . . [v.27], servants will no more obey their masters . . . [v.28], children will scorn their parents . . . [v.29], and there will be a severe drought . . ." [v.29]. As for the events that most immediately precede the Mahdi's advent, these included: "An invasion of Mecca by Iraq which will fail . . . [v.31], an invasion of the Sudan by Egypt . . . [v.32], an invasion by the peoples of the Barbary Coast . . . [v.33], an invasion of Jordan by Arabia . . . [v.33], and the destruction of the walls of the mosque at Qupa"[7] [v.35]. Climaxing all this, on the day of the Great Id,[8] there will be war and a man will emerge from the west, a leader who will lead a counterattack, which will culminate in the murder of "a great holy man" in the Ka'aba: "Then the angels will be angry and the people will beg for the coming of the Mahdi/ Who will be shown to them, and recognised [v.43]/ Good fortune will then return, but fear and war/ Will be the fate of all unbelievers [v.44]/ The poem is finished with thanks to God/ I bid farewell to all True Believers [v.45]. Thus Hadiza's work served a very specific purpose within the Muslim community, inspiring piety and unity among those concerned about the destination of mankind and the Muslims' role within it.

Aisha Fodio (1829–1870)[9]

On a less dramatic, but perhaps more immediate note, a poem by Aisha, daughter of Abdullahi b. Fodio[10] addresses the issue of forgetfulness in prayer. Prayer is one of the five pillars of Islam and its form was prescribed by the Prophet Muhammad in the year before the Hijira, so in its present pattern it has been in existence for more than thirteen hundred years. It is immutable; "Establish regular prayers/ At the sun's decline/ Till the darkness of the night/ And the morning prayer" (Qur'an 17:78). Commentators understand here the command for the five daily canonical prayers—the four from the declination of the sun from the zenith to the fullest darkness of the night, and the normal early morning prayer" (Ali 1946, fn. 2275, 716).

A very serious approach to prayer[11] is demanded of the worshipper, and he or she must follow a prescribed pattern of bodily movements[12] in the course of which certain phrases and some parts of the Qur'an, must be uttered or said silently.[13] Nothing can be changed or omitted, nor can the preparatory ablutions,[14] nor the absolute necessity to face towards Mecca. Children are trained to pray correctly and can usually do so by the time they are ten or eleven years old. Men pray alone, or with their neighbors or workmates in small, unroofed mosques, or in the large congregational mosques on Fridays and other occasions. Women pray in their own rooms, dressing carefully to cover all but their faces, feet, and hands. Prayer is vitiated if the prescribed formulas are deliberately disregarded: however, in the case of forgetfulness, there were ways to make amends. "It was reported that the Prophet said: 'I am but a human being; I may forget as you may. If I do, remind me.'"[15]

This work of Aisha's is important as a teaching device for a community of new converts who were probably more likely to hear the poem chanted than to read it. It is neat in construction, and tells how to deal with five omissions, five additions, and forgetting to face towards Mecca. The opening doxology is followed by a notice of the subject of the poem: "We must all strive to say our prayers correctly/ for if they are accepted then all is well [v.4]/ Mistakes can be amended by means of / the *sujada kabla*" (the prostration of omission; *sujada ba'ada* = "prostration of addition") [v.5][16] Following this, she listed the mistakes of omission: for example, "If the sura of the Qur'an is omitted / you must perform the *sujada kabla* [v.6]/ If the "Allahu Akbar" is not said twice/ then perform the *sujada kabla* [v.7]/ If the speaking is said silently when it should be said aloud/ then perform the *sujada kabla*" [v.8]. Then follow the errors of addition, the remedy for which is the prostration of *ba'ada* made after the salam at the end of the prayer. The errors included, for example, the following: "For forgetting how many prostrations have been made/ the remedy is to perform *sujada ba'ada* [v.16]/ If the opening sura of the Qur'an is said twice/ then perform the *sujada ba'ada*" [v.17]. Aisha ends by clarifying the reason for this work, and includes the standard closing doxology to God: "We hope this poem will help you to correct/ mistakes made when praying [v.21]/ It is finished, I thank God and pray/ for Ahmada the Defender" [v.22]. This poem clearly serves an important function, educating new Muslims about the requirements and flexibility of Islam. Poetry has long been a prime vehicle of instruction in the Muslim world, and was crucial to the education of the masses at this time.

Maryam Fodio (1810–1890)[17]

Maryam, youngest of the children of the Shehu, was born circa 1810 and was the very last to die.[18] She was described by Waziri Buhari, who lived in the colonial era as "a saintly woman" (Hiskett 1975, 76). Widowed early in her life,[19] she married as her second husband Ibrahim Dabo, Emir of Kano, who reigned 1819–46. When he, in turn, died, she returned to Sokoto and left behind a reputation for piety and wisdom while taking with her a sound knowledge of Kano politics. That she kept abreast of events over the years is shown by the way in which she was consulted during the Kano succession dispute in 1882. At a time of deadlock, when neither the Caliph nor the Waziri could agree who the next Emir of Kano should be, Maryam advised the appointment of Muhammad Bello[20] who went on to reign from 1883–92.

Written proof of her involvement is found in the reply she sent to a query made by Muhammad Bello concerning the wave of migrants moving east towards Mecca. "Has the time for the evacuation of Hausaland come?" he asked. In reply she said:

> The answer is as follows: such people [the migrants] are utterly mis-
> guided and completely ignorant of their religious and worldly af-
> fairs. . . . Indeed, the Shehu, my father did mention that we shall emi-
> grate from Hausaland but he did not specify the time. . . . But when it
> comes it will be like a fire on top of a mountain and will not be hid-
> den from anyone. . . .[21]

Implicit in this exchange is the fact that Maryam did not live a life of pious seclusion, the kind of purdah believed by many commentators on Islamic affairs, and many Muslim husbands, to be fitting for a Muslim woman. She was involved in society, leading the women's education movement,[22] distributing alms, and apportioning horses to fighting men.[23] In these circumstances, therefore, it is not surprising that she was consulted on a wide range of current issues, some of which as we have already seen were not commonly within the experience of many people, men or women.

Her unusual poem on the office of *Limam* was either written to advise a group of elders who were about to choose a prayer leader, or to help break a deadlock in a dispute over the issue. For no other reason, it seems, would anyone compose a poem of such a technical nature. It is also a mark of her authority.

After a only single verse of doxology, she launched immediately into detail stating that whereas a Limam must be a true disciple of the Prophet, nineteen categories of people were not suitable for appointment, and of these, six were totally unacceptable. The six included transsexuals, "neither male nor female", unbelievers, women, madmen, and children. The next category she labelled as "doubtfuls"; they were: "The partially paralyzed, amputees, a man with suppurating sores [v.5]/ Pimps, slaves, the incontinent of faeces and urine [v.6]/ Complete strangers, the emasculated, the uncircumcised [v.7]/ Any man shunned by his colleagues" [v.8].

About some cases she said, scholars were undecided; these included the blind, lepers, members of a different sect,[24] anyone unable to correct mistakes made in prayer,[25] and the womaniser.

Finally Maryam listed the kinds of men most suitable for the office of Limam:

The man who knows the Hadith, the scholar/ He who is Godfearing and pious [v.15]/ The man who wears clean garments and washes frequently/ The family man, surrounded by relatives—he is the most favored [v.16]/ Others are the local ruler and the head of the house in which prayer/ is to be said, and the man who guards himself from sin[v.17]/ If you follow the leadership of a Limam in the forbidden categories/ be sure your prayer is negated [v.18]/ It is better to have no Limam at all/ if there is no one suitable [v.19]/ Prayer which is led by Limams in the recommended categories/ is acceptable [v.20].

And there the poem ended. Clearly this is the voice of authority. Her abbreviated opening doxology and certainty of terms underlines the urgency and force with which she put across her message. Although it is ironic that Maryam herself was disqualified by her gender from holding the office of liman, this poem reveals a woman who was neither hesitant to clarify religious rules for others, nor tentative in her means of communicating those rules.

Hussaina bint Dabo (1846–circa 1900 A.D.)[26]

War poetry written to commemorate victory, the loss of comrades, to express joy, and lampoon the enemy was a popular genre among the jihadist writers. Abdullahi b. Fodio, the Shehu's brother, at times wrote with emotion. In his poem on the near disaster at Alwasa he opened with the words: "O God give help to a heart with which/ is mixed care and sadness [v.1]/ On the night of the full moon from morning/ to evening [v.2]/ For the loss of friends who passed away in/ their holy war" [v.3].[27] But Abdullahi, like his colleagues, also enjoyed a joke and wrote one of his works about the battle of Tabkin Kwatto in a satirical vein. His Hausa poem[28] is in short lines with much word play to amuse the victors, which regretfully does not translate well.[29] Caliph Muhammad Bello also used satire. In his poem about the Battle of Papara,[30] he said, "I send a message which all the world may hear . . . we have wounded the pride of your manhood . . . we have pulled out the horns of your ram, we have gelded him."

Such poetry was written not only as one might expect by the men who had fought on the battlefields, but by the women too. Nana Asma'u wrote six poems about warfare,[31] none of which could be described as fainthearted in tone. In "Destroy Mayaki" her two opening verses are as follows: "God the Beneficent destroy Mayaki and Nabame[32]/ Destroy them completely [v.1]/ O God drive them out of this land/ For the sake of Muhammad, the Chosen One" [v.2] (Boyd and Mack forthcoming, 148). In Asma'u's "Battle of Gawakuke," there is the following: "On that Tuesday, paganism was overthrown/ The corpses of their leaders were hacked to pieces [v.54]/ The vultures and hyenas said to each other/'Who does this meat belong to?'/ And they were told, 'Its yours. There is no need to squabble today'" [v.55] (Boyd and Mack forthcoming, 172).

The parallels between these verses and those of Hussaina,[33] daughter of the Emir of Kano, Ibrahim Dabo, are plain to see. Writing about a victory (in which the "hyenas laughed aloud") over the pagan stronghold of Ningi,[34] she wrote with delight: "I write this poem of joy in happiness/ That Haruna has been soundly defeated [v.3]/ Haruna and Ibru[35] stand disgraced in the eyes of the world/ And the Hereafter: they have been made to suffer [v.4]/ They came with a great army, in all their pride/ To confront Abdu,[36] but their attempt failed [v.5]/ A thousand of the enemy were killed/ Abdu ordered their corpses to be made an offering to the eagles [v.6]/ And the hyenas, who laughed aloud/ And thanked the young warriors of the Truth [v.7][37]/ It was between Rumfa and Jambo/ That Haruna's men were decimated" [v.8]. No shrinking violet, this woman takes as much pleasure in the defeat of the enemy as the warriors who fought the battle. Praying for God's help, she asked that Haruna be flushed from the rocky terrain[38] into which he had fled and ended with a message to the people to stop complaining and feeling jealous of each other. "Pull together," she said, "and we will overcome the unbelievers" [v.17].

In her closing doxology she drew together the names of the leading personalities in Sokoto and Kano; these were people she would have known, if she had indeed been married to the Shehu's posthumous son, the famous poet Isa, as is believed: "Spare for us, Emir Abdullahi, O God./ Grant him a long life is our plea [v.19]/ With the blessing of our Shaikh Usumanu Fodio/ Who waged the Jihad and was resolute in the Truth [v.20]/ And preserve his daughter[39] O God/ Give her a long life, for You are Omnipotent [v.21]/ And prolong the life of Caliph Abubakar[40]/ That the people of Islam may dwell in peace" [v.22]. Hussaina's poem is a news bulletin as well as victory cheer for the community. It indicates clearly that she knew what was happening on the battle field and off, and that she felt comfortable in speaking about the event with the authority to illustrate vividly her perceptions of this event, in which Muslims defeated the enemy.

Hauwa Gwaram (b. 1937)

In Kano, the tradition of Muslim women writers has continued through the twentieth century. Hauwa Gwaram, from the village of Gwaram, was trained in Islamic scholarship and poetic verse by her late father, who was himself an imam. She completed primary school, and received training in education. After moving to Kano with her husband for a while in the 1960's she worked as an itinerant teacher,[41] following the tradition established by Nana Asma'u's *Jajis*, the itinerant women teachers.[42] She worked in the educational program (*Yaki da Jahilci*, The War on Ignorance), that was instituted to help the North train sufficient numbers of people quickly enough to replace the British in skilled positions at the time of independence. Another aim of this policy was to promote unity among Northerners (see Paden 1986, 252). To teach women about community efforts, hygiene, political events, and religious obligations, Hauwa Gwarma used poetic verse whose mnemonic device allowed women to chant it while going about their daily chores. She was careful to follow specific metric and rhyme schemes, as she had been taught in the Arabic poetic style. Through her work she became well known and was invited to join a circle of poets in Kano known as the "Hikima Kulob" (*Hikima* [Ar.] = wisdom).[43] Whenever the club met, the members shared with one another poems they had written for the meeting. They critiqued each other's work with attention to facility in rhyme, meter, and turn of phrase.

In a newly independent Nigeria,[44] Hauwa Gwaram felt moved to speak to the issue of women's solidarity in northern Nigeria. Echoing some of Nana Asma'u's prime concerns, this poem describes the community work and teaching that was being carried out by Northern Muslim women at the time. All such efforts were crucial to the welfare of the new nation, as Hauwa Gwaram makes clear. After a brief opening doxology, Hauwa Gwaram moves quickly to the point of the work:

> Many people are asking me/ The reason for an association in the North [v.4]/ I want to enlighten everyone/So that they will know about the association of the North [v.5]
> We have come together to help each other/Together with the women of the North [v.6]/ Authorities of Kano, we ask that you/ Show us the way for the women of the North [v.7].

In her effort to inform, Hauwa Gwaram goes on to explain that this association involves the pooling of women's money for the welfare of the North [v.9], and the pooling of possessions in friendship among women of the North [v.10]. A sense of solidarity is the focus of this work, which conveys an urgency to improve the community.

This pooling of resources is to benefit the women who join this association, as well as the needy around them: "We pool our money to help ourselves/ And for our freedom, women of the North. . . [v.24]. We make purchases and take them to the orphans/ We give them to the destitute, women of the North. . . [v.26]. We buy towels and plastic bags and blankets/ We buy milk for the orphans of the North [v.29]/ Well we now have our own land/ We will begin building, women of the North" [v.30]. Ultimately, however, this work is for the strengthening of the new Nigeria. With the confidence of Maryam, who wrote over a century earlier, Hauwa Gwaram appeals to those in leadership positions, naming names in public praise of those who have contributed, presumably shaming others into joining the effort: "The Kano magistrate, the governor, the district officer/ And the Emir, please help the children of the North [v.31]/ Governor of Kano, Alhaji Audu Bako/ Has helped us, the association of the North [v.32]/ He gave us four bales of cloth, its true/ To give to the destitute from the women of the North [v.33]/ When we divided the cloth into nine piles/ We took it to the countryside to help the Northerners. . . [v.34]./ The association of Kano, with the self–help that was done/ Gave us eight hundred naira for the women of the North [v.40]/ The community department of the Local Government Authority of Kano/ Gave us three hundred naira for the women of the North. . . " [v.41]. She names the woman who heads the organization, and explains exactly what kind of work was done: "Our leader is Hajiya Ladi Bako/ With her and other ethnic groups of women of the North [v.35]/ We went to the Mil Tara hospital and gave them things/ To Shahuci, the place for destitute Northerners [v.36]/ To Kumbotso, Bichi, and Ungogo, and to Yadakunya. . . [v.37]/ We went to Wudil, even to Dawakin Tofa. . ."[v.38].

Just as Nana Asma'u directed her energies toward the education of women by women, and the betterment of the entire community, so, too, Hauwa Gwaram emphasizes that no matter where one's talents might lie, they are to be directed toward the benefit of the North—the community of Muslims in Nigeria. Indeed, there existed an acute feeling of northern solidarity after the 1966 coup, resulting in a strong compunction to pull together. This is clearly reflected in her poem: "There are those with money and those who teach/ In the association of women of the North [v.11]/ There are market sellers in the association/ And common people in the association [v.12]/ There are those who teach reading/ In Hausa and English . . . [v.13]/ We teach weaving shirts and hats/ And sewing by machine . . . [v.14]/ We teach child care and hygiene/ We teach cooking. . . [v.15]./ We teach the art of conversation, and headscarf tying/ We teach proper behavior. . ." [v.16]. The association provides these benefits to all, and welcomes as members everyone, without discrimination: "From the association no one is excluded . . . [v.20]/ There are the affluent, and those from the government . . . [v.21]/ There are teachers . . . /And ordinary folks in the association [v.22]/ There is no discrimination between us. . . " [v.23]. The message of solidarity and charity is clear. Further, the image of the strong, active Muslim woman is a distinct parallel to that created by Nana Asma'u's work to strengthen the Muslim community after the jihad of the nineteenth century. In Hauwa Gwaram's case, the call to (social) arms comes as the newly independent nation embarks on a new future. This society needs to be organized and uplifted, just as post–jihad society did.

Hauwa Gwaram's work is set in specific meter and rhyme, in keeping with traditional Arabic poetic style. Her doxologies, albeit brief, set the work clearly in the Islamic poetic mode, as she appeals to God for help in conveying her message: "In the name of God, I will compose a song/ About the solidarity of women in the North [v.1]/ I invoke God's aid, may He increase my insight/ That I may compose a song for the women of the North...[v.2]/ It is ended, with praise to God, here I'll cut it short. . . "[v.45]. She weaves her own signature into the last few verses—"If anyone asks you who wrote this song . . . /It is I, Hauwa Gwaram, who composed this song/ On women in the association of the North" [vv. 46–47]—a technique common to the genre. She leaves the audience with no doubt that she is active in the work she describes, and that her poetic composition is but one of her many endeavors for the betterment of society.

Hajiya 'Yar Shehu (b. 1937)

Hajiya 'Yar Shehu is the daughter of the prayer leader of the mosque at Dambatta, outside Kano, Imam Shehu. Born in 1937, she grew up under the tutelage of her father, whose teaching and example instilled in her the drive to confirm her faith by seeking knowledge. She completed her Qur'anic education and primary school before going on to a women's district school in Sokoto. Following that, she worked in a hospital in Kano in 1953, taught primary school, and then joined Nigerian Airways, eventuially rising to become the head of the gound crew for the company. Through her association with the airline, she accompanied many flights to Mecca during the Hajj periods, acting as an Arabic translator for Hausas on pilgrimage, to help them through Jedda. Upon retirement, finding herself with time on her hands, she established a concrete block company across the street from a house she had had built in Kano.

Hajiya 'Yar Shehu's energy is exhibited in her poetry, which was a valued part of the repertoire of the Hikima Kulob in the 1960s and 1970s in Kano. In keeping with local poetic traditions, she reworked long poems by other scholars (one on the hajj), composing her own on topics as widely varied as a eulogy for slain leader Sir Ahmadu Bello, and the Nigerian civil war, as well as a song of modern times. No matter what the topic, Hajiya's strict Islamic education and upbringing are evident in the tone and technique of all her poems. Hajiya is a woman whose confidence to live on her own after divorce, and to work in the public sector, is founded on the knowledge of her devotion to Islam. No one in Kano would dare to suggest that this is any less than a serious woman of great faith. Her strength of conviction that living a right life is the path one needs to follow is evident in her poetic work as well as in her day to day endeavors.

It is not surprising that Hajiya 'Yar Shehu believes in the importance of informing the public about current events, and setting them in a context suitable for a devout Muslim. One of Hajiya 'Yar Shehu's poems, "The Census of the People of Nigeria" (1973),[45] sought to inform people made suspicious by years of colonial taxation that this time the count was being made for the benefit of the nation. Beginning with a long doxology, she sets the work in context, appealing to God and all the saints for assistance and credibility: "Let us begin in the name of God, I begin in the name of the Lord/God Almighty—may He be exalted—the King of Truth [v.1]/ You are omniscient, You hear all, You know all/ Protect us from evil, from the world's wicked ones [v.2]/ For the sake of Mohammed, the leader of all on earth/ And of the afterlife too, if You grant it to him [v.3]/ For the sake of the prophets, the companions, those who were sent/ And for all the relatives of the apostle, the exemplary one [v.4]/ Grant me protection/You who are our wall, who cannot be eroded" [v.5]. With such a beginning, it would be difficult to doubt the sincerity and credibility of the message; surely no one would appeal to such authorities with other than pious intent in mind.

She continues to weave appeal to God and his saints into the next verses, even as they illuminate the aim of her work: "I will compose on the census of the districts/ Of the North and of all our country together [v.6]/ Oh God, the wise, Your wisdom suffices/ Make us understand so that we may explain the Truth . . . [v.7]/ Here is my warning for kings and teachers:/ Stand firm, to defend the North!" [v.9]. Like Maryam before her, who advised emirs, and like Aisha who instructed the masses about prayer, Hajiya 'Yar Shehu speaks unabashedly to both high and low, advocating cooperative behavior in the matter of the census. Indeed, she is aware of her connection to women writers from the Fodio community—especially Nana Asma'u and Maryam—and in writing felt she transgressed no rules of propriety, as she appeals to her audience in the Shehu's name: "Wasn't it to you that Shehu 'dan Fodio gave his banner/ For the trust of all the North, united? [v.11]/ Because it is thus, get up and help/ In counting all of our states together" [v.12]. Continuing this line of reasoning, she follows a theme that is both implicit and explicit in much of the writing that came out of the Fodio community, focusing on the need to follow the ways of Truth and justice: "May God have mercy on those former great ones/ Oh Emir, protect us from all the fears of the North [v.14]/ Lest we hear Satan's shouting/ And the trickiness of those who eschew the Truth [v.15]/ Let not ignorance entangle us/ Clinging to our legs, yes, and our necks . . . [v.16]/ God protect us from doing this [wrong], brothers !/ The remedy for it is to tell the Truth . . . [v.22]/ All those who refuse to participate in the count, you know/ Will be ashamed among Nigerians [v.40]/ They will become ugly, wicked, and ignorant/ Helping thus to cheat the North [v.41]/ Well censustakers, I warn you, [to cooperate]/ For God's sake, for the Messenger, the apostle, the exemplary one. . . "[v.42]. In the 1970s truth and justice had to be concerned with secular matters, whose impact on the Muslim community was going to be monumental. Taxes collected by the national government were to be divided according to population. Therefore, for the Muslim North to shrink from its full participation was to handicap it in terms of receiving services later. Hajiya 'Yar Shehu appeals to the Muslim North for their full and honest participation in this matter.

Getting to the basic steps involved, Hajiya 'Yar Shehu instructs both those who would be counted and those taking the count, urging each to particpate openly in the process: "If someone comes to count us, let us be sure to come/ And report to them all our family members [v.17]/ Men and women, even small children/ Including the babies who are but one day old [v.18]/ And even the old people who don't go outside;/ For God's sake, report all of them, don't miss one [v.19]/ Because leaving one out is not wise;/ It is expelling him from among the people of Nigeria . . . [v.20]/ [Well, census–takers] Don't get irritated. Have lots of patience./ And when you are counting, don't be slapdash [v.43]/ Go softly, so carefully, without causing apprehension/ And without harassing people with questions [v.44]/ [Yet] if someone asks you a silly question/ Answer them straight, don't be annoyed, you hear? [v.45]/ Do your jobs honestly, according to the rules/ In the town, the countryside, and in Qur'anic schools . . . [v.46]/ Well headcounters, we're really expecting/ To see all the work done right. . . "[v.49]. She explains not only how to do the job, but like a good teacher, explains also the reason for the project, clarifying the purpose behind such a census. She tells how the numbers will determine how to divide the nation into states [vv. 28–30], and how the census will determine the division of revenue for hospitals, schools, and other public works [vv. 31–33]. Furthermore, as Aisha made clear in her work on the obligations of prayer, Hajiya 'Yar Shehu emphasizes that there is humane leniency in this plan as well, just as there is in the practice of Islam: "The sick and the mad will not pay,/Truly, tax is from the healthy people" [v. 34].

Throughout the poem Hajiya 'Yar Shehu plants appeals to God, like the following, to insure the upright behavior of the populace: "I leave it to the Lord God—may He be exalted and glorified/ He knows everything before it enters your hearts. . . "[v.48]. Her long closing doxology continues this perspective, establishing her poem solidly in the pattern of Islamic verse: "Thanks be to God I am thankful/ For the desires of the Almighty— may He be exalted—the One king [v.55]/ It is finished, with thanks to God the song is done/ The song of the census of a unified country . . . [v. 56]/ I thank God and the apostle, our example/ God, his companions, the followers and the saints [v. 59]/ It has sixty verses, less five, do you hear ?/ I close in the name of He who need not boast" [v.60].

This poem on the census of Nigeria has clear political implications relevant to the time, as has been the case for the poetry of other Muslim women, discussed above. The census had importance as far as the well being of the Muslim community was concerned; failing to be counted meant fewer Northerners qualifying for a smaller piece of the Federal cake, which in turn meant fewer resources for the sustenance of the people. Thus, it sets a citizen's obligation to cooperate in religious terms. The mode of expression is that which has been used for the promotion of Islam in the region. Therefore in both form and content, Hajiya 'Yar Shehu's contemporary poem is very much within the established Islamic framework of the community, serving the same purposes of instruction and appeal to right behavior that were exhibited in like works of more than a century earlier.

Conclusion

For nearly two centuries[46] Muslim women in the region of northern Nigeria have been writing poetry in the Arabic mode. Their works have focused on issues pertinent to the Islamic community—matters of leadership, politics, orthodoxy, and community behavior. In the twentieth century, with the coming of Nigerian independence and a secular government, the concern for the Islamic community did not diminish, but changed with the times. Contemporary women continue the tradition of writing on social issues, using a poetic style they have learned through their religious education. These writings point to the scholarship of Muslim women, and their active involvement in the community, ministering to those in need, whether they are orphans, war veterans,[47] or simply women who are in seclusion temporarily during their childbearing years.

The women writers described here have a characteristic that is shared: they all wrote with good intention. This may seem to be a trite remark, or even patronizing; however, intention (*niyya*, Ar.) in Islam must precede every act of piety (*ibada*, Ar.) such as prayer, pilgrimage, giving of alms, fighting the Jihad, or writing a poem, especially one using God's name in its doxology. The Shehu put intention before five other rules of procedure in the Jihad (Shehu b. Fodio 1978, 83) and Asma'u said her students must set out to visit her with the right intention.[48] Aisha, Hauwa Gwaram, and the others did not set out to boost the egos of rich patrons with bombastic praise (*kirari*, H.), nor did they publicly discuss the shortcomings of well known people without mentioning their names (*habaici*, H.). They aimed instead to encourage people to act in accordance with the declared policies of the Muslim leaders. They wrote well, harnessing the rules of poesy with great skill, which is why their collective voice continues to be heard and is still acceptable. There is every expectation that the poetic tradition focused on the welfare of the Islamic community will endure into the next century.

Notes

1. This and all subsequent dates are given as A.D. unless otherwise noted; Islamic calendar dates have not been included, and the authors apologize for any inconvenience this might cause readers.
2. For a detailed study of Nana Asma'u, see Boyd 1989.
3. Hadiza's date of birth is accurate within five years; her date of death is sometime after 1842, because there exists a poem of hers dated 1842.

4. "It was in the hearts of the Muslim multitude that the Faith in the Mahdi found its resting place and support. In the midst of growing darkness and uncertainty—political, social, moral, theological—they clung to the idea of a future deliverer and restorer and of a short millennium before the end." *Encyclopedia of Islam*, p. 113.

5. This, and all citations of works by Hadiza, Aisha, Maryam, and Hussaina are from Jean Boyd's private collection, now housed in the Archives of the School for Oriental and African Studies (SOAS), University of London, Ref. PP MS 36 WW.

6. It is not clear who this person was.

7. Possibly Qubbat as–Sakhrah, Dome of the Rock in Jerusalem.

8. The Feast of Id al–Adha (or Greater Beiram Festival) to celebrate Abraham's willingness to sacrifice his son; the time of the Hajj.

9. Abdullahi b. Fodio was the ruler of the western half of the Caliphate: the history of the women of his family and their contribution to Islam has not yet been explored. The date of Aisha's birth is not certain.

10. The subject of women and Islam in Gwandu, the twin half of the Caliphate (the other being Sokoto) is, as far as we know, unexplored.

11. In addition to the five daily obligatory prayers there are others, including the Friday Prayer, Funeral Prayer, the Prayers at the two Ids, and certain extra supererogatory (*nafl*, Ar.) prayers.

12. For example, the two hands are raised, opened flat, to shoulder height at the beginning of the prayer when the worshipper says "Allahu Akbar" (God is Great). During prayer the worshipper is recommended to place his or her feet to the right of the body, placing the left foot under the right foot when seated.

13. For example, the opening *sura* of the Qur'an is recited at each "bending" (*rak'at,* Ar.).

14. The ablutions, which must be performed whenever possible with unpolluted water, involve washing the face, hands and forearms, wiping the skull and washing the feet.

15. "Abu Hurayrah reported: We were performing the noon prayer congregationally with the Prophet. He performed the Salam, after only two *rak'at*s. One of the worshippers called Dhul–Yadaya asked the Prophet whether he had forgotten or shortened the prayer. The Prophet said, 'Neither.' When we told him it was true he stood up and we all resumed the prayer with him, completed it by performing the other two *rak'at*s and performed the Sujud of forgetfulness after the *salam.*" (Sambo and Higab 1974, 106).

16. The prostration is made before the salam which is the saying of "Assalam Alaykum" (Peace be upon you) with which the worshipper closes his or her prayer.

17. These dates are accurate to within five years.

18. She died in the reign of Caliph Umaru (reigned 1883–91), Waziri Junaidu, personal communication, 1970s.

19. Her first husband was Malam Ade b. Gi'da'do by whom she had a son and a daughter.

20. For an account of Kano politics, see Fika 1978.

21. The translation is taken from al–Hajj 1973, page not noted.

22. She headed the movement after the death of her sister Nana Asma'u. When she herself died, the leadership went to her daughter Ta–Modi.

23. Untitled poem by Ilyasu b. Abdullahi b. Abdulkadir b. Shehu written circa 1880, found at Kware where descendants of her family live.

24. Waziri Junaidu said this meant those affiliated to Madhhabs other than Maliki, i.e., Shafi'i, Hanbali, or Hanafi Madhhabs (personal communication circa 1978).

25. The precise disposition of each part of the body during each section of the prayer cycle is important.

26. Hussaina's date of birth is not certain, but it predates her father's date of death, which is 1846. Her date of death is not known.

27. Fodio 1963, 118. The collection contains many poems about the various battles of the Jihad.

28. Fodio 1804, unpublished. Incorrectly titled "Murnar cin Birnin Alkalawa " in Sa'id 1973, 180.

29. The poem is still used in badinage.

30. Fodio 1811, 89, (unpublished translation into English by Jean Boyd).

31. "Give us Victory" (Work 3); "Victory at Gawakuke" (Work 9); "Caliph Aliyu's Victory" (Works 25 and 26); "Destroy Mayaki" (Work 31); "The Battle of Gawakuke" (Work 38); "Destroy Bawa" (Work 47), all in Boyd and Mack, forthcoming.

32. Mayaki = Chief of Gobir; Nabame = Chief of Kebbi.

33. Hussaina was a twin, as her name indicates. She may have been married to Isa b. Shehu who lived at Kware near Sokoto. However J . Boyd recorded the name of Malam Isa's wife as Hassana who would have been Hussaina's twin half. The matter is unclear.

34. Verification of the events in this poem are found in Palmer 1928, 130.

35. Haruna = Chief of Ningi; Ibru = possibly the given name of Dan Maji, father of Haruna.

36. Abdu = Abdullahi, Emir of Kano.

37. Warriors of the Truth = the army of the Emir of Kano.

38. The cavalry of Kano could not easily penetrate the region as horses are not adept at rock climbing.

39. Maryam, daughter of the Shehu.

40. Caliph Abubakar 1873–1878.

41. The national "War on Ignorance" program was part of a development policy for Northernization established in the 1950s by the Sardauna of Sokoto; it involved education programs for every age group, including adult literacy training and advanced vocational/technical programs. See Paden 1986, 257.

42. *Jajis,* the leaders of groups of women teachers, organized these groups to go to Nana Asma'u for conference and to further their knowledge on certain topics. See Nana Asma'u's "Elegy for Hauwa'u," Work 42 in Boyd and Mack, forthcoming, in which Nana Asma'u pays tribute to Hawa'u, who was a *jaji* in the mid–nineteenth century.

43. The club was led by Alhaji Mudi Sipikin, a well–known poet in the Kano region.

44. This poem was composed in 1967, seven years after Nigeria gained its independence from Britain. It has not yet been published, but is among

Mack's collected field materials. She recorded it as performed by Hauwa Gwaram in 1979. All the verses cited here are from the version in the Mack collection.

45. Mack recorded this as Hajiya 'Yar Shehu performed it in 1979. The complete poem is in the appendix of Mack 1981. All the verses cited here are from this source.

46. And perhaps longer, although we have yet to find further written evidence that might give us specific dates.

47. Mentioned in Hauwa Gwaram's poem, v. 27.

48. "Elegy for Hawa'u," Work 42 in Boyd and Mack, forthcoming, v. 7.

Chapter 12

▼▼▼▼▼▼▼▼▼

Islamic Influences on Oral Traditions in Hausa Literature

PRISCILLA E. STARRATT

Some of the tension and dynamism that develops between African societies and Islamic culture values is reflected in African language literature. This literature in Hausa societies comes in many different genres. Some are oral and some are written. Some genres are in prose and some in verse. Some are more likely to be Islamic in content or form than others. Some have been in use for centuries, others arose under colonial influence. Some appear to have been African in inspiration and form, while others were inspired by Arabic literature, both popular and classical.

Although Hausa religious scholars have been literate for hundreds of years, until the nineteenth century this literary tradition was reserved for writing classical religious subjects in Arabic. A more recent innovation has been the use of the Arabic script to write in African languages like Hausa, Tamasheq, Fulfulde, or Kanuri which are then called *ajami* (ie. "Hausa *ajami*," "Fulfulde *ajami*"). This practice became important during the nineteenth–century religious revolutions of the western Sudan as religious reformers tried to spread Islamic faith and government more widely by using the vernacular languages and vernacular genres and forms.

Neil Skinner presents the range of literary genres of Hausa in his study *An Anthology of Hausa Literature* (1980, 5–6). Among the genres that preceded colonial inspiration were tales (*tatsuniyoyi*), traditions (*labarai*), praise songs (*kirarai*), plays (*wasani*), proverbs or idioms (*karim magánganu*), songs and poems (*wak'ok'i*), and riddles (*ka–cinci ka–cinci*). Variations of *labarai* include dilemma tales or fables (*labarin wasa k'wak'walwa)*, and religious tales about prophets, angels, or jinn (*k'issoshi* or *hik'ayoyi*) (Yahaya 1979, 324). Mervyn Hiskett provided a magnificent collection of Hausa poetry in *A History of Hausa Islamic Verse* (1975), and Skinner himself preserved and translated many tales in his *Anthology* (1980) and *Hausa Readings: Selections from Edgar's Tatsuniyoyi* (1968). Skinner (1980, 2) noted the scarcity of published examples of the genre of traditions called *labarai* except for those in his *Hausa Tales and Traditions III* (Skinner 1977) and *Maganar Hausa* (Schön 1886). This chapter will add to the number of translated Hausa *labarai* in print and provide a sampling of the rich blend of Islamic and African literary traits in Hausa literature.

Labarai are oral traditions about current events or the past that are reputedly factual when compared with *tatsuniyoyi* which are fantasy tales of ogres and spirits or animals. Both genres are didactic. While it has been noted elsewhere that *tatsuniyoyi* are usually told in the afternoon or evening by women to children, and *labarai* are usually told by men to colleagues or young scholars (Skinner 1980, 1–2), these gender distinctions always bear more careful scrutiny. Skinner (1980, 119–120) also comments that the genre of *labarai* was most influenced by Islam:

> Islam did not much affect Hausa literature until the mid–nineteenth century. . . . The characters in the oral literature were changing. Particularly the character of the malam was becoming important. Jinns were added to the inventory of supernatural characters, previously made up of *dodos* [monsters/masquerades] and *iskas* [Hausa spirits]. Also the morals or proverbial endings were changing, and Islamic themes were being incorporated.

> *Labaru*—even more than *tatsuniyoyi* —became imbued with Islam, and centered on the Muslim heroes and saints of the recent past. In Hausa, as in Swahili and Somali, the element of miracles serves to legitimize the hero. In these three literatures there are many stories of saints and holy men, and in Hausa literature a particularly large number of stories focus on Shehu 'dan Fodio.

In Hausa literature, as in other literatures of Muslim Africa, writing in Arabic has traditionally been largely reserved for more strictly classical religious subjects: law, Qur'anic exegesis, the study of the unity of God, and the traditions and biography of the Prophet. This has left local Hausa lore to be passed on primarily in oral forms. Sometimes these oral traditions are then written down. Materials from written Arabic literature, or even from local literature in Hausa or English, in turn get incorporated into Hausa oral traditions. The scholars who are the most educated in the Islamic and/or western scholarship also tell oral traditions or *labarai* . The usual setting is in the scholar's entry way after class or the evening meal when these traditions are told for entertainment, relaxation, and moral instruction. Another occasion is during

zamam makoki or, the three days of sitting in sympathy with the be-
reaved at funerals. *Labarai* are also told during Islamic preaching or
wa'azi, and in Ramadan when *tafsiri* or Qur'anic exegesis is recited
(Yahaya 1979, 348). The *labarai* are used to illustrate religious principles
in the Qur'an and reflect the religious ideology of the *mai tafsiri,* or
Qur'anic commentator.

The purpose of the Hausa religious *labarai* are multiple and include
entertainment, political indoctrination, Islamic religious socialization, and
personal moral instruction. Furniss noted that the structure of Hausa literature was much less important than the moral message conveyed in the
story (1989, 27). He suggested that the meaning of Hausa narratives lay in
their biases and that outside scholars should concentrate on their rhetorical
content (1989, 24). Recent analysis of some historical *labarai* in Kano, Nigeria, suggested that the rhetorical meanings of the traditions can be analyzed on many levels (Starratt 1993). The *labarai* have rhetorical meanings
that are specific to the profession, particular Islamic ideologies, and resi-
dential quarter of each narrator, and at the same time they address the
larger political and religious ideology of the huge trading and scholarly
center of the city of Kano.

Labarai are both historical and literary at the same time. While *labarai*
could be about contemporary rulers, or saints in a neighboring city, many
are historical and they are all believed to be historically true. In fact, there
is a Hausa phrase that expresses the concept of historical Hausa oral traditions quite precisely: "the traditions of the people of the past for which the
ear exceeds the grandparent." The concept refers to the idea that traditions
are passed from generation to generation and so extend back before the
time of one's grandparents. While certain elements in *labarai* may be one or
two hundred years old, it is just as likely that new elements are inserted in
the *labari* as the audience, setting, and current events dictate. Each telling is
then a *mélange* of ancient and modern elements that have been remixed for
a fresh narration.

The materials for this study were collected in Kano from 1985 to
1989. If the Hausa societies of Niger, Ghana, Saudi Arabia, or the Sudan
had all been studied, the preferred genres and subject matter might have
differed. Because Kano is a great center of trade, political power, and
religious scholarship, these interests have shaped the content of oral traditions of that huge city of roughly two million people. The principal
concerns of the religious traditions presented here are stories about Islamic rulers, scholars, saints, sufis, and sharifs, categories that often overlap. These traditions were collected mostly from old men and women
and reflect the emphasis on sufi Islam that dominated northern Nigeria

for centuries. Sufis are Muslim mystics who, like mystics in other faiths, use fasting, meditation, withdrawal, vigil, repeated prayer segments, and rhythmic breathing to produce ecstatic experiences and sensations of closeness to and intimate knowledge of God.

While not all mystics achieve the reputation of saints (Hausa s. *wali/ waliyi*, pl. *waliyai)*, most saints are reputed to be mystics. Pious rulers are reputed to have been saints. The knowledge of who is and who is not a saint is believed to belong only to God. Lesser beings have to make do with the evidence of miracles. For each reputed saint there is usually a miracle story. Because the stories are unusual, and memorable, they act as mnemonic devices for oral narrators. As time passes, the size of the saint's school, the names of his prominent pupils, the way he lived or treated his family, even his or her real Islamic name is often lost. All that remains is the miracle story and the saint's nickname. Sometimes the nickname too comes from the miracle, and other times he or she is named for the type of tree that first grows from the saint's tomb. Most of the saints and sufis made their livings by being scholars. Some are remembered by the physical existence of the descendants, pupils, houses, tombs, schools, or books they left behind. Others, just by their miracle stories.

The first oral tradition translated here is about a scholar. While there is no direct mention of sufism, most scholars like the one described here who know and practice the art of astrology are also sufis or mystics. Surely the scholar who saved Katsina from becoming a non–Islamic city would have been thought of as a saint. The tradition claims to tell the story of a contest between the followers of Bori, the spirit possession cult, and the *malamai* or scholars of Islam. The narrator is Malam Sabo Lawan Kabara who is a well known astrologer in Kabara Quarter. He combines an interest in Hausa pharmacology with astrology. He traces his family origins from Andalusia (Muslim Spain) via Agades (Niger) and Katsina to Kano. He had studied at the Shahuci Judicial School, worked as a school teacher, and had a genuine interest in Kano history.

"God Indicated the One He Likes"

> So, I interrupted you to tell you history. All of these, these great servants of God that you are mentioning, all of them, the majority of them came from Katsina. All of these saints, indeed, that I just told you about, all stayed at Katsina. But the event which brought them to gather at Katsina and after to keep on scattering to the districts of the states of Nigeria took place in the time of one Ruler. But I forgot the name of the Ruler.

The Ruler was from Katsina. I think the remainder of his house is there until today and perhaps even the remainder of his family. He was an unbeliever.

By that time, except for that Bori business of fetish worship nothing was being practiced. You know Bori, don't you? So there were also some *malamai* in the country of the type who came to trade. These servants of God who kept coming to trade were bringing Islam, until Islam spread in the land. So this Ruler said he wanted to see what was the truth. Was Islam the truth? Or was it this Bori here that was being practiced? Indeed, he must understand.

So even before then, these servants of God had gathered in parts of this land to spread Islam. So in the middle of the night, he made his slaves build him a hut. And when they built him the hut, he brought a horse in order to put it inside. Then he unsheathed his sword and all those who had done the work here, then he beheaded them. So he killed them. So you see, there was no one who knew what thing was in that hut, other than God, except for himself.

So when the day dawned, then he said that the *malamai* and the Bori priests should come. So when they came he said, "O.K., I want to know what is in this hut." This was so he would know by which method he would know what was the truth. So the Bori devotees did their Bori business to the accompaniment of their music made by two–stringed instruments. They rode the *jinn* [spirits]. Then they said, "What is in the hut is something alive." He said, "What? Many things are alive, so what live thing is it?" So they returned to their Bori riding. Their leader flew to a great white silk cotton tree and fell back down. He came to the door of the hut and said, "There is a horse inside."

So they said, "What about the Muslims?" So it was said that by that time there was one *Malam* whose name I was even told, but I forgot it. As for him, he was a *Malam* who knew the science of astrology. So you know that until the end of time that Islam [he corrects himself], that knowledge is always accompanied by jealousy. If you know something, then there is always someone who doesn't know that thing. So they had isolated him in one spot. So by that time, it was only if they saw there was no alternative that they would return to him. So they returned to that *Malam*. They gathered and they said, "What are we going to do?" He said, "O.K. What we will do is that we must really exert ourselves because here we are going to work for Islam. It exceeded this expertise. This one exceeds the skill, so we are going to work for Islam. If we don't do it with all our effort, Islam will never be able to spread here. And finally, even if we shall all be killed, no one will return to Islam in this land."

He gave them the order that everyone must do prayers of two prostrations: '*Ta Abuddilillahi*'. Everyone must do prayers of two prostrations in order to look for closeness to God. They said, "Let him come and do what he can." Then he said, as for him, he said, "It's something alive inside." The Ruler said, "How can you say it is something alive when they've said there is a horse inside?" He [the *Malam*] repeated a prayer of two prostrations. He petitioned God. Then he said, "It's a bull inside, white, with horns." The ruler laughed. He said, "So, if it is opened, what if it is not a bull"? He [the *Malam*] said, "Anything you see fit to do, anything you want to do, do it to me, but it's a bull inside." As for the Ruler, he already knew it was a horse inside. The matter was finished. So the Ruler said to demolish it. And when the building was demolished, there stood—[he pauses to build the suspense] a bull, white, with horns. The ruler was utterly astonished. He said, "So, you Bori people must be patient. You knew the truth. I'm certain of what I put inside it. But it so happened that God changed it to be a bull. Even if your ways are true, God indicated the one that he likes, since he removed the horse and he changed it and put a bull in its place.

It was said that the horse was put aside for many years, thinking that, no [he corrects himself] that the bull was put aside for many years as he was thinking that it would change back into a horse, until he grew tired of keeping it. I don't know, but I never heard about the day that it changed back into a horse.

He was at Katsina, that Ruler, the one that did this. As for that, you'd never think anyone would come looking for it, so as for me, I forgot his name. He was before 'Dan Marina [A Katsina saint, said to be the author Ibn Sabbagh d. circa 1655 CE. 'Dan Marina means "Son of the Dye Pits."]. It was before that saint, 'Dan Marina. This story that I am telling you is more than a thousand years old. Shortly after the death of the Prophet. So that was it.

Only the proclamation remained. He said, "Don't revert to listening to the talk of the Bori. Only Islam. Islam alone." So he gathered the *malamai*. He told them to say what they wanted him to give them. Every *malam* was given a house, he was given slaves, he was given concubines, he was given land where he could farm. Anywhere a *malam* was in this world, if he met someone he would say, "So you are here suffering, look where there is enjoyment at Katsina. Get up and go there. Go to Katsina." Every *malam* who took up his loads and came to Katsina, the Ruler gave him a house, he gave him slaves, he gave him concubines, he gave him land where he could farm.

So that was how, that was how, *malamai* gathered inside Katsina until it reached the point where they had every type of Islamic knowledge there, none was missing. So from there they kept on scattering, they kept on scattering, they kept on scattering like that until we came to Malam Kabara [Umaru Kabara reputedly came from Mali to help with the 19th C. *jihad* and settled in Kabara Quarter, Kano which is named for him]. He stayed at Katsina. He stayed at Katsina. He stayed at Agades. Everyone of these servants of God that I heard about, when they came scattering to this land, they had all stayed in Katsina. It was the trade entrepôt, the headquarters of trade. So together with trade, Islam entered our land. That's what I know.

From the perfectly symmetrical structure of this tradition, it is clear that it had been told and retold many times. It also had a clear didactic message: Islam is the one true religion: follow it. The antithetical message is also clear: the Bori priests have real knowledge. Many good, practicing Muslims also visit Bori specialists in Kano when Western and Islamic medicines have failed to work. They are especially astute in curing mental illnesses and treating skin cancer. Many Bori specialists are Muslims themselves and have performed the pilgrimage to Mecca. The tradition also celebrates the profession of astrology, practiced by the narrator, and the reputation of the founder of Kabara Quarter where the narrator resides in Kano. It furthermore celebrates the city of origin of the narrator which is Katsina. Despite the well worn oft repeated nature of the tale, it would appear that its ultimate Islamic motif comes from another legend of a mental duel between a Bori priest and a *malam*. The setting for this legend was, however, in Gobir where the Islamic reformer Shehu 'dan Fodio and a Bori priest contest to identify the true religion (Skinner 1968, 108–110). Sarkin Gobir finds that God changed a female calf to a male calf. It would appear that the miracle of God changing an enclosed animal in a Bori priest vs. *malam* contest has been moved from Gobir to Katsina. No doubt this Islamic episode could be found in narratives in other places in West and North Africa too.

The city of Kano abounds with the tombs and traditions of ancient saints. In the same fashion as the city of Timbuktu, the old city of Kano is nearly ringed with saints' tombs. Recent research turned up the memory, history, or tombs of more than seventy–five Kano saints. Often the tombs are very large; some have elaborate borders or fencing. One of the most famous of Kano's saints is Abdullahi Sik'a. He is said to be buried in the Qadiriyya Islamic primary school in Gwale Quarter known as Ma'ahat ad–Din. After having studied in both the Fezzan and Agades, Abdullahi Sik'a was said to have established a mosque in Zawaciki and to perhaps have written the book, *The Gift of the Giver Al–'Atiya al–Mu'ti*. As an eighteenth–century sufi, Abdullahi Sik'a was most likely to have been a member of the Qadiriyya mystical order or *'darik'a* . In a survey of Hausa oral narrative, Westley wrote that "Saint's legends, for example, what Yahaya refers to as *hikayoyi* (s. *hikaya*) have never been treated to the best of my knowledge" (1991, 4) That they can still be found, is clear from the following four examples about Abdullahi Sik'a. The first of these is also narrated by Malam Sabo Lawan Kabara.

"Abdullahi Sik'a," No. 1

> As for Abdullahi Sik'a that people say was from Zawaciki, that's just mere talk. He wasn't from Zawaciki. He wasn't from Zawaciki. Abdullahi Sik'a—anyone who says "See from where he appeared, see from where

he came, see to where he was going"—it's all mere talk, it is. No one knows from where he came.

As for Abdullahi Sik'a, what explains why he came—he was passing by, that's all. Here at the side of the Native Authority buildings [erected for the Colonial administration just south of the Emir's entrance to the Palace at K'ofar Kudu] by then there was a kapok tree, many huge kapok trees. On that Friday he came passing by in the morning. Then he stopped to do his ablutions. From his satchel hung his small loads. [Scholars carry their books in decorated leather satchels.] He was going to perform the Walaha prayer [an optional prayer done 9–10 AM]. You know what the Walaha prayer is, don't you? Then he saw a certain man. A villager. He had come with chickens slung over his shoulder. He had come to do his prayers, to do his Friday prayer [the congregational prayer held in special mosques early Friday afternoons], sell his chickens and go home.

So then his chickens shit on the shoulder of this villager. So the children laughed at him—a villager who put his chickens on his shoulder and they shit on him. Then a certain man said to him, "Servant of God, the children are laughing at you because you have come to pray but your chickens have shit on you."

Then he said, "Oh, so that's it—well as for this chicken shit, I will not even wash it off. And it's not a lie, I will go to pray with it still on me. No one has ever forbidden someone with chicken shit on him to pray, have they?" He said, "These chickens are even fenced in. They don't eat rubbish that's thrown anywhere. They don't eat human flesh, or anything forbidden."

So all this that was happening, Abdullahi Sik'a was listening to it. Then Abdullahi Sik'a said (to himself), "No," he said, "This was a villager [urbanites are presumed to be more sophisticated] but so much knowledge [about Islamic law] was found with him. So then, what about the man from inside the city?" [Surely they will be even more amazingly enlightened!] So he said, better not to pass by this city. He said "See the simple villager who has so much learning with him. If one entered the city how would it be there?"

That was it. So he came and entered and came here to Gwale [a city quarter west of the Emir's Palace]. Then he built a house in this place. As for him, where he built his house, where his tomb is, here is his house. . . .

As for me, I know that Abdullahi Sik'a, by the time—before he died, he did a petitionary prayer that if he died and he was buried, God should level his tomb. So his tomb, when he died and was buried—after they had gone, no one entered his tomb. Perhaps he forbade it so that no one would come and turn his tomb into something to be worshipped [Many scholars dislike the controversial ritual practices that go on at tombs: i.e., all night prayer vigils, using leaves from the trees that grow out of tombs for medicines and washing with or drinking water set out in pots near the tomb to catch the saint's holiness]. But no single person could say see where the tomb of Abdullahi Sik'a lies— no one. It's only a guess. It's only a guess. Since the time when he was buried no sooner had they left when God sent down a powerful rain. Amazing!!!! The type where the whole place became a river completely. And after the rain stopped, you couldn't say where his tomb was. You could only guess.

The second miracle story about Abdullahi Sik'a [here pronounced Suka] confirms his role as a scholar and a religious leader. But again, the emphasis of the *labari* is on the details of the miracle. The narrator makes note of his *albarkaci* or holiness, an attribute of saints. It is narrated by Malam Sa'idu Limanin Sabuwar K'ofar who is a Tijani mystic, but also had Qadiri teachers. He was raised in Borno but studied in Zaria, and is the teacher and *imam* of a small local mosque.

"Abdullahi Suka," No. 2

We heard the legend of the saint Abdullahi Suka. He was here, near Goron Dutse [in the northwest of the city]. He lived in this Gwale here. When he was a teacher, he built one small mosque by the door of his home.

So there was a certain villager who had bought meat, the type for making soup with it when he went to his house. So when he came, it was at bright day time of Azahar [a prayer time between 2–3 P.M.] They had done ablutions and they were about to do prayers. This Saint [Abdullahi Suka] was going to lead the prayer for these people.

So he [the villager] said to himself, "I've met the communal prayer [It is considered more meritorious to do the Azahar prayer in a mosque with others, than alone]. Let me stop here and do my prayers." So he did his ablutions and he took the bag of—that is—this parcel of his with that meat. He came and set it down near him. Then they came and did their prayers. So when prayers were over, people bid good–bye. They came out [of the mosque] and said good–bye to the Malam [Abdullahi Suka]. He said, "So Malam, I'm going." So the Malam said, "May God preserve you. May God preserve you. "

So when he came, they tried to cook this meat, but it wouldn't cook. They added fire, they added fire, they added fire, they added more fuel to the fire, they added even more to the fire; the meat never cooked. As for this meat, they plucked it out of the soup and set it aside. They cooked the soup like that and ate it without any meat.

So the next day, he came to explain to the Malam saying, "Something happened that surprized me yesterday. When we went home from here, there was a small amount of meat that I had bought. So when I came it was cooked. It was cooked raw to make soup with it. We got worn out trying to cook it. So when I had been going home, we were going to do prayers, so I had set it close to me and did my prayer.

So the Malam said "Ah, my brother, you forgot that every servant of God that put down his forehead [to pray], that prostrated with us, or who is even just together with us in this small mosque, the fire of this world won't burn him. Likewise, the fire of the next world won't burn him. As for you, God forbade that the fire of this world or the fire of the next world should touch your meat."

So you see, this was a miracle. The miracle of a saint. You know meat is food. Bringing blood into a mosque is an unseemly mistake. Since he was not going to eat it. He was only bringing it and setting it aside. Since he knew it wasn't cooked, he should have set it aside outside. So because of that, anything that was brought into the Mosque of Malam Abdullahi Suka, fire couldn't burn. Even you here, if you came and entered in order to say God preserve you, if you wore this wrapper of yours [speaking to the listener who was wearing an African cloth wrapper, the normal clothing for women] be sure that fire would never be able to burn it.

He had holiness that enveloped the place completely. His holiness enveloped the whole of this place. So he and any who came after him or any person who went inside.—You see, this Saint, I said, indeed we received his history. Indeed it was miraculous. It was a miracle. Indeed.

The third story about the Kano saint, Abdullahi Suka, is narrated by Malam Yusuf Abdullahi of Makoradi Quarter. He had travelled extensively throughout the Islamic world with Malam Nasiru Kabara, the head of the Kano Qadiriyya community. Malam Yusufu was his deputy and had studied many Islamic disciplines.

"Abdullahi Suka," No. 3

Yes, Abdullahi Suka, indeed—he was the predecessor of them all. That Abdullahi Suka was the predecessor of all of them [the saints of Kano]. He appeared before them. He was the great saint of Kano.

Also, [as for] Suka, you should say: Sik'a. It's a rank in the discipline of *hadith* studies. The person who did many, who memorizes *hadith*. I hear it was ten thousand *hadith* that he memorized. He knew them because they were repeated, repeated, repeated . . . until he memorized them by heart and everything. By that time, the term "Suka" was a type of title. So he was Abdullahi Suka, indeed. Yes it was malams who award it [the title]. The ones who are your elders, when you get to this rank, then they give it to you. There is one type there [for *hadith*]: "Suka" and one there [for memorizing the Qur'an]: "'Hafizu.'" So they were awarded, they were awarded like that.

So that Abdullahi Suka, there at Gwale, there was—. There once was a Ruler here, [rather] the son of a Ruler: Shehu. So no sooner had he reached to Abdullahi Suka's place when his horse died. When his horse died, then he [Shehu] had him brought behind Abdullahi Suka's house. He said, "Conceal it here. [It will just look like] the horse just ran away." When Abdullahi Suka saw it, he said, "Horse, get up from here." When it shook, he said, "Wham! By the Grace of God—return home and die there!" So he no sooner said "Wham! By the Grace of God," when the horse got up and returned to its tethering post and died. It didn't [begin to decompose and] smell here. It was because he [Shehu] showed that he was out to cheat him [Abdullahi Suka].

As for Abdullahi Suka, he came before those [saints] like Mai Kargo [a Kano saint who reputedly saved the lives of the ruler and the inhabitants of the city from a seventeenth–century invasion. His tomb is very prominent] a little. He preceded them a bit.

One common theme of Islamic hagiographic literature is the oppression of the scholar class by tyrannical rulers. These themes are particularly useful [politically correct] if the rulers happened to have been in the former, Hausawa dynasty. Here, in the third legend about Abdullahi Sik'a, the saint performed the miracle of reviving a dead horse to prevent the ruthless prince from polluting his home, mosque, and school with the horrible odor of a decaying horse.

Another noticeable Islamic influence in this tradition is the Islamic vocabulary. Several Arabic words are used that cannot be found in any existing Hausa dictionary and are a good example of *malamanci*. *Malamanci* is the practice of speaking like an erudite Islamically educated person. To demonstrate this background, the narrator sprinkles his story with Arabic words, just as people with western education sprinkle their Hausa with English words in Nigeria or French words in Niger. In Malam Yusufu Abdullahi's legend, the words "predecessor," *masaabiq* in Arabic is rendered *masaabik'i* in Hausa, and the description of the title of Suka is described as a *rutuba* in Hausa from the Arabic *rutba* or rank. Here is an example of how Islamic influence affects even the vocabulary of the Hausa *labarai,* when scholarly narrators use the traditions as a forum for demonstrating the prowess of their linguistic skills in the Arabic language.

The last episode about the legendary saint Abdullahi Suka comes from a written source: the Kano history *Kano ta Dabo Cigari* written by the late Wazirin Kano, Alhaji Abubakar Dokaji in 1958 (1978, 28–29). The episode places the life of Abdullahi Sik'a during the reign of the last Hausawa ruler of Kano: Sarkin Kano Muhammadu Alwali [1781–1805]. Although it was preserved in a written form, this last episode was no doubt based originally on an oral narration too. The tradition is very similar in theme to the third episode about Abdullahi Suka.

"Abdullahi Suka," No. 4

In his time [Sarkin Kano Alwali's] there was a memorable event with regard to a certain great saint by the name of Abdullahi Suka. The event that took place annoyed the heart of the saint until he performed a prayer whose influence extended until the Fulani dynasty and which did not dissipate until the time of Sarkin Kano Abdullahi Bayero [1925–

1953]. What we heard was that Alwali had a son named 'Dan Mama. He was turbaned with the title Ciroma at the age of 7 days old. When he grew up, one day, he went out riding with other mounted young calvary as his companions. They went to the farm of Abdullahi Suka at Gwale where their horses destroyed the crops for fodder—not a pretty sight. So when the saint saw what they had done to him, he petitioned God asking that this boy should never succeed to his father's throne. That was it. It became like a custom, that anyone with the royal title of Ciroma would never obtain the throne of Kano. [It lasted] until our time. It was only during the reign of Sarkin Kano Abdullahi Bayero 'dan Abbas that the effect of his prayer was dissipated.

The purpose of this episode in the reputed life of the Saint Abdullahi Sik'a is political. The story is used to justify and explain the circumstances of the deposition of the old Hausawa dynasty. The Hausa ruler, Sarkin Alwali, is portrayed as practicing *zalunci* or tyranny or oppression by appointing infants to important positions of state and then allowing them to oppress the scholar class by disrespecting their property. The messages are clear: Abdullahi Sik'a was a saint; rulers must respect scholars; oppressive rulers who are not god–fearing are overthrown. These morals are thoroughly Islamic in content at the same time as they support the political status quo. The legend is entertaining and memorable. Miracles are mnemonic devices in themselves. Finally the legend explains why things are the way they are: why in the past Ciromas seldom became Sarkis and why the oppressive Hausawa were overthrown. That the tradition was recorded by a Wazir or prime minister serving in the Kano government of the Fulani dynasty that succeeded the Hausawa in 1805 C.E. is no coincidence.

The next category of the concluding two oral traditions concerns mystics or sufis. These mystics came and organized local branches of international mystical organizations, notably the Qadiriyya and the Tijaniyya, the Sanusiyya, the Salamiyya, the Shaziliyya, and the Arosiyya. The Qadiriyya *'darik'a* stretches from Morocco to India and was the oldest and most widespread of the mystical organizations in Kano. These two traditions feature sharifs who are also sufis. The sharifs are the reputed descendants of the Prophet Muhammad and have a great deal of prestige in many Muslim countries. When they perform religious miracles, they are also regarded as saints. Many of them were important sufis and scholars. So often the individuals who personify the four genre of Islamic traditions considered here: scholars, saints, sufis, and sharifs, overlap.

While the first tradition tells the story of the sufi leadership of particular mosques and is Islamic in its miracle theme, the second tradition is Islamic in both content and form. The tradition, "Myrrh Fell from His Mouth," is narrated by a woman, the late Malama Fa'dimatu Abdulk'adir, who resided in Ciranci on the Chalawa Road. Her late husband had been a member of the Qadiriyya. Here is the case of a woman contradicting the received gender roles by telling a *labari* about a saint.

"Myrrh Fell From His Mouth"

> Sidi Muhamman of Alfindik'i [a quarter to the south of the central market]? As for him? The Sidi Muhamman who established the mosque at Alfindik'i. That was Sidi Muhamman, wasn't it? He was a sharif, a sharif. And it happened that when he established the mosque, they were doing Qadiriyya, doing Qadiriyya, doing Qadiriyya. If they ran short of myrrh to put on the hot coals, for incense—they were doing the Qadiriyya like that—if he opened his mouth—ha!—myrrh would fall from his mouth.
>
> Then they put it on the coals for incense. If they said the myrrh is finished, there is no incense, then he cleared his throat and the myrrh fell out. That was the Sidi Muhamman who set up the mosque.
>
> It was a long time ago. The one who established the mosque—they aren't here anymore. Only their grandchildren, or rather the children of their grandchildren. That was the first Qadiriyya mosque of the old city. The Halla Halla Mosque. Yes, it was the Halla Halla Mosque. So he was the first to set it up, was that Sidi Muhamman.
>
> After that, there was that one at Dala [the other tall hill inside the Kano City walls]. Alhaji Bishir. The Mosque of Alhaji Bishir. He was the one who established it. It was Qadiriyya at Dala, Shatsari [a quarter by Dala Hill]. As for Alhaji Bishir, he wasn't a sharif. No he wasn't a sharif. He was a Ghadames [a major trade entrepôt in north western Libya] man. The ones who are sharifs, aren't they the same with our master 'Ali [the son-in-law and cousin of Prophet Muhammad]? And isn't our master 'Ali the same with them? So they are the same type as he is. So when it was established (the mosque), they were doing it [Qadiriyya], they were doing it, they were doing it. So now the whole of the walled city have taken it up. They are all establishing Qadiriyya mosques.

This tradition not only reportedly gives the history of the spread of the Qadiriyya *'darik'a* (Ar., *tariqa*) or mystical organization in Kano, but it also includes a miracle story of the founder of the mosque, Sidi Muhamman of Alfindik'i Quarter. It is a beautiful story of a sufi sharif who founded the first Qadiriyya mosque in the walled city of Kano and who could bring incense out of his mouth when it was needed for the worship of God. It includes a typical reference to early Islamic history with it's mention of 'Ali, the Prophet's son–in–law and cousin who fathered, by his marriage with the Prophet's daughter Fatima, the Prophet's grandsons, Hassan and Husain. References to early Islamic history are common in Hausa *labarai* .

A knowledge of early Islamic history is an essential element for the classic Islamic subject of *tafsiri* or Qur'anic exegesis. Hausa *labarai* then are full of references to other events in early Islamic history: the battle of Karbala, the military exploits of Uqba ibn Nafi, the wisdom of Umar ibn al–Khattab or the struggle between the houses of Mu'awiyya and Yazidu.

The next tradition is about the spread of the Qadiriyya in Kano, and is Islamic in form as well as content. It was narrated by a prominent Qadiri scholar of Bakin Zuwo Quarter, Malam Hassan Muhammad "'Mai Bita," who got his nickname from helping other students with their studies. He is very knowledgeable about Qadiriyya history in Kano and has traveled widely in Nigeria.

"He Gave Them the Qadiriyya"

The Qadiriyya preceded the Tijaniyya in this town, in this country of ours, Nigeria. And indeed, the one who brought the Qadiriyya to this land of ours, Nigeria, the one who came with it was Shaikh Maghili. Shaikh Maghili, indeed, he came with the Qadiriyya about nine hundred years ago, more or less [Abd al–Karim al–Maghili from Tlemsen, Algeria thought to have died c. 1503 C.E., only five hundred years ago]. He was the one who brought the Qadiriyya, that Shaikh Maghili. He came to our land, Kano. He lodged with the Saint Malam Bawa Masha Fura Wuri [Malam Bawa's name means he lived on only one cowrie shell's worth of millet paste ball a day. His tomb and mosque are in Gwammaja Quarter.] The Saint Bawa Masha Fura Wuri accommodated Shaikh Maghili. The Saint, Bawa Masha Fura Wuri accommodated Shaikh Maghili. He gave him the Qadiriyya order. Shaikh Maghili gave the Saint Bawa Masha Fura Wuri the Qadiriyya.

So the Qadiriyya order was here. It was spreading, It was spreading. It was spreading until it reached the time of the Saint Malam Musa. The Saint Malam Musa, the one who was at Alfindik'i. The one who was in Alfindik'i Quarter. The Saint Malam Musa took the Qadiriyya order from the hand of the Saint Bawa Masha Fura Wuri. He was doing Qadiriyya. He was doing Qadiriyya. But the Qadiriyya order here, the way they were doing it, never spread extensively until Malam Shaikh Sa'al came. Indeed, Shaikh Sa'al came.

Malam Shaikh Sa'al—a message came from Baghdad [Baghdad, Iraq is where the headquarters of the Qadiriyya mystical order is located] to say to appoint Shaikh Sa'al as the *muk'addami* [initiator] for the Qadiriyya here. Shaikh Sa'al took the Qadiriyya order from the hand of the Saint Malam Musa. He gave him the Qadiriyya order. After he gave him the Qadiriyya order, then he revived the Qadiriyya in this town of ours of Kano. He was doing the Qadiriyya.

During that time, by that time, there was Bubakar ibn Atma, the one who was in Shatsari Quarter. There at his house they were beating *bandiri* [drums that look like tambourines without metal clappers. The drumming is a trademark of the Qadiriyya in Kano.] By that time, from the house of Shaikh Sa'al, it was the house of Bubakar ibn Atma. They were doing, they were beating *bandiri* by that time.

So from that time the Qadiriyya order was spreading, the Islamiyya [probably the Salamiyya] order was spreading, because they were Islamiyyawa. They came from Libya. They settled in this town, in this Quarter of Shatsari. So when they settled, they spread the Islamiyya order. Also, the Islamiyya then joined with the Qadiriyya. It was going, it was going, these two mosques [Alfindik'i and Shatsari]. They were the only two in all the town, the whole breadth of Nigeria. From here the Qadiriyya order and the Islamiyya began to take hold, it took hold everywhere. Yes, his mosque in Shatsari, the mosque of Shatsari. This mosque of Sharif Sidi Muhamman, is the mosque from which they spread the Islamiyya order. But the house of Bubakar ibn Atma, which is at Shatsari, here the *bandiri* was being beaten before this mosque was built. So when they built the mosque, they returned, they were spreading Islamiyya here, they were doing Qadiriyya.

The second sufi *labari* presents roughly the same history as the previous narrator: the foundation of the Qadiriyya mosques of Alfindik'i and Shatsari Quarters. But the first enjoys an embedded miracle story of the myrrh that fell from the sharif's mouth while the second appears to have no story at all. The second version is not very satisfying to our ears. It has no story line, no plot, no dilemma, no sub–climax, no climax, no episodes, no miracles, no suspense and no humor. But it is extremely satisfying to the ears of a Muslim sufi because it is a *silsilat*. A *silsilat* is a chain of transmission of scholarship, of knowledge of subject matter, or of mystical initiation. In this case, it is the initiation into the Qadiriyya *'darik'a* and its special knowledge which has been passed from Shaikh Maghili down to Malam Shaikh Sa'al of recent memory. The narrator here has used an Islamic form which had been passed to oral listeners from readings of the Kunta Qadiriyya *silsilat* from Algeria found in Muhammad b. al–Mukhtar al–Kunti's *Kitab al–tara'if wa al–tala'id*. In this oral Kano *silsilat*, the Algerian Shaikh Maghili whose writings were so important to the intellectual justification of the nineteenth–century jihadists physically comes to Kano and brings the Qadiriyya *'darik'a* with him. This selection is thoroughly Islamic in both content and form, despite the fact that the Kunta Qadiriyya *silsilat* has now been totally localized in Kano. The localization of the events or contents of North African works of writing is apparently a standard practice for Hausa *labarai*.

On the other hand, the *silsilat* includes the discussion of the *bandiri* drums. Use of these drums, while disliked or prohibited by puritanical orders of Islam, have allowed African Muslims to express their love of God and their love of music and rhythm at the same time. The drums are used to accompany the singing of religious poetry as well as the weekly sessions of *dhikr* recitation. So although it is Islamic in form, some parts of this *labari* are very African in content. While the drumming was no doubt introduced from North Africa (the Arabic word *tunbur* also means drum, and a *tunburi* is its player), its adoption and performance by Africans has been enthusiastic for many cultural reasons.

The last genre of oral religious prose in Kano considered here is sharif tales. Both of the sufi tales given above also fall into this genre. In the first, the sharif Sidi Muhamman, is the founder of the Alfindik'i Mosque. In the second, Shaikh al–Maghili, is the progenitor of the Kano *sharifai*. Sharifs or in Kano, *sharifai*, are believed to be descendants of the Prophet Muhammad (d. 632 C.E.). Sharifs are found wherever Islam has spread. In Kano, there are many people who claim to be sharifs. Some of them live in the *Unguwar Sharifai,* The Sharifs' Quarter. It was said to be founded by an Algerian Shaikh or religious teacher, Abdulkarimu al–Maghili. Al–Maghili wrote two books for the Kano ruler Muhammad Rumfa on how to be a better Muslim ruler. Because his books and legends about him can still be found in Kano, many people believe that he personally came to Kano and established the clan of local sharifs. Other Kano sharifs do not claim descent from al–Maghili. Many sharifs are sufis and were or are reputed to be saints. But whether or not they receive public recognition as saints, sharifs are thought to have their own miracles, that prove their sharifian identity:

> It was believed that their noble descent conferred on them powers of healing, of telling the future, of interpreting dreams and of especially effective prayers (Ar. *du'a*) asking God's help for those on behalf of whom they prayed. It was by using these gifts that the *shurafa'* mainly lived, although many of them also engaged in commerce.
>
> While many *shurafa'* were learned, their contribution to the spread of Islam in West Africa was for the most part at the popular level. It was the *shurafa'* who were the most successful practitioners of Islamic divination and medicine. The Islam of the illiterate and semi–literate masses in West Africa was largely formed by contact with the *shurafa'* (Hiskett 1984, 55).

Conclusion

As an important center of Islamic trade and scholarship in the western Sudan, the Kanawa developed their own narratives about Islamic rulers, scholars, saints, sufis, and sharifs during the same period as (or sometime after) they converted to Islam and adopted its academic disciplines, its mystical orders, and its social and political institutions. Newer Islamic institutions and ideologies and newer forms of entertainment and media will likely soon change the content and form of Kano's oral Islamic stories. Then the old tales of Muslim rulers, scholars, saints, sufis, and sharifs may fade away. Younger, western educated storytellers today already narrate traditions with new nation–building themes about constitutions, ombudsmen, and universities (Starratt 1993).

The seven examples of Hausa *labarai* given above show that Islamic influences affect this Hausa genre in many ways. Entire Islamic motifs are borrowed and incorporated into the Hausa traditions, and stock miracle stories are moved about from Gobir to Katsina. References to well known events in early Islamic history provide prestigious time markers. If the Middle East and North Africa were going to have didactic legends about sufis, scholars, saints, and sharifs, then a thoroughly Islamic city like Kano would have to develop them too, to socialize its listeners to Islamic identity, concepts and lessons for living. The influences go so deep that even Islamic forms like the *silsilat* or chain of mystical leaders and Arabic vocabulary are borrowed and incorporated into Hausa traditions. In some local legends, North African written texts are the models or inspiration of local oral legends. The contents have to become localized and the action of the texts moves to a Hausa location. Because the Hausa *malam* class of educated scholars was so dedicated to acquiring Islamic knowledge, Islamic elements of style, form, narrative themes, early Islamic history, miracle episodes, and even Arabic vocabulary are prevalent in Hausa oral traditions or *labarai* . On the other hand, standard elements of African oral narrative are also present: frequent repetition of patterns, the use of shock and the unexpected for humor, and the development of a symmetrical form constructed from bipolar opposites after many narrations. *Labarai* are examples of Afro–Islamic storytelling at its best.

Chapter 13

▼▼▼▼▼▼▼▼▼

The Quest for Orthodoxy in
Ibrahim Tahir's The Last Imam

AHMED SHEIKH BANGURA

> Diamourou, the old griot who was irritated by all that, sometimes said
> what he felt about it: "A pagan of Balla's ilk in a village of Allah like
> Togobala! A sorcerer! A caster of evil spells, a public enemy of Allah, well
> then!"[1]
>
> AHMADOU KOUROUMA, Soleils des Indépendances
>
> This is a Muslim Kingdom and the Word of Allah must be kept.
>
> IBRAHIM TAHIR, The Last Imam

Sub–Saharan African writers of the Muslim tradition, like Camara Laye,
Sembène Ousmane, Ahmadou Kourouma, and Ibrahim Tahir have in varying degrees illustrated a consciousness of Islamic orthodoxy in the societies
they depict in their novels. Our introductory epigraphs underscore this
consciousness. Ibrahim Tahir's The Last Imam (1984) thematizes the intractable conflict between Islam and the pre-Islamic Fulani–Hausa cultures of
Muslim Northern Nigeria. The all-pervasiveness of the Islamic ethos in
Ibrahim Tahir's work is unmistakable; utopia is not in Africa's ancestral past,
but in puritanical Islam that sees as its vocation the erasure of that very
past. The novel is interesting not only because of its overt concerns with
orthodoxy, but also because of what it reveals about renewal movements in
Islam.

Lemuel Johnson argues in "Crescent and Consciousness: Islamic Orthodoxies and the West African Novel" (1991) that the Afro–Islamic context is primarily accommodationist (al–Mukhlit). His insistence that the
world of West African fiction is coded to be unorthodox, and that propo-
sitions of dogma in this literature are "set, modified or else ridiculed in the

contexts provided by our 'form–resisting' island" can hardly apply to *Les Soleils des Indépendances* or *The Last Imam*. Ahmadou Kourouma's novel undoubtedly depicts a heightened consciousness of Islamic orthodoxy. And Ibrahim Tahir makes the confrontation between Islam and local custom a major theme of his novel.

In *Les Soleils des Indépendances* there is an awareness of the irreconcilability between the Qur'an and *Koma*, between Islam and the Mandingo traditional belief system. The tension that this awareness engenders in Fama and Diamourou does not, however, lead to open conflict. Diamourou, the old griot of the Doumbouya dynasty, stands out in his puritanical adherence to Islam just as Balla stands out in his unequivocal loyalty to and defense of ancestral Mandingo culture. The narrative shows both him and Balla fighting to win Fama's absolute loyalties. Diamourou's efforts in this direction are more desperate, if not futile.

Diamourou's voice is a lonely one, and he is not an Islamic reformer because the stature that Kourouma gives him does not enable him to be one. He wields very little influence in his society. There is not even any mention of the possibility of *tajdid* (Islamic puritanical renewal) or *jihad* in the narrative. Kourouma's novel is nonetheless different from the other novels reviewed by Lemuel Johnson. Kourouma depicts a sharpened consciousness of orthodoxy in his fictional world and hints at the potential for conflict. It is in Ibrahim Tahir's *The Last Imam* that such a conflict is actualized and transformed into a central theme.

Ibrahim Tahir's narrative dramatizes with great realism the struggles of Alhaji Usman, the Imam of the Bauchi Empire, to implement a rigorously orthodox Islam in his personal life and in his family, and perhaps more significantly in the rest of the Bauchi Empire. Many factors, some of which are personal, but more significantly having to do with his people's unreadiness to do away completely with their pre–Islamic beliefs, stifle his efforts. His uncompromising stance on many issues affecting the lives of his followers alienates him from them. At the end of the novel he is unturbaned by the pragmatic emir who, at the same time, recognizes that his empire will never again have an Imam of Alhaji Usman's caliber. He is replaced with a spiritual leader who will be more ready to accommodate the weaknesses of the people. All subsequent "imams" will be chosen with this imperative in mind.

The biography of the protagonist is strategically linked by the author to the legend of Shehu Dan Fodio's Jihad. Alhaji Usman belongs to a lineage of Fulani scholars of great learning and devotion to Islam recruited by the emir of Bauchi during the Jihad of Shehu Dan Fodio to be the spiritual leaders of the emirate. Alhaji Usman's succession of his father as imam is consecrated by a dream when the boy is still very young. He subsequently supersedes his father's other students in learning and piety. So great is his devotion to his calling that he has to be virtually coerced at twenty-five by his father to marry a Hausa girl offered to him in an alms marriage. This marriage stifles the spiritual flame of the young Usman. He nonetheless marries three other women (this time, Fulani) in rapid succession. But his passion for Islam will only come back while he is on pilgrimage with his father.

The abstract catalyst to the spiritual rebirth is the view of the desert, but the passion itself finds concrete expression in Alhaji Usman's overpowering desire to marry Hasana, a slave girl in his household. As a Muslim, he could get a fifth consort only by kind permission of the Qur'anic verse "And take also what you may from what your right hands possess, your slave maidens" (p. 34). For the following thirteen years, Alhaji Usman, devotes himself exclusively to Hasana and the son she bears him, Kasim. He ignores the other wives and their children. This unhealthy domestic situation is made worse by the death of Hasana.

For a long time the imam is inconsolable. He feels abandoned by God and goes to the graveyard regularly to lament his loss. He just cannot reconcile God with the cruel death of his beloved. In this state of grief and near apostation, he demands to get a sign from God. When the answer finally comes, it is in the form of a "cold realization that his sadness had led him into the blasphemous hands of Sheidan and unless he repented there and then he was a sinner and an apostate" (pp. 3–4). A'isha helps to reinforce this realization. She then enjoys some measure of closeness with the imam at the price of alienating Kasim. Kasim is accused by A'isha of being disrespectful to his "mothers." The imam, conscious of the Qur'anic verse commanding believers to show deference to their parents, loses his temper and beats Kasim inordinately. He thus breaks a promise he made to the boy's mother, that he would be kind to him. Guilt-ridden, he starts going again to the graveyard to ask Hasana for forgiveness. He seeks to compensate for what he did by renewing his closeness to Kasim. The schemes of A'isha finally lead to the boy's running into the hands of a much less knowledgeable teacher whose reported maltreatment of the boy leads the people to doubt the imam's wisdom. Meanwhile the imam forces the hand of the emir to ban what he calls the heathen Hausa custom of the *gwauro*. This tradition involves the utter humiliation and torture of any married man whose wife is not home with him in the month of Ramadan.

The imam soon discovers that Malam Shu'aibu whom he has despised for his lack of learning is his elder half-brother, the son of his father and a slave girl whom his father had raped. This discovery sends the imam into a frenzy. His disillusionment with his forebears is total. He cannot accept that one of his ancestors considered to be pious and beyond reproach could have committed such an abomination. What is more significant about this revelation is that Malam Shu'aibu leads the imam to realize that he is no better than his father. By not respecting the Islamic principles regulating the days that each wife in a polygamous setting should share the night with the husband, the imam himself is guilty of what he accuses his father: "A child conceived in a stolen embrace was as much a bastard as if he had been conceived out of wedlock" (p. 177). With this realization, the imam's feeling of superiority vis–à–vis his ancestors is deflated. He seeks his wives' forgiveness and resolves to bring the empire to a strict observance of Islam's nuptial rules by giving a sermon on the nuptial and bastardy. This sermon angers many people in the Empire including members of the ruling class.

In spite of their adherence to Islam, the people of Bauchi are unwilling to give up all their ancient cultural beliefs and practices. When they hear the groan of the Bauchi hyena, they are certain that a foul crime has been committed in the land and that there will be great disasters as a consequence. Coincidentally, thunder and lightning strike for seven consecutive days, killing many people each time. No amount of Qur'anic exegesis convinces the people that the hyena's groaning has nothing to do with the tragedies. They believe that the imam's treatment of his son brought the calamity upon the people.

The people are seized with panic and some already undertake to risk abandoning their ancestral homes to flee from the curse that supposedly brought about the deaths and the imminent drought. The emir summons the imam for a final confrontation. The imam categorically refuses to bring his child home and dismisses as pagan superstition the belief that the hyena's groan has anything to do with the tragedies that have occurred in Bauchi, or that the deaths are a result of the sin committed by any one man. He bases all his arguments on scriptural exegesis. Making any concessions to the people's beliefs amounts in his opinion to catering to the fears and wishes of men and disregarding the will of God. Faced with the prospect of witnessing the disintegration of his empire, the emir judges on the side of the people, unturbans the intransigent imam and replaces him with his "bastard" half brother, who, like the other spiritual leaders to come after him, will be an agreeable imam "much better suited to the ways of some of us" (p. 241).

The personality of Alhaji Usman underscores the novel's thematic complexity. He is not only presented as an imam, he is also, in the beginning, a son, and then a husband and a father. His desire to reform the Islamic practices of his people cannot be analyzed without taking into account his upbringing, the special relationship he had with his father, which is itself later problematized in the novel; his great love for Hasana and his rather ambivalent relationship with their son, Kasim; the role of A'isha, his first wife, and the general dynamic of his polygamous household. All of these elements interact with each other to produce the difficult personality of this warrior of Islam, Alhaji Usman, the imam, the last imam. The issue of the consciousness of orthodoxy has to be analyzed within this dynamic framework.

The subject of orthodoxy is best broached by analyzing the structure of conflict in the novel. Much of the social conflict in the novel arises from the discrepancies between the Muslim ideal and the actions and beliefs of the Bauchi Muslims. Significantly, while in the novel of Alhaji Sir Abubakar Tafawa Balewa, *Shaiu Umaru*,[2] the Muslim ideal is embodied by the protagonist Shaiu Umaru, in Ibrahim Tahir's novel, the Muslim ideal remains by and large an idea that no one truly embodies. Although Alhaji Usman and his father come closest to this ideal, they themselves are shown to fall short of it. Alhaji Usman is quick to define his model: "For my part, I take my example as every true Muslim and every servant of God should do, from *Prophet Mohammad*, the Peace and Blessings of Allah be upon him" (p. 199; emphasis added). This absence of a model in the novel enables the narrative to deal with the issue of orthodoxy within a broad and general context without reducing the structure of conflict to a simple confrontation between the proponents of orthodoxy and the others.

The first conflict in the novel revolves around the old imam's desire to have his son accept the alms marriage with A'isha. He is twenty five at the time, totally devoted to his Islamic work, and insists on staying celibate in order to dedicate his life to Allah's work. What is significant in this crisis is that no one seeks to resolve it except by reference to the Sharia. The usual deference to age in general and automatic obedience to a father that one finds in African literature does not obtain here. The frame of reference remains unequivocally Islamic. The young Usman's fear that marriage will disturb his work is debunked by the evidence of his father's successful management of the duties of a husband and that of imam. On the other hand Usman's refusal is couched in religious terms: "I have told you I'm married to Allah's work and will marry nobody. That is real enough for me and I want to remain celibate" (p. 19). The old man finally prevails by using two arguments. The first one appeals to his son's love of the lifestyle of the Prophet. Just as Usman is being offered A'isha in an alms marriage so was the Prophet offered the legendary A'isha in an alms marriage. To refuse this offer will have one implication: "Will you tell the people that alms marriages are illegal, or that they are legal but that you, their Imam, disapprove" (p. 20)? The final blow comes when the father quotes a *hadith* condemning celibates as not being among the followers of the Prophet Muhammed (p. 20). Usman has to capitulate. He "dared not protest because he knew that his father's arguments were unassailable, as indeed was everything the old man said" (p. 20). This tense exchange between father and son underscores at once the predominant role that Islam plays in the world depicted by Ibrahim Tahir, and hence the power that comes with the possession of Islamic knowledge. The potential for the manipulation and abuse of such knowledge becomes more obvious in the next fight between father and son regarding a custom surrounding the taking away of the wife's virginity. According to this custom, the girl is expected to scream loud enough for her family members to hear when her virginity is being taken; that is, if she is found to be a virgin. This will mean much honor to the girl's family. One of the implications of this practice is that the first night is a public event. The narrator explains the cultural origins of this practice: "The taking away of the wife's chastity on the first nuptial night had been ritualised and had become part of the customs in the lower orders of society. . . . It was a distasteful practice that Usman's family and all houses of breeding had condemned and eschewed as a carry–over from darker days" (p. 23). "Darker days" is a translation of the Islamic concept of *Jahiliya,* which is a denigrating term designating pre–Islamic cultural practices.

The attitudes displayed here betray not only a consciousness of orthodoxy, but more significantly a resolve to erase the pre–Islamic past. Usman will have nothing to do with this custom. His father, however, does not see much harm in the practice and asks his son to do it to please the parents of the bride. To Usman the plea sounds like an invitation to honor *Jahiliya* as opposed to obeying the laws of Islam: "So you want me to disobey the laws of my faith just to satisfy a common Hausa heathen custom" (p. 22)? All attempts on the part of the old man to justify his stance only increases his son's feeling of shame that the father whose piety he clearly respects should so readily make concessions to pre–Islamic beliefs. Usman categorically denounces his father when the latter relates to his son the rumors that Usman's delay in taking his wife's virginity is due to impotence: "How can you father? It is not enough that you ask me to behave like a heathen? Must you go on to talk like vulgar market women" (p. 24)? Not even the progressive Oumar Faye in Sembène Ousmane's *O Pays! mon beau peuple* could display such irreverence towards his father.

Usman's brutal taking of A'isha's virginity is an act of vengeance directed at all those who suppose him impotent. It is this act of violence that brings about Usman's loss of his passion for his faith, which will ironically only return and be intertwined with his consummate love for Hasana when he comes back from his pilgrimage to Mecca.

This domestic saga between father and son anticipates the greater social crises that result from the conflict between puritanical concerns with orthodoxy and accommodationism. The narrator provides an interesting synopsis of the history of Islam in Bauchi. Islam arrived three hundred years back: "Yet only three hundred years ago, and maybe less, the Word of God and God Himself had not existed for the people who inhabited the land . . . For Bauchi then was no more than a rocky trough in the mountainous country of the wild savannah, a no–prophet land of pagan tribes, each with its shrine sheltering behind a rocky grove" (p. 121). After giving a description of some of the aspects of the ancient religious practices of Bauchi, the narrator portrays the triumphant arrival of Islam and its washing clean of the souls of the men "with the waters of Islam" (p. 122). Although, much as in the case of Cheikh Hamidou Kane's Diallobé, Islam becomes the real nature of the people (p. 122), some ancestral beliefs and practices resist erasure: "Even so they [the people of Bauchi] needed diversion like the *gwauro* ceremony and other rituals whose roots lay deeply buried in long–forgotten history" (p. 123). It is this major diversion of the *gwauro* ceremony that Alhaji Usman abolishes as a carry over from pagan times much to the silent resentment of the people (p. 124).

The real conflict between the orthodox quest and syncretism comes in the form of the interpretation of the world beyond the real. Legend has it that each time the hyena moans in Bauchi there is calamity in the air: "Long ago, they say, when the Hyena moaned, the emir and his entire household died" (p. 206). When the hyena emits its awesome groan, for the people it portends an ill omen. For the imam, the hyena is nothing but a beast. While the people's interpretation of this apparently unusual occurrence is based on ancestral beliefs, the imam's frame of reference remains uncompromisingly scriptural: "To show Moses his power, Allah had turned the Mount Sinai into dust, to protect him he had parted the sea and to save Joseph he had sent down a ram from the sky . . . the miracles of the past had nothing to do with superstitions. Certainly not with the moan of a hyena" (p. 207). The conflict brought about by the interpretation of the groan of the hyena is reminiscent of the legendary Askia Mohammed's report to the Egyptian scholar, Al–Maghili, on the beliefs of the Dogon whom he conquered:

> Then I released everyone who claimed that he was a free Muslim and a
> large number of them went off. Then after that I asked about the cir-

cumstances of some of them and about their country and behold they pronounced the *shahada*: "There is no god save God. Muhammed is the messenger of God." But in spite of that they believe that there are beings who can bring them benefit or do them harm other than God, Mighty and Exalted is He. They have idols and they say: "The fox has said so and so and thus it will be so and so. . . ."

So I admonished them to give up all that and they refused to do without the use of force (Hunwick 1985, 77).

Alhaji Usman, contrary to Askia Muhammed, and in spite of the militant tropes used to characterize him in the novel, is not a *mujahid*. He has to depend on persuasion and the cooperation of the emir to enforce ortho-dox Islamic beliefs and practices.

The differences between the imam's perspective and that of the people are not like those opposing Diamourou and Balla in Kourouma's novel. There is apparently no non–Muslim in Bauchi. Yet, the crisis in *The Last Imam,* resulting from differences between Muslims at different levels of commitment to Islamic orthodoxy, proves to be more intractable. Such a conflict between believers is possible precisely because the imam strategi-cally constructs a definition of the Muslim that is so rigorous that many Muslims lose their credentials as Muslims and become *Kufar* (infidels) at least in the sight of the imam.

This notion of *takfir*, the act of declaring someone to be an unbeliever, has been clearly explained by Nehemia Levtzion and John O. Voll in the context of eighteenth–century renewal and reform in Islam:

> The spread of Islam was greatly aided by a broad and inclusive definition of Muslims: whoever identified himself as such by proclaiming the *Shahada*. However, the reformists sought to separate Muslims from non-Islamic beliefs and practices and to delineate more clearly the boundaries of the Muslim community. For them, those who claimed to be Muslims but were associated with what the reformers believed to be non–Islamic beliefs and practices, were non–believers (Levtzion 1987, 12).

The process of redefining the Muslim is one that is necessary in periods of reform. In such periods the definition of the Muslim as one who believes in Allah and Muhammed is simply not useful. The re-former needs to know who the adversary is, the one who refuses to adhere to the fundamentals of the faith. It is therefore significant that the imam sees himself first as a warrior against disbelief (p. 208). To be a warrior against disbelief is, however, too abstract a formulation for a reformer. He needs to identify disbelief with those who practice it. In Tahir's novel, the imam considers as evidence of *kufr* (disbelief) the be-lief that the fate of Bauchi and its people lies in the moan of a hyena.

He thus creates an unbridgeable opposition between this belief which he considers idolatrous and the embracing of the Word of God (p. 209). His sermon during the special prayers of rededication makes his new definition of the Muslim unambiguous: "And the men who come here and join us in our acts of dedication to God and still believe in such things (as the traditional meaning of the hyena's moan) are nothing but heathens" (p. 209).

> He leaves the fate of such people in the hands of the Islamic judge, the *Qadi,* and orders them to leave the congregation of the Muslims who are "unseduced by the temptations of blasphemy" (p. 209).

The structure of the novel intensifies the conflict. The moan of the hyena is made to precede a period of heat and the signs of a devastating drought. The people interpret the moan of the hyena as the signal for a drought. Tragedy soon strikes in the form of lightening and thunder which kill several people for seven consecutive nights. While everybody including the imam believes that the calamity is a divine punishment for some iniquity committed in Bauchi, the people are quick to believe that the culprit is the imam himself. He has provoked Allah's wrath by maltreating his son, Kasim. A'isha tells him: "The Vizir and the rest are encouraging the people in their gossip, saying that you should have known better than to mention excessive sinning when you have a major sin hanging over your head unredeemed" (p. 229).

The alleged sin, as we have already mentioned, is the imam's maltreatment of Kasim that rumor has it to be the reason for Kasim's running away from home to join Malam Shu'aibu. Rumor also has it that the malam is physically abusing Kasim. The imam refuses to bring his son home in spite of the personal pleas of the emir. When the emir, out of political expediency, unturbans the imam, the latter's reaction translates adequately the extent to which he has come to see the conflict opposing him and the people of Bauchi as a conflict between Islam and paganism: "Can you not see that it is not me that you have unturbanned, but the very Word of God that you have denied! Mohammmed himself might as well never have come into the world for the deed you have committed this day" (p. 240).

This remark also points to the thematic merger between the imam as a public religious figure and the individual. None of the positions defended or promoted by Alhaji Usman can be divorced from his own personal life narrative. He is not just a reformer imbued with an ideal to purify the Islamic practices of his people. He is himself a character in process with personal frustrations and aspirations that inform in a significant way some of his major initiatives. His passion for his religious work earlier on in his career cannot be distinguished from his passion for Hasana. His love for acquiring Islamic knowledge cannot be separated from his desire for the power that comes with scholarly repute (p. 150). His resolve to ban the *gwauro* diversion is significantly motivated by his awareness that he might himself become its victim.

To make these observations is not to suggest that the imam is a hypocrite who uses his position as imam simply to protect himself and serve his own personal ambitions. He is indeed a reformer, but a reformer that is also a person with weaknesses and a potential for pettiness. His complex characterization is first of all a testimony to Ibrahim Tahir's mature realism. It is also perhaps an indication that great historical figures do not fit single neat descriptions such as "jihadist" or "reformer."

That *The Last Imam* is imbued with a consciousness of orthodoxy even goes beyond the puritanical program represented by the protagonist. The all–pervasiveness of the Islamic discourse is first of all evidenced by Tahir's use of Islamic scriptural models and motifs. The physical appearance of the protagonist himself is, as the narrative suggests, based on the scriptural model of Moses: "He was very tall: with his long beard and his white robe hanging on so majestically around him, he looked like a Hausa or Fulani idea of Moses in all his dignity" (p. 1). This messianic appearance is stressed throughout the narrative. Moses is not the only model used to construct the personality of the imam. In fact the many tribulations that the imam faces in his life create an affinity between him and the prophet Job, although one can arguably say that the Biblical Job rather than the Qur'anic one comes out clearly in the imam's feeling of being abandoned by his God when Hasana dies (p. 3). The Prophet is also not only a personal spiritual model for Alhaji Usman, just as he ought to be for every Muslim, significant aspects of his *seera* (biography) are also used by Ibrahim Tahir to develop the character of the imam. The narrative continuously stresses the parallels between the imam's marriage with A'isha and the Prophet's marriage with A'isha, Abu Bakr's daughter. Both are alms marriages, and both women's fathers are named Abu Bakr (rendered Bukar in Hausa). Moreover, neither woman has had children of her own. Tahir's A'isha, like many of the characters in the novel, is very aware of these parallels. This awareness only increases her frustrations: "She had come into the Alhaji's hands as the bride of the Prophet Mohammed, and when she felt she needed Allah and Mohammed most, they had rebuffed her" (p. 173).

The all-pervasiveness of the Islamic ethos could also be seen in the presence of the Qur'an in the text. Ibrahim Tahir uses the Qur'an more extensively than any other sub–Saharan African writer. We find none of the "exuberant Qur'anic inversions of Yambo Ouologuem"—to use Lemuel Johnson's terms (Johnson 1981, 242)—in *The Last Imam*. Tahir's use of Qur'anic references and allusions is altogether reverential. He has used the Qur'an so extensively that his narrative would lose much of its length if all the Qur'anic quotations were removed. In no other sub–Saharan African novel does the Qur'an actually assume the status of *Furqan* (the ultimate yardstick by which all human actions are judged to be good or evil, wise or unwise). The Qur'an, and not the wisdom of men, is presented in this novel as the final arbiter. One can thus understand the power that those who have mastered its interpretation wield in Ibrahim Tahir's text. Part of the conflict in the novel is due to the fact that many believers of Bauchi still subscribe to other cultural frames of reference apart from the Qur'an, without necessarily disputing the authority of the Qur'an in their lives as Muslims.

Ibrahim Tahir's novel is, as a result, perhaps the least charitable among sub–Saharan African novels to pre–Islamic indigenous African culture. The narrator's presentation of the history of the triumphant spread of Islam in Bauchi is not only simplistic, it also translates a celebration of the wiping out of indigenous cultures by Islam. Islam is presented as a liberator and cleanser of wicked traditions. In pre–Islamic times, for example, certain days were set aside during which no man could show his face: "The man who dared to show his face, for whatever reason, was caught, at once, set upon, torn apart and ritualistically laid out in the Juju shrine for all to see and to learn, to feel the enslaving grip of their terror" (p. 122). It is such wanton barbarism that Islam came to eradicate: "And the new God arrived, emerged from hiding, banished the idols with their fetish priests and their shrines, and washed clean the souls of the men with the waters of Islam" (p. 122).

The narrator will accord little space to a more detailed presentation of the so-called Juju religion in the novel. Aspects of this culture occasionally appear between the cracks of the Islamic canvas, but then such apparitions of the past come in very grotesque forms. It is, for example, difficult for a reader to identify with the *gwauro* tradition. The ugliness of the *gwauro* is metaphorically linked to the ugliness of the ancestral deities: "When the man [the *gwauro* victim] was stood up he looked to Kasim like the pagan mask gods he had seen coming in Bauchi on Sallah and Empire day to dance their ritual dances" (p. 97). This passage is significant in many respects. First of all it supports our observation regarding the negative associations with the ancestral religion. These metaphorical associations are found in many other places in the novel. For example, the somber aspect of the wives of the imam who await their husband to tell him about their disgust at Kasim's behavior, evokes the image of ancestral carvings. The imam is reported to see on his return home "The grim circle of women sitting there like ritual carvings in a juju shrine" (p. 59).

Elsewhere ancestral religion is disnarrated.[3] The imam is not tempted to revert to traditional religious practice when he loses Hasana, his beloved:

> No ritual drums roared, no horns blew, no 'bori' spirit dancers who had held the people captive long ago came, and the *magajiva,* the spirit dance queen and arch seductress of the delinquent young and the unrepentant old, did not lay out her idolatrous mat for him (p. 37).

That traditional practices are inscribed in the narrative by negation illustrates the tendency to relegate them to the irretrievable past in Ibrahim Tahir's novel. Moreover, the constructed identification between the traditional religion and images of enslavement, debauchery and idolatry is also obvious.

One of the most peculiar characteristics of this novel is its refusal to define itself relative to anything having to do with the geopolitical realities of post–Jihad Nigerian history. Not once is Africa or Nigeria mentioned in this narrative. The *gwauro* passage is one of only two occasions in which the historical reality of the Nigerian colonial experience is vaguely and dismissively hinted at. The other instance relates to the abolition of slavery: "Her people [Hasana's] had been made free by the British, but that had been a mere technicality. To himself and to everyone, slaves not free–born could not legally wed without bringing scorn upon his own head" (p. 34).

The absence of any reference to Nigeria or Africa and the scanty reference to the Nigerian colonial experience cannot be fortuitous. It has to be read within the context of an overall denial of anything not directly related to the Islamic ideal. While for all sub–Saharan writers the question of the cultural and political rehabilitation of the continent is a major preoccupation, Ibrahim Tahir's text is primarily concerned with that part of northern Nigeria that was part of the Islamic state founded by Usman Dan Fodio in the late eighteenth and early nineteenth centuries.

Ibrahim Tahir also establishes the classical Islamic division of the world into bipolar camps of *Dar al–Islam* and *Dar al–Harb* (cf. Nyang

1984, 264). The former is the land of the Muslims. It is supposed to enjoy peace and stability and is governed by the rules of Islam. The latter, meaning literally the land of war, is the land of the non–Muslims governed by the customs of *Jahilliya*, in tension with the Muslims, and therefore unsafe. Hence in the *Last Imam* we have the dwellers of *Dar al–Islam*, primarily the Fulani and the Hausa on one hand and the others, that is the dwellers of *Dar al–Harb*, on the other. The latter are lumped under the anonymous designation of the *Asabe* or men of the South. When Kasim runs away from home and spends a night in the jungle, these are the men he fears most: "Child thieves, too, were lurking in the jungles, ready to pounce on any stray child and sell him to the men of the South, the Asabe, as they called them" (p. 65). The image of the non–Muslim as savage and barbarian is clearly constructed in Ibrahim Tahir's text. One is left to imagine what happens to the unfortunate children who are sold to the men of the South. Will they be used as slaves or, worse still, will they be eaten?

Even Muslims who live in the periphery of the Muslim state are very readily categorized as bush men. Yako, one of the men from Kangere, who come to Bauchi to report the sighting of the new moon for the month of Ramadan, is immediately referred to as a bush man and his report is dismissed upon his failing to tell the difference between the *farli* (obligatory prayers) and the *nafila* (supererogatory prayers) (p. 87). The real news, the credible news, will have to come from *Dar al–Islam*, not from Kangere: "It was just as well to stay awake, in case Sokoto, Kano or Katsina sent wires that they had seen the moon" (p. 88). The land beyond the Muslim city state is the origin of all pagan practices such as involve the pagan mask gods who come into Bauchi on Sallah and Empire day, or at best the home of Muslims whose commitment to and knowledge of Islam is doubtful.

Beyond the use of the Qur'an, the biography and traditions of the Prophet, and the structure of dichotomy between *Dar al–Islam* and *Dar al–Harb,* one further Islamic motif dominates the entire novel of Ibrahim Tahir: the personality of Usman Dan Fodio. The reform movement that the latter started and the Islamic society that he succeeded in establishing are always invoked in the text with a sense of nostalgia. The Jihad itself is remembered as a time of valor and Islamic heroism: "It was a long time, a long time indeed since the Jihad when the men rode out to hunt down the pagans for the God of man and came back crippled, scarred and bloodied but proud in their victorious robes" (p. 144). The family history of the imam is traced back to the Jihad. His struggle to purify Islam and revive a strict adherence to its fundamentals is modeled on the cause of Usman Dan Fodio, who in the imam's estimation fought for the preservation of the word of God against the wills of men (p. 199). The struggle between him and the Bauchi leadership is in many ways reminiscent of the protracted struggle between Usman Dan Fodio and the Habe kings. Although the imam never considers taking up arms to uphold the supremacy of Islam as his historical model did, the tropes used to describe his personal vocation are unmistakably militant. During one of his meetings with Bauchi's political leadership at the emir's palace, he is described as a "warrior of Islam thrusting the sword into the infidel flesh and hearing the pagan's groans" (p. 77). The same image of the *mujahid* is used to describe the imam's final struggle with the political establishment bent on unturbanning him due to his radical Islamic intransigence: "I see before me fighting men in battle dress and I am a warrior King. But Allah is with me and I fight not for the glory of the world but for the Kingdom of God" (p. 242). Admittedly the war evoked here is metaphorical, but the struggle it connotes is no less real. Unlike his historical model and homonym, Alhaji Usman does not take up the sword against those he considers as enemies of Allah, and he also loses in the struggle. However, his stance against open accommodation to local practices is much better articulated than that of Diamourou in Ahmadou Kourouma's *Soleils des Indépendances*. Moreover, Ibrahim Tahir's protagonist is not totally crushed at the end of the novel. He vows to get back his son, Kasim who henceforth represents his "hope for the future" (p. 244). The struggle for the establishment of an Islamic fundamentalist state will be passed on to a new generation of Muslims. Will these new Muslims limit themselves to preaching peacefully, or will they model the struggle more concretely on legendary figures like Usman Dan Fodio, whose memory is still fresh in the mind of Muslim northern Nigerians? The Yan Tatsine insurrections of the 1980s and the violent inter–religious conflicts of 1987 in Kaduna portend a future of militant Islamic activism in Ibrahim Tahir's real northern Nigeria.

The foregoing analysis demonstrates that sub–Saharan African writers of the Muslim tradition textualize varying degrees of consciousness of Islamic orthodoxy in their works. Ibrahim Tahir most fully articulates this consciousness and makes it the central theme of his work. *The Last Imam* is bound to be categorized as fundamentalist and totalitarian by many. It comes as no surprise that critics have been reluctant to approach it. Given the current trend towards radical Islam in sub–Saharan Africa, however, *The Last Imam* needs to be studied. Indeed, Diamourou's definition of Togobala as a village of Allah, where pagans should not be

welcome, and Alhaji Usman's insistence that Bauchi is a Muslim kingdom in which Allah's laws must be observed are a fictional translation
of the growing radicalization of Islamic consciousness and of calls for
the implementation of Sharia in a number of sub–Saharan countries.

Notes

1. "Le vieux griot Diamourou, que tout cela agaçait et qui disait parfois ce qu'il
   en pensait: "Un Cafre de la carapace de Balla dans un village d'Allah comme
   Togobala! Un féticheur, un lanceur de mauvais sorts, un ennemi public d'Allah,
   alors! Alors!"
2. In his introduction to Tafawa Balewa's novel, p. 4, Hiskett observes that the
   character of Umar, the protagonist, "is both an Islamic and Hausa ideal."
3. In "The Disnarrated," p. 2, Gerald Prince defines the *disnarrated* as a category
   that includes "all the events that do not happen but, nonetheless, are referred
   to in a negative or hypothetical mode by the narrative text."

Chapter 14

▼▼▼▼▼▼▼▼▼

The View from a Mosque of Words: Nuruddin Farah's Close Sesame *and* The Holy Qur'an

MAGGI PHILLIPS

It is not for the sun to overtake the moon, nor can the night outstrip the day. All of them float in an orbit.

The Holy Qur'an, Ya–Sin, 41.

Nuruddin Farah writes exclusively about his estranged Somalia with literary techniques and a linguistic receptiveness that reflect his cosmopolitan lifestyle. No stranger to postmodernist manipulations, re–mapping and fictional play, Farah forages, too, through archaic symbols, myths, and oral legacies in order to give expression to the Somali life and thought of his age. He attributes his polyvalent style initially to his "schizophrenic" education wherein his—exclusively oral—mother tongue mixed with sacred Arabic script and the languages of the colonial Italian and British masters (Farah 1990, 1264). Attending university in India and his forced exile since 1972 widened his experience of the inordinately varied cosmos and nurtured his belief in a "plurality of truths" (Farah 1988, 1597). His writing, he claims, revolves around doubt: "I usually doubt almost everything, and therefore, because I doubt, I would look at different possibilities of looking at the same thing" (Pajalich 1993, 63). This shifting form of semantic analysis would seem to bring Farah close to the traditions of Hadith exegesis as described by Michael Fischer and Abedi Medhi, except that Farah's preoccupations lie in interpretations of secular and sacred ideas of the twentieth century. *Close Sesame* (1992) describes the Islamic faith in a Somali setting by filtering through the symbolic complexes found, concurrently, in *The Holy Qur'an* and in the streets of Mogadiscio.

A tattered copy of Ya–Sin, sura 36 of the *Qur'an,* retrieved from the pockets of a dead man contributes unlikely intertextual references to close a trilogy entitled *Variations on the Theme of an African Dictatorship.* Yet, contrary to expectations, Farah's choice of the sura and its placement at the conclusion of *Close Sesame,* the trilogy's third volume, attests to his artistry and to his significance in any discussion of the role of Islam in African literature. Regarded as "the heart of the *Qur'an,"* Ya–Sin becomes one of the significant symbolic materials indicative of an alliance with Allah that pervades this novel's stand against the General's totalitarian regime. It is the favored sura of Deeriye, an aged and infirm Muslim whose final days and reflections the novel records. Further, Ya–Sin generates sub–textual information pertinent to Deeriye's failed assassination attempt and contributes alternative meanings for the superficially hapless death. Through such techniques, Farah breathes life into archaic symbols and concepts and creates a thoroughly Islamic novel, a metaphorical mosque of words in which the puzzles of creation and sanctity are contemplated and praised anew.

Farah invests his relatively straightforward plot of one family's involvement in conspiracies to assassinate the General with sepulchral motif designs. The dialectic established between the surface level of the narrative and this design tests human perception and ideation against sacred referents. While human knowledge is subsequently affirmed, Farah's emphasis lies in the imperfections, or incompleteness of that knowledge, in contrast with the all–knowingness of Allah. The movement from a state of partial knowledge to one of wholeness in the sacred embrace evokes a fundamental Qur'anic truth wherein human nature is seen as a secular entity, made in the likeness of God and imbued with His spirit. For believers, the earthly journey is a stage in a process that will eventually lead to a unification with the sacred whole. This differs from the division of human nature into body and soul, inasmuch as there are no quantitative parts that either end or continue. Thus, Farah interprets the secular as being of the same substance as the sacred but only containing, as it were, half of what is possible in the totality of the sacred condition. Deeriye contemplates this transition from incompleteness to wholeness as his daughter–in–law Natasha drives him through Mogadiscio: "time was travel, the journey each undertook so that *another* arrived, because each would eventually reach his or her destination having become *another*" (p. 94). Ambivalent and unmarked—except for its italicization—in the fertile jumble of Deeriye's thoughts, the line is a metaphor of Deeriye's story and the very substance of *Close Sesame.*

If secular knowledge is theoretically informed in part with an ultimately sacred potential, then, narratives created from that knowledge will, accordingly, be partial or unfinished, a position that Farah makes manifest through Deeriye's engagement with issues of secrecy, uncertainty, and error. Therefore, *Close Sesame's* description of Deeriye's final days depends on what it is possible to know about the incidents and actions that embroil his family in politics as well as the gaps and obscurities discovered in his interior profile. The former covers the events that draw Deeriye into political intervention to vindicate justice and his son Mursal's death. Mursal is one of four conspirators whose plots to assassinate the General fail and result instead in death and imprisonment. Likewise, Deeriye's inner journey encounters mistake and misapprehension, except that here frailties lead to insight and transcendence, phenomena that finally exert more power than any the General can engineer.

Close Sesame's conceptual incompleteness is echoed in its diffuse narrative style and in the subject matter itself. For example, details of the central political struggle between the four conspirators and the General are curtailed on both sides. Secrecy is a vital weapon for the associates because their subversive activity is predicated on surprise and non–attachment. On the other side, distorted and withheld information are propaganda mechanisms whereby the General maintains his authority. These limits are further exacerbated by the narrator's location, for the major part of the novel, in Deeriye's consciousness. While this position privileges insight into Deeriye's thought, it confines the narrative to a single point of view, further impaired by the blackouts that Deeriye suffers during asthmatic attacks. All these restrictions on human communication and perception are discovered to be but metaphors of the basic human limitations in relation to the sacred. Yet, as any half presupposes a whole, the limits imply God's ineffable presence and, thus, provide the phenomological profiles of the hidden actor in this deeply theological and structurally unified novel.

In Deeriye, Farah draws a fine portrait of a devout Muslim who, in spite of his illness and the inhibiting political situation, continues his disciplined devotion to Allah with much joy in his heart. As well as demonstrating *Close Sesame's* orientation towards language as a negotiable phenomena, the following extract acts as a key to Deeriye's relationship with God and His Qur'an. "Deeriye was sitting in his favourite armchair, listening with elaborate relish to his favourite litanies of the Koran being recited by his favourite sheikh: each Koranic word created crests of waves of its own, curiously rich with the wealth of the interpretation the hearer heaped on them: Deeriye's heart danced with delight" (Farah 1992, 20). Conscious that Muslims value words for their aural effect, Farah transposes oral qualities to the written word in a process that is not unlike the passage of his chosen source, the Qur'an, wherein the uncreated book is conveyed to the illiterate Muhammad through a vision heard in the heart. Joy, rather than a humbled sense of submission, transforms the participant during the act of prayer in which each word possesses multiple symbols whose subsequent interpretation lies in the partnership between the word and its interpreter. This veneration of the living vigor of words is emblematic of Islam, wherein devotion through and towards the words of the Qur'an enables the faithful to apprehend God.

While developing Deeriye's intimate relationship with his God, Farah places a constant emphasis on Deeriye's divided attention. Though one part of his life is devoted to Allah, he is also a benign and monogamous patriarch who, after his dear wife's death and toward the end of his own days, is still genuinely interested and concerned in family and social matters. Moreover, Deeriye's family brings different points of view together into a unit that advocates equality between generations, sexes, and different ethnic roots: there is the religious Deeriye, the legal Mursal, the scientific Zeinab, the celestial Nadiifa, the Jewish daughter–in–law Natasha, and Samawade, the young and innocent translator. On a metaphorical level, Deeriye's storytelling places the family cluster within the traditional continuum that carries oral wisdom through generations, while Nadiifa's spiritual leadership provides a channel for sacred wisdom to illuminate the family's secular state.

The expansive egalitarian nature of this family lies in direct opposition to traditional clan and male hierarchies that form the infrastructure of the General's authority. Thus, Farah criticizes not only the regime's crimes but its organizational structure, derived equally from colonial imperial systems and Somali clan traditions. A political alternative, held by Deeriye throughout his life, is but an extension of the equilibrium practised within his family unit: the trust between clans, which his elders had impressed on his mind, forms a blueprint for an egalitarian society that respects diversity and difference in all people within the Somali nation and, by extension, all peoples in the states and societies of Africa. For this principle of trust, the young Deeriye refuses to betray a confidence and, consequently, suffers his first stint in prison under the Italians. At that time, his stand so incites the Italian officials that they massacre his clan's cattle and thus inflict unwarranted hardship on an innocent people. Ironically, his nonviolent withdrawal from action—which instigates a counter–violence—gains him the reputation of a national hero and, as is later revealed, provides the key to a symbolic explanation of his asthma.

When Deeriye compares himself with his hero, Sayyid Mohammed Abdulle Hassan, an ostensible link is established among all fighters against oppression: the Sayyid against the British in 1912, Deeriye against the Italians in 1934, and the group of four against the General in 1981. However,

background knowledge of the Sayyid together with Deeriye's partial ac-
knowledgment of his own errors of judgement indicate that truth is fal-
lible. Deeriye's understanding of the Sayyid glosses over—or demonstrates
his ignorance of—the many Somalis who condemn the "mad cleric" for
his attacks on religious men and his "brutal and humiliating methods of
forcing his will on others" (Andrzejewski 1985, 353). The date of the
Sayyid's poem, "Death of Corfield," is confounded and matched, instead,
with the year of Deeriye's birth in 1912. More importantly, as Derek Wright
points out, the two personalities are at variance: "The modes of resistance
employed by Deeriye and the Sayyid, and their respective effects, have very
little in common" (Wright 1994, 119). Despite the Sayyid's eventual failure, the myth founded on the Sayyid's militancy on behalf of his God and
country led him to be accepted, in the Somali consciousness, as the father
of the nation. Only in the assassination attempt does Deeriye approach
anything like the Sayyid's aggressive style, although, paradoxically, its inept
delivery saves Deeriye from committing an unforgivable crime against his
faith. The effects of Deeriye's act are not described, yet Farah implies that
the kind of mystique that obscured the violent actuality of the Sayyid's life,
will likewise be accorded to Deeriye's abortive heroism. Although rife with
irony, Deeriye's martyrdom promises to keep alive a resistance that works
against all repressive forces, whether they be the Quraysh who originally
opposed Muhammad, the British, the Italians, the General or the corrupt
forces yet to be born.

Despite Deeriye's serious intentions to give a proper account of his
place in history, he continues to be beset by perceptual error. For example,
though he occasionally benefits from his reputation as a national hero,
Deeriye is well aware that his claim to fame is overrated: "I was taken away,
saved—this is the irony of history—by the Italians who threw me into
prison and by that action turned me into a hero, something I don't believe
I am or will ever be" (p. 230). On the other hand, Farah's authorial voice
informs the reader, through dialogue and the respect accorded to the old
man, that Deeriye's moral courage is exceptional. The situation, at the time
of the encounter with the Italians, required that the young Deeriye, as
leader of the clan and guardian of inviolate clan allegiances, keep his promise of asylum to the unlucky man sought by the Italians, even if this meant
endangering his own life. That the Italians chose to punish his fidelity to
principles with imprisonment and the massacre of the clan's cattle was,
ultimately, beyond his control. Moreover, Farah counteracts the disastrous
aspects of the crisis with Deeriye's first direct experience of God, and thus
demonstrates that events are the result of a conjunction of many influences,
values, and contradictions, which no one human perspective can describe,

much less overcome with unilateral heroism. The point to note is that even men of God can be wrong, simply because they are men. This said, Deeriye is perspicacious about issues of truth's plurality within his human limitations.

A plurality of truths emerges from the events and symbolic associations that surround Deeriye as, for example, in the coincidence of the conspirators' names with those directly involved in the delivery of the Qur'an to humankind.

> "Mursal, Mahad, Mukhtaar, and now Jibriil. What a fine set of names. And what suggestions! What a wealth of possibilities! Listen to this: the Messengers; the divine message; and the chosen one."
>
> Deeriye's mind dwelled on the paradox and paradigmatical complications of the names. What could that mean? Mukhtaar, the chosen one, leaving a message for the messenger Mursal; and Jibriil wishing to bring forth the dawning of a new era by delivering the divine message to the messenger. Down with that infidel of a General, amen! (p. 76).

At first glance, the juxtaposition of names appears sacrilegious but, leaving aside the numinous aspects of God's message, politics played a major role in the birth of Islam. Muhammad was obliged to protect the sacred message from the pagan Quraysh of Mecca who rejected his plea for widespread religious unity. Thus, the Prophet was a political as well as a religious leader who, in fidelity to his principles, overthrew tribal groups that contested his power on material and cultural terms. The activities of the four men in Mogadiscio in 1981 suggest a repetition of events that took place in Medina and Mecca between 610 and 630 A.D. Yet Deeriye is also aware that names handed down from religious forebears do not carry the same valency in 1981, where motivations are driven by secular, rather than sacred justice.

Imagination expresses that which is, by definition, beyond its grasp through symbolism and paradox. Seizing on these techniques, Farah explores the extent of their viability through two antithetical motifs: on the one hand, there is a contradictory stone imagery one finds in Islam and, on the other, an extensive symbolism of the breath that binds *Close Sesame* to its holy origin in the Qur'an. The former, though rendered meaningless by contradiction, nonetheless, establishes a model of interconnections essential to the latter's semantic unity. The stone imagery becomes the topic of family conversation when Yassin, the grandson of the unneighbourly neighbours, hits Deeriye with a stone. In Islam, the Black Stone of Ka'aba, the "symbol of th[e] covenant made between man and God," is worshipped as the spatial centre of Islamic faith, "the *axis mundi* and therefore the foundation for the rest of creation" (Nasr 1985, 26). Stones, therefore, are symbolically vital to the practical and metaphorical expression of Islamic sanctity. In sharp contrast to this association, stone is identified with Satan or *jinn* and other creatures who err from correct conduct. Known as "The Stoned" (*rajim*), Satan is said to have been stoned out of heaven by angels with "piercing shooting stars" (Al–Tabari 1987, 47). Alternatively, "the stoned" are culprits who are reviled by verbal stoning. The contradiction of verbal and physical stoning by believers who are thought to be exemplars of devotion and nonviolence, is central to the debate on justice in *Close Sesame*. Deeriye describes it himself:

> There is a whole lot of material on the symbolic and religious significance of stones. Idols of stones, which were worshipped, had to be discarded and they gave way to an All–present, Omni–this or–that, complemented with a sacred word and code of behaviour which still had room for stones: the Wailing Wall, the Kaaba and the making use of stones to chase Satan and his hangers–on. Madmen, with whom a saintliness of a kind is associated, are stoned by children—but not by adults; for in children, in a manner of speaking, dwells the divided and unseasoned man or woman. Nobody ever stones the object of one's love (p. 62).

But is this so? Somalis stone crows, Deeriye informs Zeinab, the "crow used to be worshipped once even by Somalis . . . [and] the Somali word for God is *waaq* because it is the sound the crow makes" (p. 62). How can stoning be defined against such a mass of contradictions?

On a metaphorical level, the satanic General insults the nation with his autocratic word games. Yassin successfully stones the innocent Deeriye and inverts Mahad's symbolic failure to hit his target, the General. It seems as if the Somali saying, "a stone thrown at a culprit hits but the innocent," (p. 67) is valid, because even the Prophet was stoned when his revelation of God's words were taken for the ravings of a reactionary madman. On yet another level, stone is the structural material of the sacred cave wherein Muhammad received the visions that conveyed Allah's words. Caves are implicated in the novel's title, since "open sesame" is the magical appeal to stone in *One Thousand and One Nights*: there words are spoken and freedom is gained. The inversion of this command, "close sesame," suggests a negative closure, yet signs of an exhausted resistance to dictatorial variations must be considered alongside the notion that the promised revelation from God abides within the stone. Consequently, the title, too, bears contradictions in its single and divisible symbol.

Finally, the contradictory stone symbolism appears in the lyricism of Farah's art. When Farah depicts Deeriye as "a cairn of clothing wrapped in reverence" (p. 147) and Natasha as "simply a float–stone in this his sea of contradictions" (p. 51), he employs the mystical language of paradox, used traditionally to articulate the inexplicability of God. In this respect, the poet and the mystic are one, because "paradox is a way of understanding the otherwise nonunderstandable" (Yusa 1987, 194). In overview, the stone symbolism intellectually concretizes the contradictory nature of language and overtly comments on political ironies, but, as extensive as it is, it remains a surface indicator of the novel's internal motif schema.

This schema can be conceived as that which shapes the narrative into a three–dimensional semantic field. Motifs interrelate and join echo to echo in an ongoing process and, gradually, a literary cosmos is revealed, wherein the surface metaphor is message, its atomistic unit is breath and its ceiling is revelation. Messages, whether of Qur'anic origins or generated from the political past and present, permeate the novel and their resonances reach far back into antiquity and outwards to timelessness. Biologically and symbolically, these messages are borne on the phenomenon of breath. When the Qur'an speaks of creation, archaic signs are invested with Allah's indelible authority: "Then He fashioned him and *breathed into him of His spirit*" (S.XXXII.10, Khalifatul II 1988; my emphasis). The properties of air, wind and breath provide a paradigmatic metaphor for divine essence *par excellence*, since the prevailing features of these phenomena are invisibility and omnipresence. Further, in his work on Ibn al–Arabi, William Chittick explains that the "Breath of the All–Merciful" is "the exhalation of God within which all created beings take shape, just as words take shape within human breath" (Chittick n.d., 56). Breath thus leads to the word, the central icon of Islam, evoked in the intricate arts of calligraphy and architecture as in the practice of prayer and Qur'anic chanting. The messages and revelation of the Qur'an and the conception of humankind through the benefaction of God's breath are the inspirational foundations of Farah's motif scheme.

Farah maneuvres these symbols in much the same way that architects construct mosques around the shapes, patterns, and inscriptions of the sacred Arabic language. He breathes through God's symbols and creates a motif design that involves breath, lungs, mouths, voices, asthma, words, messages, recitation, prayer, chant, oral poetry, tape recordings, telephones, and stories. Speakers and orators, news readers and storytellers, devotees and listeners, and most significantly, messengers are all caught up in an architectonic configuration whose highest point is marked by the visions that carry revelation.

Islam claims that revelation is necessary from time to time because "although a theomorphic being [Man] is by nature negligent and forgetful; he is by nature imperfect. . . . Revelation is there to awaken man from this dream and remind him of what it really means to be man" (Nasr 1985, 22–

23). At the same time, Islam is peculiarly insistent that revelation ends with Muhammad, the last prophet, as if the act and the gift of the Qur'an could banish imperfections forthwith. Yet, as Farah clearly demonstrates, humankind's vulnerability did not disappear with the advent of the Qur'an. And this is where, for many Muslims, the Cult of Saints plays a role. Orthodox Islam takes a hard line on saints or *walis* (friends of God), yet, history is witness to the various charismatic figures who, after death, act as intermediaries to God in the human imagination. Saints do not dispute the absolute authority of the Prophet, but they do relieve people of the austerity occasioned by the Qur'an being the final direct communication with God. In this way, Nadiifa is Deeriye's private saint. More significantly, Farah expressly designs Nadiifa's feminine spirituality to correct the general imbalance of gender within his native Somali society. In the Pajalich interview, Farah emphasises the roles of women in his fiction:

> It is as if women in my novels determine the pace at which life is lived; whether they are absent or present they seem to determine how men should operate or should look at them or how they should view them. . . . *I create conditions in the imagination in which women reign absolute* (Pajalich, 70; my emphasis).

Where better to reign absolute than in spiritual leadership?

The ambiguity that Farah attributes to Nadiifa calls for two possible readings of a single phenomenon that are equally valid and must be understood as such. For instance, in Deeriye's memory of the crucial events that triggered the cattle massacre, he places his wife, then alive, within his first experience of visions:

> He had been kneeling down, saying one prayer after another, when he heard a voice call to him, a male voice from somewhere outside of himself and which told him to persevere, hold on to his principle. But when he opened his eyes, he found his wife by him. . . . *And* he was not alone. God had returned, Nadiifa had come to him . . . (p. 38).

Farah differentiates God and Nadiifa by name and sex, but not by action. God's presence is Nadiifa when filtered through Deeriye's consciousness, although Deeriye does not grasp the implications of his own phrasing. Deeriye thinks in terms of God and *then* Nadiifa, sensing that they are of the same community, but Farah writes, "God had returned, Nadiifa had come . . . ," possibly implying that there are two names for one phenomenon. Time and again, Deeriye slips from the female, earth–formed Nadiifa to the male, abstract God, without disturbing the mysterious semantic unity of the two disparate subjects. Farah does not overstep the bounds of religious ethics by this provocative puzzle. Nadiifa's visions retain an air of mystery, returning us again to the central premise of the relationship between the secular and the sacred, because Nadiifa is the pillar that bridges the two worlds. Likewise, Nadiifa's symbolic counterpart, the madman Khaliif, inhabits that altered state of consciousness that represents the threshold to the sacred.

The novel's polemic on madness includes religious and cosmological explanations of the condition that may be marked by two complementary attributes: madness enables communication to occur between spiritual and earthly worlds; and in specifically Arabic terms, "all people who receive wisdom from the mouths of the mad remain sane" (Jaggi 1989, 182). Khaliif, who is written into Deeriye's every waking hour, is an enigmatic figure whose insane behaviour is curiously powerful and prophetic. The balance between divine inspiration and behavioral incoherence is emblematic of his divided nature as he strides out of dawn, "half his face painted white and the other half dark" (p. 14). Madness, metaphorically, corresponds to the characteristic divided nature of the novel's themes, and it is, as we shall see, the liminal state through which transition is affected.

Improbably, asthma complements the cluster of half–states and half–visions. Farah claims that asthma "is a symbol of that enclosure, of refusing, in view of old age, and the political situation, to come out and be free" (Jaggi, 185). But, asthma's most potent function within the novel is to represent the notion of the seamlessness between presence and absence. As a result of his twelve years in prison, which separated him from his family and diminished his contribution to political resistance, Deeriye is much preoccupied by absence. Asthmatic blackouts further compound his sense of absence, although, when viewed more closely, absence is seen to be but a sign of presence. Like light and darkness, absence and presence can only be defined through recourse to their binary opposites, wherein absence *is* where presence *is not*. Therefore, Deeriye's absence from the family photograph is equal to his presence in prison, or, in the vast cosmic scheme, Allah's absence from an assumed corporeal form equals a presence in the mysterious other–time and other–world. At the novel's end, when Nadiifa's spirit sets Deeriye free, asthma proves to be more of a spiritual failing than a biological disease. This disclosure ties asthma to the novel's half–truths.

Another form of absence, Mursal's disappearance and subsequent death, elicits a change of pace in a novel whose structure and subjects are principally contemplative. Instead of confining himself to family deliberations on political actions that take place outside the home, Deeriye is forced to participate in those events. First, there is the spontaneous act of apology and compassion extended to Natasha, whose confusion and sense of isolation at Mursal's disappearance has turned to anger. When Deeriye hugs Natasha's knees and begs her forgiveness in a language that she understands, he dispels the emotional pressure of the moment and draws the fragmenting family together again. This incident suggests that Deeriye is instinctively preparing the women and children for the time when they must continue the struggle alone. Second, Nadiifa surfaces in the narrative, not only as his "secret–sharer," but to direct him into action: "Avenge your son. Let the powerful heat of your anger persuade you, don't wait until it cools. *Then come and join me*" (227). Here again, Farah's phrasing and italicization significantly separates the act of revenge from that of death and gives death the greater value. The rendezvous with Nadiifa equals the final and sacred destination of life's journey, described as "having become *another*" in Deeriye's earlier reflections during the drive through Mogadiscio. Both define death as the threshold to the next journey wherein human reality may realize another, greater potentiality. However, the most vital change concerns the "turn–about" revelation, which Nadiifa pre–empts when she informs Deeriye that "your lung is your soul" (p. 226). I have chosen the term "turn–about" to denote the peculiarity of this revelation that, as will become apparent, both informs Deeriye of his perceptual failing and alters the focus of the text.

After an unexplained visit by a uniformed and sober Khaliif, Deeriye leaves the house for the last time, still fearful that an asthmatic attack may forestall his plans. Yet, in the narrator's final perusal of Deeriye's thoughts, that fear gives way to a confidence implied by the prophetic Khaliif–like tone that Farah attributes to Deeriye's resolution of the puzzling connection between his lungs and his soul.

> "All our lives, mortals that we are, we misname things and objects, we misdefine illnesses and misuse metaphors. Why, it is not my lungs: my face! Why, this suggests a loss of face, the loss of reputation, and nothing more than that! Why, this doesn't suggest the loss of faith, the spiritual loss, the spiritual famine which envelops one—right from the moment hundreds of heads of cattle rolled. I didn't lose face: I lost faith, yes, faith, in my own capability, faith in my people. . . . Nadiifa," he said to himself silently now, "spoke of my lungs as my soul; she didn't speak of my lungs as though they were my face. Which perhaps means that she believes that my soul is struggling, has been struggling to free itself and join its Creator from the day the Italians made the cattle's heads roll . . . so it can join Nadiifa and prepare for the eventual rollcall of names of the pious when these souls will be one with their Creator" (p. 235).

In a swift redefinition, the "turn–about" revelation changes the plot into a tale of one man's discovery of his innermost spiritual nature: a truth had lain in the psychological blind–spot of his asthma since that day when abhorrent human behaviour had shaken his faith. Instead of political justice, the question on which the novel turns is Deeriye's ailing faith and its symbolic analogue, his lung disease. The General and his politics are still formidable foes, but Deeriye's crucial enemy is his human spiritual blindness.

Nadiifa's message intimating the state of Deeriye's soul illuminates Farah's complex symbolic art and leads Deeriye on to the General, or, more correctly, to his Creator through his love of Nadiifa. At the high point of Deeriye's revelation, Farah removes narratorial privilege and leaves Deeriye's destiny to rumour and imagination. Details of his movements are locked in a puzzle: the only information available with certainty to the reader, from the moment Deeriye presses the unidentified doorbell to the report of his death, concerns Deeriye's communication with Khaliif and the uniform that they seem to share. As previously suggested, Khaliif is the novel's symbolic figure of half–truth, who continually reflects Deeriye's state of mind. Given this divided identity and Farah's concern with the secular as but half the human potential, it would appear that Khaliif's schizophrenia functions as a ritualistic threshold across which Deeriye must pass to attain his destination. Deeriye's act of vindication must be an inspired act of madness, performed with sacred eloquence and human frailty. Through this act, the secular half of human nature and its madness is sloughed off, releasing Deeriye to undertake "*another*" departure toward the sacred whole.

On a more pragmatic level, the ostensible failure of Deeriye's plan clears the way for the paradoxical power of martyrdom, which "aims to reduce political authority to ineffectiveness by challenging the basis of the legitimacy of the adversary authority," provided the catalytic act is public (Klausner 1987, 231). Arguably, Deeriye's end could be interpreted as the delusions of an old man who tried to be a hero. However, God's beads, superimposed on the revolver, can be seen as a sign of Allah's condemnation of the General, and this, added to Deeriye's reputation as a national hero, raises Deeriye's act to the level of martyrdom. Once rumors circulate on the death of a hero clasping Allah's signal, the people of Mogadiscio have a martyr and a powerful symbol to challenge the General's legitimacy. At the same time, Deeriye's heroism metaphorically blesses the women and children of his family and their guardianship over the earthly continuity of morality and love.

Like forensic evidence, the contents of Deeriye's pockets are further clues to the meaning of *Close Sesame*'s parting messages. The list encapsulates those things that Deeriye intended to be made public: his self–assured identity and political affiliations; his devotion to his wife and Somalia's traditional saintly heroes; and, before all else, his submission to God. Beneath these public messages, Farah continues to generate symbolic meaning, most markedly through Deeriye's tattered copy of Ya–Sin that, as indicated at the beginning of this essay, manifests interconnected attributes that are central to *Close Sesame*. Ya–Sin reiterates "the central figure in the teaching of Islam and the central doctrine of Revelation and the Hereafter" and is, thus, an appropriate companion for solemn ceremonies after death (Yusef Ali, 3.1168). This indicates Deeriye's cognizance of his death as he prepared to confront the General. At the same time, the "Abbreviated Letters *Ya–Sin*" are usually construed as a title of the Prophet, although "it is not possible to be dogmatic about the meaning" (Yusef Ali, 3.1168). Ambiguity is central to textual incompleteness and, in this instance, denotes a close relationship between Deeriye's life and the Prophet's name that secrecy conceals. Jean–Pierre Durix consolidates the connection between the two men, at opposite ends of Islamic history, through his reading of Ya–Sin: "Deeriye in his mission as dreamer, visionary, prophet of Truth and sacrificial victim, evokes Allah's envoy who in the thirty–sixth sura of the Koran, was nearly stoned to death for preaching the Divine Word" (Durix 1989, 134). Although certain Qur'anic commentators believe Muhammad to be the parable's "messenger," the allusion is not specific. I am more inclined to believe that Farah models Deeriye on the single old man among the disbelievers:

> [He] was just a simple honest soul, but he heard and obeyed the call of the apostles and obtained the spiritual desire for himself and did his best to obtain salvation for his people. For he loved his people and respected his ancestral traditions as far as they were good, but he had no hesitation in accepting the new Light when it came to him (Yusef Ali, 3.1176).

If Deeriye's change of heart from nonviolence to active participation is equated with the lone man's conversion to a new Islamic faith, then Deeriye is, indeed, modelled on the candid soul of the parable. Nonetheless, the two old men, symbolic of all pious Muslims, resemble the Prophet, for all are receptacles of God's messages and all hold their submission to Allah as their most valued human trait. Consequently, *Close Sesame* reinvokes, if enigmatically and personally, the coming of God's word to humankind.

Close Sesame is a record of Somalia's political crisis of the 1980s, a polemic on time and language, but it is first and foremost a story of a vibrant sacred heritage. Farah describes secular natures and evokes human sanctity through half–realized and plural visions. Like breath, the novel's atomistic motif, paradox, and "absence" move within and with-out the text, reaching for the parameters of puzzles whose solutions are ultimately denied. Nevertheless, the view from Farah's mosque of words affirms sacred presence and implies that secular phenomena, like the re-gime, are assigned to a half–truth that will never become whole. In death, Deeriye achieves sacred unity and, at the same time, he abides, figuratively, in people's small yet perpetual acts of resistance against in-justice. Farah's partial and human narrative is wholly Islamic and its open–ended revelation reiterates the quintessential message of the sacred in concept and metaphor for the ongoing imperfections of a twentieth–century world.

Chapter 15

▼▼▼▼▼▼▼▼

Mapping Islam in Farah's Maps

ALAMIN MAZRUI

If Africa were to produce its own Salman Rushdie—the writer who became the subject of Ayatollah Khomeini's death *fatwa* after the publication
of his controversial novel, *The Satanic Verses* (1988)[1]—it is likely to be the
Somali novelist, Nuruddin Farah. It may be mere coincidence that Rushdie
is one of the critics who praised Farah's *Maps* (1986), describing it, on the
back cover, as "the unforgettable story of one man's coming of age in the
turmoil of modern Africa by one of the finest contemporary African novelists"; and indeed, Rushdie may have been referring specifically to Farah's
artistic achievements. But one cannot help notice in *Maps* the seeds of
Rushdian sentiments which ended up provoking the rage of many Muslims all over the world.

Most sub–Saharan Muslim African writers have generally been
guarded in their criticism of Islam. Their tendency has been to condemn the abuses of Islam by certain powerful interest groups, rather
than the doctrine of Islam itself. The writer who may have gone far-
thest in this regard is perhaps Ousmane Sembène, the Senegalese novelist and film–maker.[2] As a Marxist, Sembène has sometimes tried to show
how the religion is used as a legitimizing ideology of the ruling class in
their quest for politico–economic hegemony. This, too, seems to be the
position of some other Muslim writers like Tayeb Salih and Nawal el–
Saadawi.

To Farah, however, it is not the misuse of Islam by any particular dominant group that is the overriding problem in Afro–Islamic societies. It is,
rather, the inherent moral bankruptcy of the religion itself whose manifes-
tations are equally visible among members of less privileged groups. In this
regard, Farah seems to be informed by a brand of Eurocentric ideology
that has considered Islam as retrograde in its cultural dispensation, and as
socially and historically decadent in its doctrines.

205
▼

Farah's peculiar projection of Islam in his *Maps* takes place along four different parameters: the identitarian, the spiritual, the moral and the canonical. What is the relationship between Islam and African identity? If Islam is averse to materialism, is it a fulfilling experience in its spiritual provisions? Can Islam serve as a bulwark of morality against human weakness and social decay in a crumbling political order? Does the Qur'an encapsulate the word of God, or does it merely mask the spirit of Satan? It is to these questions, as addressed in *Maps*, that we must now turn.

Islam and Identity

There are certain societies in Africa in which Islam as a cultural expression is virtually an indispensable attribute of their ethnic identity. The Hausa of West Africa and the Swahili of East Africa are cases in point. It is perhaps possible to have a Hausa or Swahili person who is not a Muslim in religious faith, but it is far less conceivable to have a Hausa/Swahili individual who is not Islamic in cultural practice.

The Somali, whose identity constitutes a central theme of Farah's *Maps*, are like the Hausa and the Swahili in regard to the identitarian role of Islam. In the words of David Laitin and Said Samatar,

> Although traces of pre–Islamic traditional religions are clearly visible in Somali folk spirituality . . . Islam today is deeply and widely entrenched not only as the principal faith of the Somalis, but also as one of the vital wellsprings of their culture. A pervasive sense of a common Islamic cultural community contributes vitally to Somali consciousness of a shared national identity (1987, 44).

This pervasiveness of Islam and the massive infusion, into Somali society, of the Arab culture that came with it, has supposedly generated such an attachment to the religion that, in the opinion of Laitin and Samatar, an elaborate genealogical myth has been "fabricated," tracing Somali origins to the Arabian peninsula, the cradle of Islam (1987, 44).

Farah clearly recognizes Islam as an integral part of Somali society. The novel itself is virtually saturated with Islamic cultural practices, from the employment of clichés like "Ma–sha–a–llah," to actual performance of the Islamic *salat* [prayer]. At the mythical level, the boundary between what is Islamic and what is Somali in the story of Adam and Eve, with its obvious Biblical and Qur'anic roots, has become blurred in the minds of some characters like Hilaal (1986, 229). And at the more symbolic level of identity, conversion to Islam, together with infabulation rights, were essential processes towards the Somalization of the Ethiopian immigrant girl, Misra (1986, 69).

At the same time, however, Farah's position about Islam betrays some ambivalence. In spite of all the suggestions in the novel about the interconnection between Islam and Somaliness, there are definite counter–allusions that the religion is, in fact, foreign to Somalia's body politic.

As regions, East Africa (which includes Somalia) and West Africa naturally differ in the cultural orientations towards Islam. In West Africa, Islamization followed a quiet process fostered by trade and other contacts with Berbers, rather than by an encounter with Arabs. As a result, Islam in West Africa became gradually indigenized, manifesting a dynamic interplay of tensions and accommodations between the religion and other indigenous traditions.

In East Africa, on the other hand, partly because of the proximity of the Arabian peninsula, the Arabic influence has been more pronounced. The arrival and expansion of Islam in this region was coupled with visits and settlements by Arabs from the earliest days down into the twentieth–century. Culturally, therefore, East African Islam probably retained an Arabic character to a greater extent than did West African Islam. And this, in turn, may have promoted the perception, alluded to in *Maps*, that Islam is essentially a foreign religion.

But, for Farah, this seeming "foreignness" of Islam in Somali society appears to be an issue only to the extent that it is linked to imperialism, to alien cultural impositions that have supposedly confounded Somali identity. This thesis, that Islam in Somalia is a form of cultural imperialism, becomes clearer when one looks at Farah's views on *writing* (using the Arabic script), in particular, and the *Arabic language*, in general—two foundational, historical imperatives of the religion of Islam.

Much of sub–Saharan Africa was characterized by the oral tradition prior to its encounter with the Arab–Islamic world. For a number of African societies, therefore, Islamization also brought an induction into the art of reading and writing. While Muslims believe that the Prophet Muhammad could neither read nor write, Islam itself holds the written word in the highest esteem. Partly as a result of this religious influence, therefore, African versions of the Arabic script, like the *ajami* of West Africa, emerged and, in time, contributed to the creation of a new literary tradition.

But the process also involved the acquisition of Arabic as the language of Islamic ritual, and the language in which the Qur'an was revealed to the Prophet Muhammad. And this intrinsic religiosity of the Arabic language has been important in forging a collective consciousness of the Muslim *umma* all over the world. In sub–Saharan Africa, its impact was felt in the formation of Afro–Islamic languages, like Hausa and Kiswahili, indigenous languages of predominantly Muslim communities which became highly infused with Islamic idiom.

In Muslim Africa, therefore, writing in Arabic characters and the Arabic language are two dimensions of Arab culture which have always been part and parcel of the legacy of Islam. Southern Sudan is perhaps the only region in sub–Saharan Africa in which Arabization, i.e., the spread of Arab culture, seems to be proceeding faster than, or independently of, conversion to Islam. But in the rest of sub–Saharan Africa, Islamization and Arabization were twin and, often, fused processes. Literacy and the Arabic language, therefore, are among the aspects of Arab culture which clearly contribute to the construction of a new African Islamic identity.

Within Muslim Africa, however, Somalia presents a rather anomalous case. Despite their geographical proximity to the Arab world, and centuries of exposure to the Arabo–Islamic culture of literacy, the Somali people have remained passionately attached to the oral heritage. The greatest poetry in Somali literature has been primarily in the oral mode. Orality has sometimes been invoked in the quest for cultural authenticity in the attempt to construct an identity that could be considered truly African. But, for Somalis, the orality–identity dialectic is not merely a quest. It is a living reality.

Perhaps partly as a result of this patriotic embrace of orality, Farah seems totally unaffected by the unique veneration and virtual divinity that Islam accords to the written word. Farah recognizes, of course, that the "miracle" of the written word is canonized in the Qur'an itself. When Askar was receiving his first lesson in written English, he remembered reading in the Qur'an in his childhood how Allah swore "By the pen and that which it writes," and how He ordered the Prophet Muhammad to "Read" in the name of the Most Bountiful "who taught by the Pen!" (1986, 169). Despite this sacralization of the written word, however, Farah would seem to regard all writing as merely a question of power and domination as far as Somalia was concerned. It is in this regard that Hilaal asks his nephew, Askar:

> Are we in any manner to see a link between "This is a book" and the Koranic command "Read in the name of God," addressed to a people who were, until that day, an illiterate people? In other words, what are the ideas behind "pen" and "book?" It is my feeling that, plainly speaking, both suggest the notion of "power." The Arabs legitimized their empire by imposing "the word that was read" on those whom they conquered; the European God of technology was supported, to a great extent, by the power of the written word, be it man's or God's (1986, 169–170).

Somalis, then, are supposed to have come under colonial domination of the neighboring Amharas, Muslim Arabs, the Christian Europeans, partly through the instrumentality of the written word of man or of God.

Does this mean that writing should be rejected because of its presumed imperialist role and connections? No. Rather like the Most Royal Lady of Cheikh Hamidou Kane's *Ambiguous Adventure* (1963) who advocated the pursuit of the secular education introduced by colonial invaders, Farah's Hilaal encouraged the acquisition of literacy as a key to the kind of knowledge that would eventually lead to the liberation of the African people (1986, 168). Writing as part of the Arabo–Islamic legacy, then, is not seen as making a constructive contribution towards a new identity—as it is in many Afro–Islamic societies—but as a weapon of subversion against foreign domination.

With regard to the Arabic language, Farah assumes a quasi–Whorfian position—the relativist position that language influences perception in a culturally specific manner. Benjamin Lee Whorf claimed that a person's basic ontology or worldview is structured or determined by langauage. Each language is supposedly encoded with a particular mode of thought, a metaphysics, that affects the speaker's experiences at the level of perception. As a "foreign language," therefore, Arabic is regarded by Farah as a reservoir of "alien concepts and thoughts" which are imposed forcefully on the minds of Somali children, presumably as part of the process of cultural colonization (1986, 84). Of course, the "alien concepts and thoughts" which are supposedly inherent in the Arabic language must include Islamic thoughts and concepts, for it is in the Arabic language that the Qur'an itself was revealed. In the words of the Muslim Holy Book, "We have sent it down as an Arabic Qur'an, in order that you may learn wisdom" (Qur'an 12:2).

Should the Somalis, then, reject Arabic together with the Arabo–Islamic worldview it necessarily implies, or as with writing and literacy, should they seek to acquire it with the eventual aim of subverting Arabo–Islamic hegemony? Farah's position on this matter is not explicitly articulated in the novel.

Islam as a Spiritual Force

The binary opposition between the spiritual and the material, between the Word and the world, has been a central theme in Islamic thought. There are sayings attributed to the Prophet Muhammad to the effect that a pious Muslim is one who strives for this world as much as for the hereafter (al–Suhrawardy 1980, 91). Despite the unambiguous supremacy of the Word in Islamic doctrine, therefore, the religion is interpreted by some as urging its followers to maintain a rather delicate balance between their spiritual and material worlds, between the quest for spiritual salvation and the striving for material welfare.

There are versions of Islam, however, in which the veneration of the spiritual entails, at the same time, the debasement of the material. Ultimate salvation is measured in part by the extent to which a person has managed to shun the material in pursuit of the spiritual. Human labor is to be expended in the service of God even if it means relying exclusively on charity for one's subsistence. Some sects of Sufist (mystical) Islam clearly belong to this religious legacy.

Ch. Hamidou Kane's *Ambiguous Adventure* (1963), for example, is partly informed by this Sufist ideology. The disciples are expected to demonstrate their anti–materialism not only by devoting their labors entirely to the service of Allah and living in the most deprived of material conditions, but also by bringing the body under spiritual control. Bodily senses which interfere with the development of a complete communion between the person and the Word, between the spirit and Allah, must be subdued. And Samba Diallo's excruciating experiences under Thierno's tutelage demonstrate that the quest for the spiritual "ultimate" makes physical pain not only bearable, but almost desirable and, certainly, purifying. Thierno subjects Samba Diallo to extreme physical torture when it appears to him that his bodily senses interfere with his pronunciation and mastery of the Word.

Samba Diallo's reaction stands in marked contrast to that of Askar in Farah's *Maps*. Like Senegal, Somalia, the setting of *Maps*, has a mystical brand of Islam with Sufi orders which include the Qaadiriyya, Ahmadiyya and Saahiliyya. In the opinion of Laitin and Samatar, the vast majority of Somalis belong to some mystical order and their Islam "is characterized by saint veneration, enthusiastic belief in the mystical powers of charismatic roving holy men, and a tenuous measure of allegiance to Sufi brotherhoods" (1987, 45). But what this ideology spiritually provided for Samba Diallo, it completely failed to provide for Askar.

As in Senegalese society, in Somalia there is the belief that a disciple may have to undergo physical suffering in the process of acquiring the Word. When Askar was first taken by his uncle to Aw–Adan, the "priest," for Qur'anic instruction, the uncle reminds the teacher that:

> Askar is part bone and part flesh. The flesh is yours and you may punish it to the extent of it letting or losing a bit of blood. Teach him the Word . . . show him the light which you've seen when he is still young (1986, 81).

Inflicting pain on the body for purposes of inculcating the Word of God is seen as a natural part of the process of training the spirit.

Unlike Samba Diallo, however, Askar does not quite accept this religious connection between physical mutilation and spiritual salvation. Of course, as a child, societal and familial pressures led him to pretend that he did espouse this ideology. In Askar's words:

> I behaved as though I were convinced that being caned by Aw–Adan was part of the ritual of growing up, that in a way, it was for my own good—didn't learning the Koran form part of the ritual of growing up spiritually? (Farah 1986, 85).

In reality, however, he could not come to terms with this painful path towards Islamic spirituality. Physical pain led Kane's Samba Diallo to perfect his Qur'anic recitation; but with Askar it had the reverse effect. "The letter *alif*," said Askar, "because I was hit by Aw–Adan and I bit my tongue, became *balif*; and *ba* when struck again sounded like *fa*; whereas the letter *ta*, now that my mouth was a pool of blood, was turned by my tongue into *sha*" (1986, 82).

To Askar, then, Islam and the Qur'an lacked the spiritual substance that could prepare him to endure bodily pain. He believed that "no verse in the Koran could've reduced the pain or even eliminated it altogether" (1986, 89). While Muslims are generally urged to read the Qur'an in moments of psychological and emotional stress, Askar felt that he could not depend on the Word to fill his own void: "The Word, I said to myself, was not a womb; the Word, I convinced myself, wouldn't receive me as might a mother, a woman, a Misra" (1986, 86–87). Far from being touched by the Word and deriving strength from it, therefore, Askar actually felt deserted by it.

Partly because of the Word's "failure," then, Askar's physical suffering turned into a compulsive hate against Aw–Adan, the priest. According to Askar:

> I hated him more when he caned me, because I thought that each stroke struck a blow, rending a hole in the wall of my being. When with him, when at school that is, I uttered every sound so it was inlaid with the contemptuous flames meant for him. Which was why I shouted loudest, hoping he would burn in the noises—ablaze with hate (Farah 1986, 77).

The priest, then, became the target of the very pain he inflicted on Askar, partly because the Word and the Islamic doctrine had failed to grip Askar and uplift him spiritually.

Islam as a Moral Code

But there was another, somewhat Freudian, reason why Askar hated Aw–Adan so intensely; and this had to do with the nature of the priest's relationship with Askar's adoptive mother, Misra. Islam is not only a spiritual path; it is also a way of life. It encompasses certain values and mores which help guide the social conduct of the believers. If Islam has failed as a spiritual guide—in Farah's conception—has it fared any better as a moral code? Are the custodians of the Word, like Aw–Adan, also the moral conscience of society?

In this regard, Kane's *Ambiguous Adventure* and Farah's *Maps* again offer contrasting perspectives. Thierno, the teacher in Kane's novel, is a model of morality and social uprightness. In his society he is regarded with utmost honor and veneration. Apart from devoting the most minimum amount of time in the field to procure his extremely frugal nourishment, the "rest of his days and nights he consecrated to study, to meditation, to prayer, and to the education and molding of the young people who had been confided to his care" (1963, 7). The custodian of the Word in *Ambiguous Adventure*, then, is unambiguously the epitome of Islamic morality.

The priest, Aw–Adan, in Farah's *Maps*, however, presents a dramatically different picture. In spite of his thorough knowledge of Qur'anic law and the trust that the community has placed in him to serve as a spiritual and moral guide for their young, Aw–Adan engages in one of the few crimes against Islamic morality, adultery, that is punishable by death. Jealously, Askar explains to us how he saw Misra, his adoptive mother, and the Islamic priest lying naked in bed, and how Aw–Adan's artificial, wooden leg

> was dropped and how fast another between his legs came to raise its head, jerkily, slowly and how the whole place drowned in the sighing endearments of Misra who called him . . . yes him of all people . . . "my man, my man, my man!" (1986, 32).

This seemingly prolonged illicit relationship between Aw–Adan and Misra started when he was teaching her the Qur'an.

Aw–Adan's moral standing had become so low that Askar wondered if, in fact, he, the "master," had not once acted altogether sacrilegiously in his affair with Misra. Was Aw–Adan not guilty of violating the very Word for which he served as custodian by making love to her as she was reading the Holy Book? "Did Aw–Adan make her read the Koran," wondered Askar, "and, while she was busy deciphering the mysteries of the Word, did he insert *his* in?" (1986, 52). The Muslim priest's reputation was so negative, then, that one could think the unthinkable of his moral conduct—committing adultery in the very process of imparting the Word.

This negative portrayal of the priest as essentially immoral and hypocritical is, in fact, extended to other characters who espouse an Islamic ideology and who are still attached to the more non–westernized dimension of Somali traditions. Qorrax, Askar's paternal uncle who sent him to the priest to receive the Word and to be shown the light while still young, engages in the same kind of adulterous affair with the same woman, Misra, as Aw–Adan. Again, Askar tells us how Qorrax "came after nightfall and made his claims on Misra," how he threatened to hire another woman to take care of Askar and dispense with her services unless she offered herself to him, and how "Misra suffered the humiliation of sleeping with him" so she could continue being with Askar (1986, 28). The uncle who is so concerned about Askar's Islamic and moral upbringing, then, is himself so morally decadent as to force Misra into an illicit affair through sheer coercion.

On the other extreme of the morality continuum are Askar's maternal uncle, Hilaal, and his wife, Salaado. Though intensely nationalistic towards Somalia, these two are anything but Somali in their socio–cultural disposition. As intellectuals who are highly educated in the Western tradition, they have become completely alienated from their "cultural Somaliness" in the process. They have, in fact, become highly Westernized and, in their attitudes and behavior, seem to espouse an "extreme" brand of Western liberalism that even questions the boundaries of gender.

But precisely because they have become more liberal in the Western tradition, Hilaal and Salaado have become less Islamic in social orientation. It is perhaps possible to be a Westernized liberal in political and economic terms without being less Islamic in politico–economic ideology. It is, however, less possible to be a Westernized liberal in cultural terms without violating some of the basic canons of Islam. Western media has created the impression that all politically active Islamic groups are "fundamentalist" with overall aims and objectives that are incompatible with liberalism and democracy. But, the polysemy of the term "Islamic fundamentalism" notwithstanding, it is in fact possible to have Islamic–oriented politico-economic action that is not antidemocratic or antiliberal, and which advances the political aims of liberal democracy.

Perhaps less compatible with Islam is a cultural liberalism in the Western mold. Some of the most basic values of Western liberalism are diametrically opposed to Islamic doctrine. The cultural values of Western liberalism would accommodate, for example, a multiplicity of religious views and beliefs—from fundamentalism to agnosticism to atheism. In Islam, however, such a wide range of liberal opinion in religious affairs is likely to enter into the realm of apostasy. It is perhaps for this reason that some followers of Islam who reject what is seen as excessive Westernization[3] often react more violently towards cultural symbols than towards political and economic symbols of the West. They are more likely to target a Western theater showing western–style films than a Western–style legislative assembly following Western–derived procedures of deliberation, or a Western factory producing Coca Cola.

The cultural dimension of Hilaal and Salaado's Western liberalism thus implies a certain degree of cultural divergence from Islam. Their behavior has ceased to reflect anything Islamic, and the Islamic learning that they grew up with has been all but forgotten. During Misra's funeral, for example, where verses from the Qur'an were recited in chorus by those present, Salaado reports that she could not remember a single verse from the Holy Book, not even from such a basic chapter as the "Faatihah." Salaado acknowledges that this may have been due, in part, to her mental state precipitated by the shock of Misra's death; but she then goes on to add that "even now" she doubts if she could remember anything from the Qur'an (1986, 241).

Yet, it is precisely these two characters, who have apparently been de–Somalized and de–Islamized through a process of cultural Westernization, that are projected extremely positively in terms of their conduct. The two are morally upright and deeply sensitive people who have transcended the parochial confines of "tradition" in their humanism. What Islamic ideology failed to provide to the likes of Aw–Adan and Qorrax, then, Western liberal ideology succeeded in providing for Hilaal and Salaado.

The Qur'an

Historically the most widely read book in its original language, used at least five times daily in formal worship by millions of people, the Qur'an is regarded by Muslims as Allah's direct revelation to His Prophet Muhammad. There are, in fact, many Muslims who believe that the Qur'an is so sacred that one must be in a state of ablution before handling it, and that it must always be stored in a place that is compatible with its supreme honor. Contrary to these beliefs held by a wide section of the Muslim population, however, Farah's views on the Qur'an are, at best, ambiguous, betraying a mixture of seeming reverence and what borders on sacrilege.

Many of the Muslim beliefs about the Qur'an are, in fact, contained in the Qur'an itself, and some of these are articulated in *Maps*. To Muslims the Qur'an is the ultimate miracle from Allah, and there are several verses which point to its inimitability. But equally important among God's miracles is nature, and the Qur'an repeatedly calls on the unbelievers to look at the various aspects of nature—the mountains and the seas, the moon and its "accompanying" stars, the sun and its orderly movement, and so forth—as miracles of God's creation in their own right. And this is perhaps the essence of Askar's suggestion that in Islam, Nature . . . is conceived of as a book, comparable, in a lot of ways, to the Holy Koran: a genus for a sura, a species for a verse, and every subspecies shares a twinship with the *alif*, *ba*, and *ta* of mother nature—*maa shaa Allahu kaana*! (1986, 128).

In *Maps*, therefore, as in popular Muslim beliefs, the Qur'an and nature join to serve as a testament of the existence and boundless power of God.

Equally important to Islam is the idea that, despite its great clarity on all fundamental issues, the Qur'an is also a reservoir of hidden meanings known only to the Almighty. Following the bizarre murder of Misra, Askar suggests that the priest supervising the burial should have recited, among others, verse sixteen of Sura *Luqmaan* (1986, 242) which reads: "O my son! if there is but the weight of a mustard–seed hidden in a rock or anywhere in the heavens or on earth, God will bring it forth: for God understands the finest of mysteries and is well acquainted with them." Like a good Muslim, therefore, Askar seems to turn to the mysterious aspect of the Word of God in the quest for a resolution to his own inner conflicts and for some light on his enigmatic past and the direction of his destiny.

Muslims also regard the Qur'an as a form of healing. Verse 82 of Surat *Banii–Isra–il* proclaims to the world: "We sent down in the Qur'an that which is a healing and a mercy to those who believe . . . ." Of course, the Qur'an regards itself as a healing for broken spirits; but there are many Muslims who regard it as a cure for physical ailments as well. And it is this popular belief rather than the doctrinal position of Islam which is invoked when Askar falls sick and Aw–Adan offers "to read selected verses of the Qur'an over Askar's body astraddle the bed in satanic pain" (1986, 102).

Is the appearance of the words "verses" and "satanic" in the above quotation a mere coincidence, or, like Salman Rushdie's *Satanic Verses*, is it, in fact, intended to have an allusive significance that pits God, on one side, and Satan, on the other? Askar promptly and categorically rejected Aw–Adan's offer to recite the Qur'an over his body. He feared that the priest may read the "wrong" passages from the Holy Book, "passages, say, which could turn him into an epileptic" (1986, 103). The idea that one could maliciously or inadvertently invoke the "wrong" verses from the Qur'an that could end up harming an innocent person is alien indeed to the belief system of the Muslim *umma*, and would amount to an attack upon the Book for possessing an evil dimension that is incompatible with its Godliness. But, to Askar, the Qur'an does seem to encapsulate both Godly power that could heal the sick and "satanic" power that could harm the innocent.

Farah further explores this interplay between the Word and the world of Askar through two symbols, one sexual and one unsanitary. The prospects of circumcision and the fear of being separated from Misra thereafter lead Askar to sleep with the slate containing Qur'anic verses *between his legs* to serve as a much needed extension of his body—a penis perhaps?—as he "chanted selected verses of the Koran whenever Aw–Adan called on Misra, as he was accustomed to doing after dusk, verses which promised heaven for the pious and a hellish reward for the adulterous and the wicked" (1986, 86).

Later, when Askar was being given a bath by Misra, the Word moved from its position between his legs to intermingle with the filth from his body. As Misra lovingly splashed water on his face, Askar tells us, "I jumped up and down in glee, oblivious of the fact that the Koranic writings had ended up in the same baaf as the dirt between my toes. I decided I wouldn't hold the slate between my legs that night, and the following night too. Misra and I slept in each other's embrace and the slate was left in a corner until after I was made a man" (1986, 88).

With a somewhat Freudian twist, the Qur'an reassures Askar about his sexual existence when there is some distance between himself and Misra; but when the two are joined again, the Word becomes peripheral to his life and even meaningless, as it is cast aside in a neglected corner or allowed to wallow in the same water as the filth from his feet. At least until Askar became a man!

And what happens when Askar is initiated into adulthood? In his sojourn in the land of pain immediately after his circumcision, he tells us: "The waters of the rain washed the slate on which I had written my prayers and the thunder drowned my chanting of the verses which praised the traditions of Islam" (1986, 92). As Askar enters a new psychosexual stage of his life and becomes his own man, so to speak, after belatedly outgrowing his oedipal inclinations he realizes that he no longer needs Misra. Nor, indeed, does he any longer need the Word. The Word gets washed away and drowned like any material thing on the ground, as he himself physically moves away from Misra to his new home, Mogadisho.

Conclusion

Farah's *Maps* portrays a complex social web that is heavily intertwined with Islamic symbols and idioms. This has arisen, in part, because his fictional world of the Somali people is, after all, predominantly Islamic in faith and culture. However, this is a culture and a worldview that Farah seems to reject in quite explicit terms. But Farah goes beyond rejecting Islam. He satirizes it. And it is in this respect that one can draw a parallel between him and Salman Rushdie. He does not, for example, go to the extent of describing the Prophet Muhammad as Mahound and his wives as prostitutes. But, in addition to debasing the religion and its Book, through the metaphoric and symbolic strategies discussed above, he does make sex a primary feature of the relationship between the Prophet and his wives. Even the Prophet, then, is "sooner or later" expected to engage in sex partly as a way of subduing his wives (1986, 223–24). In his satirical projection of Islam, therefore, Nuruddin Farah has clearly taken the path of a cultural apostate.

Notes

1. Like Rushdie, but to a lesser extent, Farah's novel raises once again the problematic question of the conflict between faith and fiction, between the freedom of the writer and the integrity of the community of believers. For a more extensive coverage of these issues, see *The Rushdie File*, edited by Lisa Appignanesi and Sara Maitland (1990).

2. Mbye B. Cham describes Ousmane Sembène as an apostate, and seemingly the only one among Senegalese Muslim writers (1990, 178–83).

3. In the words of Ali Mazrui, "there is a heavy responsibility on the shoulders of Islam as the one culture that clearly produces rebels against western hegemony. . . . It is the vanguard against western cultural hegemony. Whenever we complain about Muslim fundamentalists, let us remember that that is a term which describes a rebellious mood against being assimilated by the majority culture in the world" (1990, 225).

Glossary

▼▼▼▼▼▼▼▼

Abtar: To be without a male descendant, which was Muhammad's fate

Ajami: An adaptation of the Arabic script used by the Hausa and some other West African Muslim peoples

Asabiyya: Group solidarity, the forms of which differ in primitive and civilized societies. See *badawa* and *hadara.*

Awliya' (Arabic; sing. *wali*): Muslim individuals who during their lifetime were extraordinarily pious and were (are) believed to have found such favor in the eyes of God that they could (and can) bring about miraculous things.

Bab al-ijtihad: Literally, the "gate of interpretation," an expression referring to the closure of free debate or *ijtihad* (q.v.) about the principles of Islamic doctrine

Badawa: Primitivism, contrasted with *hadara* or civilization, a distinction proposed in particular by Ibn Khaldun in the fourteenth century A.D., and which governs distinct forms of group solidarity of *asabiyya.*

Baraka (Arabic); *albarkaci* (Hausa): The holiness of a saint, believed to be obtainable through touching the saint's gown or visiting his/her tomb, etc.

Bori (Hausa): A spirit possession cult often found in association with Islam, believed to be efficacious in curing the many illnesses attributed to spirits. Called *zar* in North Africa.

'Darik'a (Hausa); *tariqa* (Arabic): Literally "path," meaning the way of the sufi mystics. The term evolved into the term for the organizations of the sufi mystics. Examples in Africa include the Qadiriyya and the Tijaniyya.

Dhikr (Arabic, "mentioning"): The ritual "mentioning" of God's name in accordance with prescriptions specific to each Islamic brotherhood (*tariqa*). Similar in meaning to *hadra.*

Dini: Religion; in this context, the formal teachings of Islam

Ecstasy: The Sufi idea of detachment from material existence in order to better grasp true reality, which is the realm of the divine. The central doctrine of Sufism is *wahdat al-wujud*, "oneness or unity of being." This is derived directly from the *shahada* which is understand not only as "there is no God but God" but also "there is no reality except Reality." One of the names for God is *al-Haqq* which means "Reality" or "Truth" (Stoddart, 43). The goal of the quest for the Unity of Being is for self to step aside and let the absolute know itself through itself. The journey begins with withdrawal from the material world. This retreat to an isolated cell in order to "remember" God is considered by many orders to be the most important of Sufi disciplines. Within all Sufi orders, a division arises between those who are in a state of intoxication (*sukr*) and those in a state of sobriety (*sahw*). The intoxicated state is a transient spiritual station that is characterized by loss of sanity and self-control. (Bakhtiar 1987, 94–95).

Essuf: Refers to the outside in Tuareg thought; a strange and dangerous space that opposes the places that are inhabited and ordered by men; this world of the strange crosses and intersects the domesticated universe and constitutes its inevitable counterweight.

Fatwa: A religious decree

Fitna: Disorder, but by connotation female beauty

Habaici (Hausa): Innuendo in verse entertainment

Hadara: Civilization, as opposed to primitivism or *badawa*.

Hadith (Arabic): Traditions or reports about the life of the Prophet, relating the deeds and utterances of Muhammad and his Companions. These Traditions have been subject to Islamic scholarly scrutiny and are part of the sources of Islamic Law (*Shari'a*)

Hadra (Arabic): See *dhikr*

Hikima (Arabic): Wisdom

Ibada (Arabic): Act of piety

Ijma: The consensus which should prevail among the community of the learned.

Ijtihad: Free interpretation of Qur'anic sources and commentary. Can be opposed to unquestioning allegiance to religious authority, *taglid* (q.v.). Also see *bab al-itjihad*

Iqra: Read or recite; God's command to Muhammad at the moment of revelation.

Imam (Arabic): Prayer leader

Insan: Man in the wide sense, "human," but also a conventional reference to Muhammad.

Inta: Inta represents the phase of harmony and absolute unity in Tuareg cosmogony; the instant of equilibrium that follows the end of one action and that precedes the beginning of another, the moment when motion harmonizes into the annihilation from which a new cycle will be born.

Isnad: The chain of transmission of Hadith (q.v.) which authenticates their veracity

Jihad: "Holy war" in some contexts, but commitment or inner struggle in others. Sometimes divided into *jihad al-sayf* ("armed jihad") and *jihad al-gawl* ("proselytizing jihad"). Pre-Qur'anic sense of toiling or laboring.

Kel Tagelmust: Those who wear the veil. The Tuareg are frequently identified by their turbans that leave only the eyes unveiled.

Kel Tamajak: Those who speak Tamajak, the language of the Tuareg

Ki-Pemba: A spirit-mediumship and possession cult in Mombasa, Kenya. Members of the cult believe that they are possessed by spirits from the island of Pemba.

Kirari (Hausa): Bombastic praise

Koma: Spirits of the dead

Labari (Hausa; pl. labarai): A genre of Hausa oral legends reputed to be historical truth or "news" about a ruler, saint, or mystic.

Limam (Hausa): Hausa term for Imam (Arabic)

Litany: A prayer consisting of a series of invocations and supplications, known as the *wird* in Islam.

Madih (Arabic): Praise poetry for God and His Prophet

Mahdi: The Muslim messiah

Malami (Hausa, pl. malamai): an Islamic scholar or teacher.

Malamanci (Hausa): Using many Arabic loan words in one's speech to exhibit Islamic erudition.

Mansoukh: Qur'anic verses that were replaced by subsequent contradictory revelation, apocrypha of sorts. See *nasikh*.

Ma-sha-Allah: "Whatever Allah wishes"

Mganga: A shaman, healer, "medicine-man"

Mila: Customs; in this context, customs indigenous to the Swahili people

Mujtahid: An accepted interpreter of Qur'anic traditions. From the same root as *ijtihad* (q.v.)

Muhkam: To be grounded or founded upon correct thought, clear in thought.

Mutashadbih: possibly illusory interpretative appearances and resemblances; allegorical, figurative, not literal.

Mu'tazila: (from the Arabic, *a'tazala*, "to take one's distance," "to remove oneself," "to withdraw.") A religious movement founded at Basra in the first half of the second/eighth century which became one of the most important theological schools of Islam, establishing the widespread use of rational arguments in the subsequent development of theology

Mzimu: A spirit-dwelling

Nafi (Arabic): Supererogatory prayers

Nasikh: Qur'anic verses that were replaced by subsequent contradictory revelation, apocrypha of sorts. See *mansoukh*.

Niyya (Arabic): Intention

Rak'at (Arabic): A "bending" in prayer

Rawiyate (sing.: *rawiya*): in Assia Djebar's *Loin de Médine*, this term refers to female transmitters of Hadith.

Salat: A prayer, as in the five daily prayers of Islam.

Sharif (Hausa, pl. sharifai): A reputed descendant of the Prophet Muhammed; they often have special privileges.

Shari'a: Islamic law or jurisprudence founded in the first instance on the Qur'an, then upon later Hadith (q.v.) and commentaries.

Sittaat: Somali praise songs for the prominent women of early Islam.

Sufi: An Islamic mystic who practices sufism, often involving group prayer, chanting, drumming, singing, or whirling, recitation of a short prayer formula, fasting, seclusion, meditation, self-denial and asceticism to obtain knowledge of and nearness to God.

Ta'a: Obedience

Tafsiri (Hausa); *tafsir* (Arabic): Quranic exegesis which is the explanation of the meaning of the Holy Qur'an in the light of the historical circumstances of its revelation and other sources of Islamic knowledge

Taqlid: unquestioning obedience to religious authority.

Tariqa (Arabic, plural *turuq*): Islamic or Sufi brotherhood with a formal organizational structure, a specific chain of spiritual leaders, and its own devotional and mystical practices.

Tifinar: The writing system of the Kel Tamajak or Tuareg; geometric decor found engraved on rocks, on leather, wood, pottery, and other objects common to Berbers

Trance: The mystical state in Tuareg cosmogony that leads to the indescribable, the inexplicable, to the harmonious step of annihilation or dissipation into the flux of the universe, to the savory state of non-being.

Uganga: the concept and practice of healing through spirit-possession

Ulama: Scholars; the community of the learned.

Umma: Community, nation

Wali (Hausa; pl. waliyai): A sufi saint who enjoys closeness to and knowledge of God, often reputed to perform miracles.

Wird: the rosary or litany that bridges the *dhikr* and the daily prayers. It comprises essentially three formulas: purification, expansion, and union with God . The *wird* is normally recited morning and evening, each formula being repeated a hundred times, for which purpose a chaplet is used.

References

▼▼▼▼▼▼▼▼▼▼

Abbot, Nabia. 1942. *Aisha the Beloved of Muhammed*. Chicago: University of Chicago Press.

Abdisalam Yassin Mohamed. 1977. "Sufi Poetry in Somali: Its Themes and Imagery." Ph.D. diss., University of London.

Abdullahi b. Fodio. 1963. *Tazyin al–Warakat*. Trans. M. Hiskett. Ibadan: Ibadan University Press.

Abun–Nasr, Jamil M. 1971. *A History of the Maghrib*. Cambridge: Cambridge University Press.

Ahmed, Akbar S. 1992. *Postmodernism and Islam: Predicament and Promise*. London: Routledge.

Ahmed, Leila. 1992. *Women and Gender in Islam*. New Haven: Yale University Press.

Albasu, Sabo Abdullahi. 1985. "A Glimpse of Muhammad Bello's Views on the Mahdi and Mahdist Expectation." Paper presented at the Seminar on Amir al–Mu'min, Muhammad Bello, University of Sokoto, Nigeria.

al–Hajj, M.A. 1973. "The Mahdist Tradition in Northern Nigeria." Ph.D. diss., Ahmadu Bello University, Zaria, Nigeria.

Ali, Abdirahman Hersi. 1977. "The Arab Factor in Somali History: The Origins and Development of Arab Enterprise and Cultural Influences in the Somali Peninsula." Ph.D. diss., University of California, Los Angeles.

Ali, Abdullahi Yusufu. 1946. *The Holy Qur'an, Text, Translation and Commentary*. Vols I and II. New York: Hafner Publishing Co.

Ali, Moulavi Cheragh. 1977. *A Critical Exposition of the Popular "Jihad."* Karachi: Karimsons.

Allen, J.W.T. 1971. *Tendi*. Nairobi: Heinemann.

Al–Suhrawardy, A.M. 1980. *The Sayings of Muhammed*. London: John Murray.

Al–Taberi, Abu Ja'far Muhammad B. 1987. *The Commentary on the Qur'an*, abridged and with introduction by J. Cooper. Oxford: Oxford University Press.

Andrzejewski, B.W. and I.M. Lewis. 1964. *Somali Poetry: An Introduction*. Oxford: Oxford University Press.

Andrzejewski, B.W. 1974. "The Veneration of Sufi Saints and Its Impact on the Oral Literature of the Somali People and Their Literature in Arabic." *African Language Studies* 15:15–53.

Andrzejewski, B.W. 1974. "Somali Literature." *Literatures in African Languages: Theoretical Issues and Sample Surveys*. Ed. B.W. Andrzejewski, S. Pilaszewiez, and W. Tyloch, 340–81. Cambridge: Cambridge University Press.

Appignanesi, L. and S. Maitland, eds. 1990. *The Rushdie File*. Syracuse: Syracuse University Press.

Arasteh, A. Reza. 1980. *Growth to Selfhood: The Sufi Contribution*. London: Routledge and Kegan Paul.

Bakhtiar, Lelah. 1987. *Sufi Expressions of the Mystic Quest*. New York: Thames and Hudson.

Bakhtin, M.M. 1981. *The Dialogic Imagination: Four Essays*. Ed. Michael Holquist. Trans. Caryl Emerson and Michael Holquist. Austin: University of Texas Press.

Balewah, Abubakar Tafawa. 1989. *Shaiu Umar*. New York: Markus Wiener Publishing.

Bali, Saley Boubé. 1993. "Hawad et la poésie de l'errance." *Ecriture 42: Littératures du Niger*. Lausanne: Révue Littéraire Ecriture, 171–83.

Bataille, Georges. 1962. *Eroticism*. Trans. Mary Dalwood. London: John Calder Publishers Ltd.

Ben Jelloun, Tahar. 1987a. *The Sand Child*. Trans. Alan Sheridan. New York: Ballantine Books. Originally published as *L'Enfant de sable* (Paris: Editions du Seuil, 1985).

Ben Jelloun, Tahar. 1989. *The Sacred Night*. Trans. Alan Sheridan. San Diego: Harcourt Brace Jovanovich, Inc. Originally published as *La Nuit sacré* (Paris: Editions du Seuil, 1987b).

Bensmaïn, Abdallah. 1986. "Driss Chraïbi, le precurseur." *Revue Celfan* 5, 2: 9–15.

Bertrand, Louis. 1921. *Les Villes d'or*. Paris: A. Fayard.

Boyd, Jean. 1989. *The Caliph's Sister*. London: Frank Cass.

Boyd, Jean and Beverly B. Mack. Forthcoming. *The Collected Works of Nana Asma'u bint Usman 'Dan Fodio 1793–1864*.

Braukämper, Ulrich. 1992. "The Sanctuary of Shaykh Husayn and the Oromo–Somali Connections in Bale." In *Proceedings of the First International Congress of Somali Studies (July 1980)*. Ed. Hussein Adam and Charles L. Geshekter, 145–66. Atlanta: Scholars Press.

Brown, Norman O. 1991. *Apocalypse and/or Metamorphosis*. Berkeley: University of California Press.

Casanova, Paul, ed. 1926. Ibn Khaldoun, *Histoire des Berbères et des dynasties musulmanes de l'Afrique septentrionale, traduite par Le Baron de Slane*, I. Paris: Librairie Orientaliste Paul Geuthner.

Cham, M.B. 1990. "Islam in Senegalese Literature and Film." In *Faces of Islam in African Literature*. Ed. K. Harrow, 163–86. Portsmouth, N.H.: Heinemann.

Chittick, William C. 1989. *Ibn al–Arabi's Metaphysics of Imagination: The Sufi Path of Knowledge*. Albany, N.Y.: State Uuniversity of New York Press.

Chittick, William C. n.d. "Death and the World of Imagination: Ibn Al–'Arabi's Eschatology." *The Muslim World*: 51–82.

Chraïbi, Driss. 1955. *Les Boucs*. Paris: Editions Denoël. Trans. Hugh A. Harter under the title *The Butts* (Washington D.C.: Three Continents, 1983).

Chraïbi, Driss. 1954, *Le Passé simple*. Paris: Editions Denoël. Trans. Hugh A. Harter under the title *The Simple Past* (Washington D.C.: Three Continents, 1990).

Chraïbi, Driss. 1956. *L'Ane*. Paris: Editions Denoël.

Chraïbi, Driss. 1962. *Succession ouverte*. Paris: Denoël. Trans. Len Ortzen under the title *Heirs to the Past* (London: Heinemann, 1971).

Chraïbi, Driss. 1972. *La Civilisation, ma mère!* . . . Paris: Denoël. Trans. Hugh A. Harter under the title *Mother Comes of Age* (Washington D.C.: Three Continents, 1984).

Chraïbi, Driss. 1981. *Une Enquête au pays*. Paris: Le Seuil. Trans. Robin Roosevelt under the title *Flutes of Death* (Washington D.C.: Three Continents, 1985).

Chraïbi, Driss. 1982. *La Mère du Printemps (L'Oum–er–Bia)*. Paris: Le Seuil. Trans. Hugh A. Harter under the title *Mother Spring* (Washington D.C.: Three Continents, 1989).

Chraïbi, Driss. 1986. *Naissance à l'aube*. Paris: Le Seuil. Trans. Ann Woollcombe under the title *Birth at Dawn* (Washington D.C.: Three Continents, 1990).

Chraïbi, Driss. 1991. *L'Inspecteur Ali*. Paris: Editions Denoël [translations John C. Hawley].

Clark, Andrew F. and Lucie Colvin Phillips. *Historical Dictionary of Senegal*. Metuchen, N.J.: Scarecrow Press, 1994.

Claudot, Hélène. 1985. "Introduction." In *Caravane de la soif*. Aix–en–Provence: Edisud.

Claudot, Hélène. 1987. "Introduction." In *Chants de la soif et de l'égarement*. Aix–en–Provence: Edisud.

Conrad, David. 1995. "Blind Man Meets Prophet: Oral Tradition, Islam, and Funé Identity." In *Status and Identity in West Africa: Nyamakalaw of Mandé*. Ed. David Conrad and Barbara Frank. Bloomington: Indiana University Press: 86–132.

Déjeux, Jean. 1973. *Littérature maghrébine de langue française*. Sherbrooke: Editions Naaman.

Déjeux, Jean. 1986. *Le Sentiment réligieux dans la littérature maghrébine de langue française*. Paris: L'Harmattan.

Déjeux, Jean. 1992. "Francophone Literature in the Maghreb: The Problem and the Possibility." *Research in African Literatures* 23, 2:5–19.

Dieng, Bassirou. 1993. *L'Epopée du Kajoor*. Dakar: Editions Khoudia.

Diop, Birago. 1961. *Les Contes d'Amadou Koumba*. Paris: Présence Africaine.

Diop, Samba. 1995. *The Oral History and Literature of the Wolof People of Waalo, Northern Senegal*. Lewiston, N.Y.: Edwin Mellen Press.

Djebar, Assia. 1975. "A Noted Algerian Writer Presents her Views of Muslim Women Today." *The UNESCO Courier* 28, 8 (Aug.–Sept): 23–28.

Djebar, Assia. 1980. *Femmes d'Alger dans leur appartement*. Paris: des femmes.

Djebar, Assia. 1985. *L'Amour, la fantasia*. Paris: J.C. Lattès. Trans. D. S. Blair under the title *Fantasia: An Algerian Cavalcade* (Portsmouth, N.H.: Heinemann, 1993).

Djebar, Assia. 1987. *Ombre Sultane*. Paris: Edition Lattès.

Djebar, Assia. 1991. *Loin de Médine*. Paris: Albin Michel.

Dokaji, Alhaji Abubakar [Wazirin Kano]. 1958, rep. 1978. *Kano Ta Dabo Cigari* . Zaria: The Northern Nigerian Publishing Company, Ltd.

Donadey, Anne. 1993. "Assia Djebar's Poetics of Subversion." *Esprit Créateur* 33, 2 (Summer): 107–17.

Dubois, Felix. [1896].1969. *Timbuctoo the Mysterious* . New York: Negro Universities Press.

Dubois, Lionel. 1986. "Les Voyages de Driss Chraïbi," *Revue Celfan* 5, 2:15–19 [translation John C. Hawley].

Dubois, Lionel. 1986. "Interview de Driss Chraïbi." *Revue Celfan* 5, 2: 20–26.

Durix, Jean Pierre. 1989. "Through to Action." *Contemporary Literary Criticism*, vol. 58, 134. Detroit, Mich.: Gale Research.

The Encyclopaedia of Islam. 1960–1993. Ed. R. Lewis, V.L. Menage, Ch. Pellat, and J. Schacht. New edition. Vols. I–VII. Leiden: Brill.

Farah, Nuruddin. 1968. *Maps*. New York: Pantheon Books.

Farah, Nuruddin. 1988. "Why I Write." *Third World Quarterly* 10, 4: 1591–99.

Farah, Nuruddin. 1990. "Childhood of My Schizophrenia." *The Times Literary Supplement* (November 23–29): 1264.

Farah, Nuruddin. 1992. *Close Sesame*. Saint Paul, Minn.: Graywolf.

Fika, Adamu Muhammad. 1978. *The Kano Civil War and British Over–Rule 1882-1940*. Ibadan: Oxford University Press.

Fischer, Michael M.J. and Mehdi Abedi. 1990. *Debating Muslims: Cultural Dialogues in Postmodernity and Tradition*. Madison: The University of Wisconsin Press.

Furniss, Graham. 1989. "Typification and Evaluation: A Dynamic Process in Rhetoric." Chapter 3 in *Discourse and Its Disguises: The Interpretation of African Oral Texts*. Ed. Karin Barber and P. F. De Moraes Farias. Birmingham: CWAS African Studies Series I.

Gallieni, Joseph Simon. 1891. *Deux Campagnes au Soudan Français*. 1866–1888. Paris: Hachette.

Geertz, Clifford. 1968. *Islam Observed*. Chicago: University of Chicago Press.

Giles, L.L. 1987. "Possession Cults on the Swahili Coast: A Re–Examination of Theories of Marginality." *Africa* 57: 234–58.

Gimaret, D. 1993. "Mu'tazila." *The Encyclopedia of Islam*. New Edition. Ed. C.E. Bosworth, E. van Donzel, W.P. Heinrichs, and C. Pellat. Leiden: E.J. Brill.

Hale, Thomas A. 1990. *Scribe, Griot and Novelist: Narrative Interpreters of the Songhay World. Followed by the Epic of Askia Mohammed Recounted by Nouhou Malio*. Gainesville: University Press of Florida.

Hale, Thomas A. 1985. "Islam and the Griots in West Africa: Bridging the Gap Between Two Traditions. *Africana Journal* 13, 1–4: 84–90.

Harrow, Kenneth W., ed. 1991. *Faces of Islam in African Literature*. London: Heinemann.

Harter, Hugh A. 1986. "Why Chraïbi? A Translator's Essay." *Revue Celfan* 5, 2: 36–38.

Hawad. 1985. *Caravane de la soif*. Aix–en–Provence: Edisud.

Hawad. 1987. *Chants de la soif et de l'égarement*. Aix–en–Provence: Edisud.

Hawad. 1987. *Testament nomade*. Paris: Sillages.

Hawad. 1989. *L'Anneau sentier*. Céret: L'Alphélie.

Hiskett, Mervyn. 1975. *A History of Hausa Islamic Verse*. London: School for Oriental and African Studies.

Hiskett, Mervyn. 1984. *The Development of Islam in West Africa*. New York: Longman, Inc.

Hourani, Albert. 1991. *A History of the Arab Peoples*. Cambridge: The Belknap Press of Harvard University Press.

Hunwick, John O. 1985. *Sharia in Songhay: The Replies of al–Maghili to the Questions of Askia al–Hajj Mohammed*. New York: Oxford University Press.

Hutcheon, Linda. 1988. *A Poetics of Postmodernism: History, Theory, Fiction*. New York: Routledge.

Ibn Khaldun. 1967. *The Muqaddimah*. Trans. F. Rosenthal. London: Routledge and Kegan Paul.

Innes, Gordon. 1976. *Kaabu and Fuladu: Historical Narraives of the Gambian Mandinka*. London: School of Oriental and African Studies.

Innes, Gordon. 1978. *Kelefa Saane: His Career Recounted by Two Mandinka Bards*. London: School of Oriental and African Studies.

Jaggi, Maya. 1989. "A Combining of Gifts: An Interview." *Third World Quarterly* 3: 171–87.

Johnson, Lemuel. 1991. "Crescent and Conciousness: Islamic Orthodoxies and the West African Novel." In *Faces of Islam in Sub–Saharan African Literature*. Ed. Kenneth Harrow, 239–60. London, Portsmouth, N.H.: Heinemann.

Kadra–Hadjadji, Houaria. 1986. *Contestation et révolte dans l'oeuvre de Driss Chraïbi.* Alger: E.N.A.L. [translations John C. Hawley].

Kane, Cheikh Hamidou. 1962. *L'Aventure ambiguë.* Paris: René Julliard. Trans. Katherine Woods under the title *Ambiguous Adventure.* Oxford: Heinemann, 1971.

Kapteijns, Lidwien. 1994. "Women and the Crisis of Communal Identity: The Cultural Construction of Gender in Somali History." In *The Somali Challenge.* Ed. Ahmed I. Samatar, 211–32. Boulder: Lynne Rienner.

Kapteijns, Lidwien. 1995. "Gender Relations and the Transformation of the Northern Somali Pastoral Tradition." *International Journal of African Historical Studies* 28, 2: 241–59.

Keddie, Nikki R. 1991. "Introduction: Deciphering Middle Eastern Women's History." In *Women in Middle Eastern History: Shifting Boundaries in Sex and Gender.* Ed. N. Keddie and B. Baron, 1–22. New Haven: Yale University Press.

Kesteloot, Lilyan. 1991. "Power and Its Portrayals in Royal Mandé Narratives." Trans. Thomas A. Hale and Richard Bjornson. *Research in African Literatures* 22, 1 (Spring): 17–25.

Khalifatul, Ilm Hazrat Mirza Bashiruddin Mahmood Ahmed. 1988. *The Holy Qur'an: With English Translation and Commentary,* Vols. 1 and 4. Islamabad: Islam International Publications.

Khatibi, Abdelkebir. 1971. *La Mémoire tatouée.* Paris: Editions Denoël.

Khatibi, Abdelkebir. 1983. "Bilinguisme et littérature." *Maghreb pluriel.* Paris: Editions Denoël.

Khatibi, Abdelkebir. 1990. *Love in Two Languages.* Trans. Richard Howard. Minneapolis: University of Minnesota Press.

Khatibi, Abdelkebir and Mohammed Sijelmassi. 1976. *The Splendour of Islamic Calligraphy.* Trans. James Hughes. London: Thames and Hudson.

Klausner, Samuel Z. 1987. *The Encyclopedia of Religion.* Vol. 9. Ed. Mircea Eliade, 230–38. New York: Macmillan.

Knappert, Jan. 1971. *Swahili Islamic Poetry.* 3 vols. Leiden: E.J.Brill.

Knappert, Jan. 1979. *Four Centuries of Swahili Verse.* Nairobi: Heinemann Educational Books.

Kourouma, Ahmadou. 1968. *Les Soleils des Indépendances.* Montréal: Les Presses de l'Université de Montréal.

Krapf, J.L. 1882. *A Dictionary of the Swahili Language.* London: Tubner and Co.

Laitin, D.D. and S.S. Samatar. 1987. *Somalia: Nation in Search of a State.* Boulder, Colo.: Westview.

Le Clezio, Marguerite. 1985. "Assia Djebar: Ecrire dans la langue adverse." *Contemporary French Civilization* 9, 2 (Spring–Summer): 230–44.

Levtzion, Nehemia. 1987. *Eighteenth–Century Renewal and Reform in Islam.* Syracuse: Syracuse University Press.

Lewis, Bernard. 1971. *Race and Color in Islam.* New York: Harper and Row Publishers.

Lewis, I.M. 1955–1956. "Sufism in Somaliland: A Study in Tribal Islam." *Bulletin of the School of African and Oriental Studies* 17, 3: 581–602; 18, 1: 145–60.

Lewis, I.M., ed. 1966. *Islam in Tropical Africa.* London: Oxford University Press.

Lewis, I.M. 1969. "Sharif Yusuf Barkhadle: The Blessed Saint of Somaliland." In *Proceedings of the Third International Conference of Ethiopian Studies–Addis Ababa* 1966, 75–81. Addis Ababa: Institute of Ethiopian Studies.

Lings, Martin. 1975. *What is Sufism?* Berkeley: University of California Press.

MacGregor, Geddes. 1987. "Doubt and Belief." *The Encyclopedia of Religion*. Vol. 4. Ed. Mircea Eliade, 424–30. New York: Macmillan.

Mack, Beverly B. 1981. "'Wa'ko'kin Mata':'Hausa Women's Oral Poetry." Ph.D. diss., University of Wisconsin–Madison.

Mallat, Chibli. 1993. *The Renewel of Islamic Law: Muhammad Baer as–Sadr, Najaf and the Shi'i International*. Cambridge: Cambridge University Press.

Mariko, Kélétigui A. 1984. *Les Touaregs Ouelleminden*. Paris: Karthala.

Martin, B.G. 1976. *Muslim Brotherhoods in Nineteenth–Century Africa*. Cambridge: Cambridge University Press.

Martin, Gérard. 1991. "Hawad: l'écriture nomade." *Notre Librairie* 107 (*Littérature nigérienne*): 82–85.

Marx–Scouras, Danielle. 1986. "Re–Interpreting Our Interpreters: Chraïbi and `Civilization,'" *Revue Celfan* 5, 2: 3–8.

Marx–Scouras, Danielle. 1992. "A Literature of Departure: The Cross–Cultural Writing of Driss Chraïbi," *Research in African Literatures* 3, 2: 131–44.

Mazrui, Ali. A. 1990. "The World of Islam: A Political Overview." *Journal Institute of Muslim Minority Affairs* 11, 2: 218–25.

McPherson, J.W. 1941. *The Moulids of Egypt (Egyptian Saint–Days)*. Cairo: H.M.Press.

Mehrez, Samia. "The Poetics of a Tatooed Memory: Decolonization and Bilingualism in North African Literature." *Emergences* 2 (1990): 105–129.

Merini, Rafika. 1986. "Women in Man's Exploration of His Country, His World: Chraïbi's *Succession Ouverte*." In *Ngambika: Studies of Women in African Literature*. Ed. Carole Boyce Davies and Anne Adams Graves, 45–61. Trenton, N.J.: Africa World Press.

Mernissi, Fatima. 1987. *Le Harem politique: Le Prophète et les femmes*. Paris: Albin Michel.

Mernissi, Fatima. 1991. *The Veil and the Male Elite: A Feminist Interpretation of Women's Rights in Islam*. Trans. Mary Jo Lakeland. Reading, Mass.: Addison–Wesley Publishing Company, Inc.

Mernissi, Fatima. 1992. *Islam and Democracy: Fear of the Modern World*. Trans. Mary Jo Lakeland. Reading, Mass.: Addison–Wesley Publishing Company, Inc.

Middleton, John. 1992. *The World of the Swahili: An African Mercantile Civilization*. New Haven: Yale University Press.

Monego, Joan Phyllis. 1984. *Maghrebian Literature in French*. Boston: Twayne.

Mortimer, Mildred. 1988. "Entretien avec Assia Djebar, écrivain algérien." *Research in African Literatures* 19, 2 (Summer): 197–205.

Moussalli, Ahmad S. 1992. *Radical Islamic Fundamentalism: The Ideological and Political Discourse of Sayyid Qutb*. Beirut: American University of Beirut.

Muhammad Bello b. Fodio. 1811. *Infakul Maisuri*. Trans. Jean Boyd. Unpublished.

Mukhtar, Mohamed Haji. 1995. "Islam in Somali History: Fact and Fiction." In *The Invention of Somalia*. Ed. Ali Jimale Ahmed. Laurenceville, NJ: Red Sea Press, 1–27.

Murdoch, H. Adlai. 1993. "Rewriting Writing: Identity, Exile, and Renewal in Assia Djebar's *L'Amour, la fantasia*." *Yale French Studies* 83: 71–92.

Nasir, Sayyid Abdalla A. 1977. *al–Inkishafi. Catechism of a Soul*. Trans. James de Vere Allen. Nairobi: East African Literature Bureau.

Nasr, Seyyed Hossein. 1985. *Ideals and Realities of Islam*. London: Allen and Unwin.

Nyang, Sulayman and Samir Abed Rabbo. 1984. "Bernard Lewis and Islamic Studies: An Assesment." In *Orientalism, Islam, and Islamists*. Ed. Sulayman Nyang, 259–84. Brattleboro: Amana Books.

Omotoso, Kole. 1984. "Trans–Saharan Views: Mutually Negative Portrayals." *African Literature Today* 14: 111–17.

Paden, John. 1986. *Ahmadu Bello, Sardauna of Sokoto.* London: Hodder and Stoughton.

Pajalich, Armado. 1993. "Nuruddin Farah Interviewed by Armando Pajalich." *Kunapipi* 15, 1: 61–71.

Palmer, H.R. 1928. *Sudanese Memoirs Vol. III.* Lagos, Nigeria: Government Printer.

Penel, Jacques Dominique. 1991. "Hawad, marcheur, poète, calligraphe." *Notre Librairie* 107 (Littérature nigérienne): 86–91.

Peters, Rudolph, trans. 1977. *Jihad in Mediaeval and Modern Islam: The Chapter on Jihad from Averroes' Legal Handbook "Bidayat Al–Mudjtahid" and The Treatise "Koran and Fighting" by . . . Mahmud Shaltut.* Leiden: E.J. Brill.

Prince, Gerald. 1988. "The Disnarrated." *Style 22* 1 (Spring): 1–8.

Rabi, Muhammad Mahmoud. 1967. *The Political Theory of Ibn Khaldun.* Leiden: E.J. Brill.

Rezzoug, Simone. 1984. "Ecritures féminines algériennes: histoire et société." *The Maghreb Review* 9, 3–4: 86–89.

Rich, Adrienne. 1972. "When We Dead Awaken: Writing as Re–Vision." *College English* 34, 1 (October): 18–30.

Robinson, David. 1985. *The Holy War of Umar Tal: The Western Sudan in the Mid–19th Century.* Oxford: Oxford University Press.

Robinson, Douglas. 1991. *The Translator's Turn.* Baltimore: The Johns Hopkins Press.

Roblès, Emmanuel. 1986. "Driss Chraïbi." *Revue Celfan* 5, 2: 1–3.

Roy, Olivier. 1990. "Les Nouveaux intellectuels islamistes: essai d'approche philosophique." In *Intellectuels et militants de l'Islam contemporain.* Ed. Gilles Kepel and Yann Richard, 259–283. Paris: Seuil.

Rushdie, Salman. 1988. *Satanic Verses.* New York: Viking.

Sa'id, Bello. 1973. "*Gudummawar Masu Jihadi Kan Adabin Hausa.*" M.A. thesis, Bayero University, Kano, Nigeria.

Samatar, Said S. 1992. *In the Shadow of Conquest: Islam in Colonial Northeast Africa.* Trenton, N.J.: Red Sea Press.

Sambo, Bashir, and Mohammad Higab. 1974. *Islamic Religious Knowledge for WASC* (West African School Certificate), Book 2. Lagos, Nigeria: Islamic Publications Bureau.

Schön, J.F. [1886] 1971. *Magana Hausa.* Nelden: Kraus.

Schimmel, Anne. 1975. *Mystical Dimensions of Islam.* Chapel Hill: University of North Carolina Press.

Shariff, Ibrahim Noor. 1984. Review article of *Four Centuries of Swahili Verse*, by Jan Knappert. In *Kiswahili, Journal of the Institute of Kiswahili Research,* 51: 156–96.

Shehu Usman b. Fodio. 1978. *Bayan Wujub.* Trans. F.H. el–Masri. Khartoum: Oxford University Press.

Skinner, A. Neil. 1968. *Hausa Readings: Selections from Edgar's Tatsuniyoyi.* Madison: The University of Wisconsin Press.

Skinner, A. Neil. 1969. *Hausa Tales and Traditions Vol. I*, London: Cass.

Skinner, A. Neil. 1977. *Hausa Tales and Traditions Vols. II-III.* Madison: University of Wisconsin Press.

Skinner, A. Neil. 1980. *An Anthology of Hausa Literature.* Zaria: Northern Nigerian Publishing Company, Ltd.

Spellberg, Denise A. 1991. "Political Action and Public Example: A'isha and the Battle of the Camel." In *Middle Eastern Women in History*. Ed. N. Keddie and B. Baron, 45–57. New Haven: Yale University Press.

Starratt, Priscilla E. 1993. "Oral History in Muslim Africa: Al–Maghili Legends in Kano." Ph.D. diss., University of Michigan.

Stoddart, William. 1986. *Sufism: The Mystical Doctrine of Islam*. New York: Paragon House.

Stowasser, Barbara. 1992. "The Mothers of the Believers in the Hadith." *The Muslim World* 82, 1–2: 1–36.

Susso, Al Hajj Papa Bunka. Interviewed by Thomas A. Hale, 10/6/94. Pennsylvania State University.

Tahir, Ibrahim. 1984. *The Last Imam*. Boston: Routledge and Kegan Paul.

Topan, Farouk M.T. 1972. "Oral Literature in a Ritual Setting: The Role of Spirit Songs in a Spirit–Mediumship Cult of Mombasa, Kenya." Ph.D. diss., University of London.

Topan, Farouk M.T. 1992. "Swahili as a Religious Language." *Journal of Religion in Africa* 22, 4: 331–49.

Trimingham, J. Spencer. 1964. *Islam in East Africa*. Oxford: Clarendon Press.

Trimingham, J. Spencer. 1965. *Islam in Ethiopia*. London: Frank Cass.

Urbani, Bernard. 1986. "La Revolte de Driss Chraïbi." *Revue Celfan* 5, 2: 27–35.

Watta, Oumarou. 1993. *Rosary, Mat and Molo: A Study in the Spiritual Epic of Omar Seku Tal*. New York: Peter Lang.

Waugh, Earle H. 1989. *The Munshidin of Egypt: Their World and Their Song*. Columbia, S.C.: University of South Carolina Press.

Westley, David. 1991. "Hausa Oral Traditions: An Annotated Bibliography." Boston: Boston University African Studies Center Working Papers in African Studies, 154.

Woodhull, Winifred. 1993. *Transfigurations of the Maghreb: Feminism, Decolonization, and Literatures*. Minneapolis: University of Minnesota Press.

Wright, Derek. 1994. *The Novels of Nuruddin Farah*. Beyreuth: Beyreuth African Studies.

Yahaya, Ibrahim Yaro. 1979. "Oral Art and the Socialization Process: A Socio–Folkloric Perspective of Initiation from Childhood to Adult Hausa Community Life." Ph.D. diss., Ahmadu Bello University, Zaria, Nigeria.

Yetiv, Isaac. 1977. "Iconoclasts in Maghrebian Literature." *The French Review* 50, 6: 858–64.

Yetiv, Isaac. 1983. "The Evolution of the Mother in the Works of Driss Chraïbi." *Revue Celfan* 2, 3: 23–25.

Yusa, Michiko. 1987. "Paradox and Riddles." *The Encyclopedia of Religion*. Vol. 2. Ed. Mircea Eliade, 189–195. New York: Macmillan.

Yusef Ali, Abdullah. 1980. *The Holy Qur'an: Text, Translation & Commentary, Vol. III*. Lahore, Pakistan: Sh. Muhammad Ashraf.

Zabus, Chantal. 1991. *The African Palimpsest: Indigenization of Language in the West African Europhone Novel*. Amsterdam: Rodopi.

Zimra, Clarisse. 1993. "When the Past Answers Our Present: Assia Djebar Talks About *Loin de Médine*." *Callaloo* 16, 1 (Winter): 116–31.

Zimra, Clarisse. 1992. "Writing Woman: The Novels of Assia Djebar." *SubStance* 69: 68–83.

Index

▼▼▼▼▼▼